nts

Spitfire Heaven - Hurricane Hell

Heavy dust covered the bodies. I looked at them – studied them. One was headless, the head had been cut cleanly away from the top of the shoulders. I didn't see the head, but I could recognise the man by his very broad shoulders.

*   'I heard a moan, so I put my hand gently on the bodies to feel which of them was alive. One of them I noticed had a hole, more than a foot wide, right through the abdomen. Another's head was split wide open into two halves, from back to front, by a piece of shrapnel. The face had expanded to twice its size. I thought of shooting him with my revolver. As I felt for it, I heard 'Bud' Connell's voice behind me. 'Look at this mess!' I put my hand against the wall, but it slithered down it. It had seemed dry with all the dust, but when I took my hand away, I found it was covered with blood with bits of meat stuck to it – like at the butcher's when they're chopping up meat and cleaning up a joint. I turned to Bud. 'For God's sake,' I said, 'don't come in here.' Then I noticed that my battledress and trousers were torn and ripped …'*

Spitfire Heaven - Hurricane Hell

Malta's Battle for Survival in WW2 By Those Who Were There

Martin W. Bowman

AIR WORLD

First published in Great Britain in 2025 by
Air World
An imprint of
Pen & Sword Books Ltd
Yorkshire - Philadelphia

ISBN 978 1 39903 339 8

Typeset in INDIA by IMPEC eSolutions
Printed and bound in the England by CPI Group (UK) Ltd, Croydon, CRO 4YY

The Publisher's authorised representative in the EU for product safety is
Authorised Rep Compliance Ltd., Ground Floor, 71 Lower Baggot Street,
Dublin D02 P593, Ireland.
www.arccompliance.com

For a complete list of Pen & Sword titles please contact:

PEN & SWORD BOOKS LIMITED
47 Church Street, Barnsley, South Yorkshire, S70 2AS, England
E-mail: enquiries@pen-and-sword.co.uk
Website: www.pen-and-sword.co.uk

or

PEN AND SWORD BOOKS
1950 Lawrence Rd, Havertown, PA 19083, USA
E-mail: uspen-and-sword@casematepublishers.com
Website: www.penandswordbooks.com

Author's Introduction and Acknowledgements

It was the chance discovery of a thrilling, yet heretofore, unpublished, wartime narrative by Pilot Officer Donald Wilson 'Mac' McLeod, an American Eagle Spitfire pilot, that inspired me to begin researching and writing this book. Dogged determination and hours of detective work – my raison d'être in a career spanning 40 years and with over 200 books published – have ensured that this work has now borne fruit. 'Mac's' diary entries that he composed while en route to Malta on SS *Queen Victoria* and almost until the end of the war, consisted of typed pages that had become almost unreadable, using as he must have done, an old typewriter and an even older ribbon that 'muddled his vowels' and produced many anomalies such as 'pianos' when further investigation revealed that he was referring to 'planes'! This breakthrough helped me to crack the 'formula' and once 'I's were replaced with 'L's, 'o's with 'e's, 'a's with 'u's etc, all was deciphered and a uniquely detailed masterpiece was saved from oblivion. Then followed hours of deciphering names as most were simply nicknames like 'Australia' and 'Canada', 'Malaya' and 'Florida'; 'Tim', 'Bart' and the two 'Jimmies'. 'Mac's' enthralling passages are the golden tableaus that form the core of *Spitfire Heaven, Hurricane Hell*.

Many people have responded generously to my requests for assistance. Aviation artist and fellow historian Mike Bailey, now

88 years old, who is still painting, advised, and loaned several of his books on Malta in the Second World War. These include two volumes, or rather 'Bibles' – *Malta: The Hurricane Years* and *Malta: The Spitfire Year 1942* by Christopher Shores and Brian Cull with Nicola Malizia; both of which were published by Grub Street, in 1987 and 1991 respectively. Among my other favourite books about the Allied pilots and the 300,000 people who bravely offered such stoical resistance and who defeated the Axis against all odds, are: *Onward to Malta* by Wing Commander T.F. Neil (Airlife Publishing Ltd, 1992); *Malta; The Thorn in Rommel's Side,* by 'Laddie' Lucas (Penguin, 1992); *Tattered Battlements: A Malta Diary by a Fighter Pilot* by 'Tim' Johnston, later Wing Commander DFC and Bar but published anonymously in 1943 by Peter Davies. It quickly established itself as a classic account of a RAF fighter pilot's war over Malta and was republished on 1 January 1985 by William Kimber & Co; *An Island Under Siege* by James Holland (Orion, 2003); *Victory in the Air* by Richard J. Caruana (Modelaid International Publications, 1996); *One Man's Window* by Denis Barnham (William Kimber & Co, 1956); *The Air Battle for Malta: The Diaries of a Spitfire Pilot* by James Douglas-Hamilton (Mainstream Publishing Co, Edinburgh, 1981 and Airlife Publishing Ltd, 1990), *185: The Malta Squadron,* edited by Anthony Rogers (Spellmount, 2005), and *Air War Malta* by Jon Sutherland and Diane Canwell (Pen & Sword, 2008).

The late Major Ronald Xuereb of Armed Forces Malta Air Wing at Luqa went out of his way to make possible my trip over Malta in an Aérospatiale Alouette helicopter to photograph the Island's wartime locations that included Valletta, Grand Harbour and Mosta, and beyond.

Last but not least, Patrick and Maggie Neil made me most welcome on my visit to see them and they kindly loaned me a copy of *Onward to Malta* (one of Tom Neil's four published titles) to read his father's stunning passages describing his experiences flying Hurricanes in the Battle of Britain and Malta.

In 2010 my colour photographic book on the Battle of Britain Memorial Flight (*The Immortal Few*) had just been published and I wanted to add Tom Neil's moniker to the dozen Battle of Britain pilots' signatures in my copy of the limited-edition and sumptuous leather-bound volumes. I managed to track down Tom via the late Wing Commander Gerry Honey OBE, who flew me in Jet Provosts and Stearman biplanes during air-to-air photographic sorties in the eastern region, and who, like Tom, was a member of the RAFA in Diss. What followed was a most enjoyable day with Tom and his dear wife Eileen at their home, not more than 30 miles from mine in Norwich.

The couple welcomed me warmly and Tom duly signed my cherished book. I listened in awe as he recounted his vivid memories of those perilous days. Eileen, it transpired, had been a WAAF ops 'B' officer at Biggin Hill, where, on 30 August 1940 the WAAFs remained at their posts throughout the German bombing (thirty-nine RAF personnel were killed). Eagerly, I asked her if she could tell me more; but her modest response was: '*I think one hero in this family is quite enough!*' Cue laughter all round!

It was at Biggin Hill in 1942 that Tom first met Flight Officer Eileen Hampton, who reached the rank of pilot officer. They had promised each other that they would marry as soon as the war was over and in 1945 the couple tied the knot.

Sadly, 'the Few' as Churchill eloquently called his RAF fighter pilots, became even fewer and now almost all the BoB veterans have passed. Eileen died in 2013. Tom died on 11 July 2018, three days before his 98th birthday. They are survived by their three sons.

Now, only a very small number of modern-day pilots can relate to, and are able to recreate, the sounds and vision, of the 'Hurris' and the 'Spits' that flew from Malta all those decades ago. RAF Coningsby is the Lincolnshire home of the world-famous Battle of Britain Memorial Flight and their restored Hurricanes and Spitfires (and Lancaster and Dakota), always a favourite with the public, especially at air shows in Britain and beyond.

I have been fortunate to be introduced to, and get to know, Squadron Leaders 'Major' Paul Day; Clive Rowley MBE RAF Retd; and Al Pinner MBE – true officers and gentleman all – who commanded the BBMF in turn until their respective retirements. I owe them a great debt, because from 1999 to 2007 I was afforded several flights in the Lancaster and Dakota to photograph the BBMF's Spitfires and Hurricanes over Lincolnshire and beyond.

When I approached Clive with a request for him to write a suitable foreword for this book, he responded with his usual alacrity and he has assiduously composed an outstanding tribute, which uniquely draws comparisons with the Hurricane and Spitfire airmen of yesteryear and the supersonic jet pilots of today.

Foreword

By Squadron Leader Clive Rowley MBE RAF Retd, author of *Lightnings to Spitfires* (Pen & Sword, 2021)

During the eleven years that I flew Hurricanes and Spitfires with the Battle of Britain Memorial Flight (BBMF), I met several wartime veterans, aircrew and ground crewmen, who had served on Malta during the Second World War and who had suffered the deprivations and extreme dangers of that ferocious cauldron of war. I had the pleasure, privilege in fact, of meeting Wing Commander Tom Neil DFC and Bar AFC AE, on a few occasions and I once discussed with him the merits or otherwise of the Hurricane and Spitfire. It was Tom's lot to fly Hurricanes during the Battle of Britain and from Malta. Later in the war, when he was OC 41 Squadron, he flew Spitfires Mk Vs and Mk XIIs, so he was well placed to give a comparative viewpoint. His answer was basically that the Hurricane was alright until you've flown a Spitfire. He also said that although in the early days the RAF pilots considered their new Hurricanes to be 'out of this world and second to none', it soon became apparent that the Germans had the better, more effective fighter aircraft and: 'We were lucky to do as well as we did against them.'

As a 'modern' ex-RAF fighter pilot I know that fighter pilots live, work, fly and fight in an extremely competitive environment of fast-moving and lethal air combat, where winning or losing may well mean the difference between life and death. In aerial combat several factors may affect the outcome, but better equipment is high up on the list.

For me, being allowed to fly the Hurricane was always an enormous privilege and the achievements of the aircraft and its pilots during the Second World War were never far from my mind. Just as those wartime pilots wrote in their memoirs, the Hurricane is an aircraft that feels strong, robust and rugged; it inspires confidence. The Hurricane is a very stable aircraft to fly and I can easily understand why the wartime pilots said it was a good gun platform.

The thing about flying the Spitfire, quite apart from its beauty and charisma, which are magical, is that from a pilot's point of view it is the finest-handling aircraft it is possible to imagine. It takes skill and finesse to fly it well, but once 'hooked up' with it the result is infinitely satisfying. The performance of the Spitfire was always better than the Hurricane in terms of climb rate and top speed, and that improved further with later marks.

If I had been fighting in the Second World War and if I had the choice between a Hurricane and a Spitfire, I would choose the Spitfire, not that anyone was given the choice. However, when it comes to landing, especially on a rough strip or in difficult wind conditions, give me a Hurricane every day!

Chapter 1

Hurricane Hell

*If we could get out of this jam by giving up Malta and
Gibraltar and some African colonies, I would jump at it. But
the only safe way is to convince Hitler that he cannot beat us.*
                                                    Winston Churchill

*The greatest of battles for supply fell upon Malta. This
was now turned into a hell. Malta was a base for British
submarines and aircraft preying on Axis lines of supply to
Libya. In the spring of 1942, the Axis decided to obliterate
that base and they wanted to starve it as well. Right through
the spring they turned such blitz upon Malta as no other island
or city had seen in the war. It was a siege of annihilation.
One after another all the great sieges were eclipsed – England
and Odessa, Sebastopol and Tobruk. Malta became the most
bombed place on earth.*
                          Alan Moorhead, the distinguished Australian war
                          correspondent, 22 July 1910–29 September 1983

The main island of Malta is only 95 square miles. It is
just 17 miles long by 9 miles wide. Approaching it from
the air, it appears like a leaf, green or brown according
to the season, floating upon the blue sea. The landscape of
this rocky island is almost biblical with flat-topped houses in

honey-coloured limestone, set against stony hills. Contrasting with this is the brilliant blue sea and sky. Malta's strategic position in the middle of the Mediterranean, 60 miles south of Sicily has made it attractive to all sorts of people – traders, colonisers and invaders – dating back to the Phoenicians. The Mediterranean island's most climactic episode was the second Great Siege of Malta during 1941–42, when it endured incessant air attacks from the Luftwaffe and the Regia Aeronautica Italiana. Benito Mussolini, dictator of Italy having declared war on France and Great Britain on 10 June 1940, after withholding formal allegiance to either side in the battle between Germany and the Allies. The Führer had already told El Duce that the time was not yet right for Italy to declare war but France and Great Britain were staring defeat in the face.

The Nazi opinion was, wrote Gerhard Engel from Hitler's HQ, that Italy was 'embarrassingly opportunistic; first of all they are too cowardly to fight with us and now they cannot join us fast enough to get their share of the swag'.

On 22 June 1940 a Gloster Gladiator on Malta scored the first victory of the war when Flight Lieutenant George Burges shot down a Savoia-Marchetti SM.79 Sparviero (Sparrowhawk) bomber, which crashed into the sea off Marsaxlokk Bay. On 3 July 1940 Flying Officer John Lawrence Waters of the Hal Far fighter flight claimed the first ever victory with a Hurricane from Malta when he destroyed a SM.79 bomber of 259ª Squadriglia, 109° Gruppo, 36° Stormo BT, which fell into the sea 5 miles off Kalafrana. Tenente Mario Squario's crew of five bailed out, but none were ever found.

Britain had initially thought, after Italy had entered the war, that Malta could not be held against determined Regia

Aeronautica, less likely Luftwaffe attack. But the events of late 1940 and early 1941 then convinced them that the Island could indeed be held, and also serve most usefully as a base from which British forces could interdict the Italian lines of communication to the Axis forces in North Africa.

During the interminable ordeal that was the siege, the Royal Navy and the Merchant Navy made almost non-stop convoys informally known as the 'Club Runs', to the besieged island during 1941–42 to resupply the islanders and the RAF contingent with food, materiel and weapons and aircraft such as Albacores, Fulmars, Swordfish, Hurricanes and Spitfires.

At Duxford on 18 July 1940, Flight Lieutenant Anthony John Trumble, a Boulton Paul Defiant pilot on 264 Squadron, was instructed to report to Abbotsinch in Scotland. On arrival he discovered that there were a number of RAF officers from other units in Fighter Command. 'The one common denominator was that we had all served in the Fleet Air Arm and we concluded that the mission was concerned with carrier operations. The next day 12 Hurricane Is were delivered to us. They were painted in desert camouflage and had tropical filters and air cleaners.'

From all over Britain, under strict security regulations, a select few pilots spent 130 hours practising very short take-offs in Hurricanes fitted under the mainplanes with 45-gallon non-jettisonable long-range petrol tanks and auxiliary pumps to pump petrol into the main tanks, before reaching a white line that seemed only a few yards distant. They were told to use 15 degrees of flap for take-off; something that was alien to them then.

'We surmised that our destination was east of Gibraltar,' wrote Tony Trumble. 'I had not flown the Hurricane before so I had a 20-minute familiarisation flight on 20 July. On 21 July the aircraft were carried by lighter to the docks and craned aboard the small WWI vintage aircraft carrier *Argus*, which was lying in dry dock. The next day *Argus* sailed down the Clyde to Greenock where we met up with our escorts, still not knowing where we were heading for. On board we were given the designation No. 418 Flight.

'We arrived at Gibraltar at the end of July, where we learned that our destination was Malta,' Trumble recalled. Operation 'Hurry' as it was appropriately called, not only because it was the nickname of the famous Hawker machines stowed between decks, but also because they were desperately needed on the Island – and quickly.

'On 2 August we were to fly off *Argus* at extreme range from Malta with two FAA Skuas on 800 Squadron.' These were flown by Flying Officer Harry Bradbury with Sub-Lieutenant William Ronald Nowell, a Royal Navy pilot, and the other was flown by Sergeant Harry W. Ayre RAF, whose navigation was left in the capable hands of Captain Keith Langler Ford RM. 'We were also told that after delivering the Hurricanes we would be returned to UK by Sunderland.'

Two Sunderlands from a detachment on 10 Squadron RAAF based at Gibraltar, followed the flight to act as 'airborne lifeboats', which would be needed if any of the pilots had to ditch. They also carried twenty-three airmen who were to service the Hurricanes on Malta.

'On the night of 30 July *Argus* left "Gib", later to be joined by Admiral Somerville's Force H; in all, a fantastic concentration of sea power and a certain amount of air power since we included HMS *Ark Royal*. We flew off at a point 80 miles west of Galite Island, about 430 miles from Malta. I flew Hurricane N2673 and the 380-mile flight in formation to Luqa took 2 hours and 20 minutes, all aircraft arriving safely but with very little fuel.'

The final aircraft, flown by Sergeant Frederick Neal 'Jock' Robertson DFM on 261 Squadron, was damaged on landing, which, according to the Scot, was all due to a 'faulty petrol gauge'. In fact, Robertson and two other pilots arrived in 'vic' formation very low over Luqa and beat up the airfield, then did a roll off the top. As Robertson made his final turn, his engine cut. The Hurricane turned upside down and went through three stone walls. Luckily for Robertson he sustained nothing worse than minor concussion and was flying again within a few days. Flying Officer Bradbury's Skua also crashed when he stalled on landing but no one was hurt.

'On arrival,' Trumble recounts, 'we were met by the Station Commander Luqa, Wing Commander R. Carter Jones and the AOC, Malta.' Air Commodore (later Air Vice Marshal) Forster Herbert Martin Maynard. Born in New Zealand on 1 May 1893 to a Church of England clergyman, 'Sammy' Maynard soon gained a questionable, yet well-merited reputation, for appropriating any aircraft and equipment that came his way!

'After the welcome, came the bombshell that we were to stay on as Malta was short of fighter pilots.'

On 12 November 1940, Operation 'White', a consignment of twelve Hurricanes in two flights of six on *Argus*, ended in tragedy. The operation was cut short by the presence of the Italian fleet at sea, which prompted a premature take-off of the fighters. This, combined with bad weather, led to only four Hurricanes reaching Malta. The first flight was led by 21-year-old Flight Lieutenant James Archibald Findlay MacLachlan DFC, who along with Sergeant John King 'Jock' Norwell, landed with only 2 gallons of fuel remaining, Pilot Officers Claud Eric Hamilton and Hugh William Eliot MiD, were the only other Hurricane pilots who reached the Island. Sergeant Richard Alfred Spyer ran out of fuel and Flight Sergeant William George Cunningham was drowned after he ditched in the sea. On 16 February 1941 MacLachlan was wounded in action. His arm was so severely damaged it was amputated, but he would return to operations in November 1941 with an artificial limb.

From the second flight, which was supposed to have been met by a Sunderland to escort them to Malta but which failed to take off from Gibraltar, all six pilots were lost after they missed their landfall at Galite Island and the bomber sent out to meet them. Finally, they became hopelessly lost. The navigator on the Skua that was to lead them to Malta radioed for help but his receiver was faulty and he could not pick up the replies.

On 9 January 1941 six Hurricanes for 261 Squadron were flown off *Furious*, a converted Courageous-class battlecruiser for the Royal Navy during the First World War, with a 160ft flight deck built along its roof, for Takoradi in the Gold Coast. From there they made the onward flight on the trans-Africa ferry route to Cairo via Lagos, Kano, El Geneina, Khartoum, Wadi Halfa and Abu Sueir; a trip of more than 4,000 miles. On 29 January the Hurricanes and two navigating Wellingtons of 38 Squadron, the latter carrying three additional fighter pilots, the kit of all nine pilots and the balance of the fighters' guns, which had been removed to save weight, were flown to Hal Far, led by Flying Officer Charles Derek Whittingham.

One of the pilots was Pilot Officer David John Thacker, who was born in 1918 in Buckinghamshire and had joined the RAFVR around July 1939. Wednesday, 12 February, marked the first appearance of Messerschmitt Bf 109s in the skies over Malta, and six Hurricanes were sent up to intercept them. Thacker's Hurricane was hit by Oberleutnant Joachim Müncheberg, one of a dozen Bf 109 pilots of 7 Staffel/Jagdgeschwader (JG) 26, newly arrived from Sicily the day before. Flight Lieutenant Roger 'Jock' Hilton Barber, a veteran pilot on the squadron, entered in his log book the immortal words; 'On this occasion the 109s were over in force.' Despite his nickname, Barber was not Scottish but had been born in South Africa and, as he put it, was of the Bushveld.

'The instruments were shattered,' Thacker wrote later 'but the controls and engine still functioned except that the latter was spewing coolant vapour. I headed back for Malta well throttled back and losing height. At about 5,000ft, when over St Paul's Bay, the engine cut, the vapour and smoke had now increased, so I bailed out.'

Barber had seen Thacker ditch 7 miles out to sea off Fort St Elmo and covered his parachute descent. '"Banjo", our control, told me all was clear but I continued to weave, probably out of habit. Then I saw this big red spinner in my mirror. I went into a very tight turn very quickly and after a couple of turns, was beginning to get inside him when he pulled up and cleared away from me not going very fast. Although out of range I gave the

109 a long squirt using plenty of deflection with no visible result however.' He stayed with Thacker until he was picked up almost an hour later by High-Speed Launch 107 based at St Paul's Bay and taken to hospital with shrapnel wounds in the buttocks and one arm.

The Hurricane pilots knew they had met their match. They reported that their Hurricane Is were so much slower than the 109s that they were now at a real disadvantage.

On 7 March Lieutenant General Sir William George Shedden Dobbie, Governor of Malta, had urged the need for rapid fighter reinforcements, and steps were soon in hand to bolster the Island's defences. Air Chief Marshal Sir Arthur Longmore, commanding the RAF in the Middle East, sent six Hawker Hurricanes fitted with drop tanks from Egypt via a forward base in Libya to Malta on 2 March, and another six followed on 14 March. With attrition continuing at an alarming rate, in mid–March 1941, on Operation 'Winch', a dozen Hurricane IIAs (plus nine Fulmars of 800X Naval Squadron to reinforce the Malta garrison and three Blackburn Skua two–seat naval aircraft to act as navigation leaders) were loaded aboard *Argus,* which sailed from the Clyde on 21 March for Gibraltar. The old carrier was escorted by the light cruiser *Sheffield* and the destroyers *Garland, Napier, Nizam* and *Ottawa. Argus* was soon screened by elements of Vice Admiral Sir James Somerville's Force 'H' (the battlecruiser *Renown,* the fleet carrier *Ark Royal,* the light cruiser *Fiji* and the destroyers *Foresight, Forester* and *Fortune*).

After arriving at Gibraltar on 29 March all the aircraft were transferred to the *Ark*. The pilots were not allowed to go ashore so a party was started in the wardroom. On 2 April the RAF contingent woke up to find 'everything vibrating like the devil', as one of the pilots described the unwelcome intrusion. The carrier sailed with an escort provided by *Renown*, *Sheffield* and the destroyers *Faulknor*, *Fearless*, *Foresight*, *Fortune* and *Fury* to a launching point 460 miles to the west of Malta. On 3 April the pilots were called at 0400 hours and they got out of bed with a real effort, followed by breakfast about half an hour later. All the knives and forks were leaping about the table when the *Ark* increased speed to 28 knots. At about 0620 hours the Hurricanes in two flights of six each eventually began taking off.

One flight was led by Flight Lieutenant Peter William Olber 'Boy' Mould DFC; the other by Flying Officer Innes Bentall Westmacott, who was born in Heybridge, Essex, on 20 September 1913. Mould had entered the RAF College, Cranwell, in 1937 and had served in France with 1 Squadron in 1939–40. He had eight victories to his name. On 30 October he had shot down a Do 17, the first German aircraft to be claimed by the RAF over the Western Front.

Operation 'Winch' went according to plan. Three Skuas guided the Hurricanes towards Malta and after about 100 miles two Sunderland flying boats on 228 Squadron met the fighters in the area of the Kerkennah Islands and led them the rest of the way. Pilot Officer Henri Ferdinand Auger, a French-Canadian from Montreal, made a bad take-off and punctured one of the auxiliary petrol tanks and broke off his tailwheel but he was able to reach the Island, where he landed at Ta'Qali, the first airfield he saw. Ta'Qali, or 'Takali' as it was commonly known in RAF circles, boasted a large house called 'Torri Cumbo', that served as the officers' mess in early 1941. All the Hurricanes arrived, although one pilot came in too fast and had to swing to avoid an obstruction at the end of his run. The undercarriage collapsed. A fellow pilot commented that 'it was really sickening to have an aircraft, which is worth its weight in gold out here, broken through damned bad handling'. The three Skuas were forced to ditch.

On 11 April between the hours of 1125 and 1155, several Hurricanes were scrambled to engage a formation of twelve Macchi C.200s of the 17° Gruppo under the command of Magg (Major) Bruno Brambilla, covered by six CR.42s from the 23° Gruppo led by Ten. Col. Tito Falconi, six CR.42s and some Bf 109E escort fighters of 7/JG 26 escorting a Ju 88 offensive reconnaissance patrol over Malta. Two of the Hurricanes on 261 Squadron, one piloted by 21-year-old Flying Officer Peter Kennett and the other by Sergeant Peter Harry Waghorn, who had arrived on the Island just eight days earlier on Operation 'Winch', got onto the tail of the Ju 88 and 20 miles north of Gozo and it was claimed as shared, probably destroyed. Tragically, the two Hurricanes were immediately bounced by the 109s. Kennett managed to get out and was seen to be swimming vigorously. However, there was a long delay in sending out a rescue launch as the raid was still on, and he was dead when eventually picked up. He had been employed as a bank clerk before the war and had joined the RAFVR in June 1939. Flying Officer Westmacott recorded that evening: 'Kennett and Waghorn killed … It is the same old story – no one was looking behind. It is frightfully difficult to make inexperienced pilots realise the necessity of even so small a formation as two aircraft keeping one up above looking out while the other is attacking the Hun ... Not very long ago, Kennett told me he was sure he was going to be killed.'

Waghorn's Hurricane was seen to crash in a field near St Paul's Bay and break up. The engine and propeller came to rest against a farmhouse while Waghorn, still strapped in his seat, was found in the road. He was born on 2 August 1920 at Hendon. Both pilots had attended Cranbrook School a year apart. They are buried next to one another in the Capuccini Naval Cemetery.

On Operation 'Dunlop', *Argus,* accompanied by the heavy cruiser *London* and light cruiser *Fiji,* departed the Clyde on 17 April after embarking pilots and seventeen Hurricane Mk Is and six Mk IIs for delivery to Gibraltar to be put aboard *Ark Royal* for Malta to form a second fighter squadron at Hal Far (185 Squadron) to work alongside 261 Squadron. The young pilots, who were under the command of Wing Commander Patrick John Handy 'Bull' Halahan DFC, a Battle of France veteran, came from all over the United Kingdom and were from many different social backgrounds.

Raymond Ottey, who would not long survive the sojourn on Malta, was born in Loughborough in 1921. He had wanted to be an actor, but war broke out and he joined the Royal Air Force Volunteer Reserve. His father, who had been with the Royal Flying Corps in the First World War, returned to the RAF as a crown sergeant, whose job was bringing crashed aircrew home. Between 1932 and 1938 Raymond was educated at Gateway Grammar School, Leicester. Raymond had two sisters, Clarice and Ellen. Ray Ottey was killed at Kalafrana during a German air raid on Malta on the night of 2–3 May 1941.

Argus reached Gibraltar on 24 April with a local escort of the light cruiser *Sheffield* and the destroyers *Faulknor, Forester* and *Wrestler.* At Gibraltar the Hurricanes, the last having been damaged in transit, were transferred to the fleet carrier *Ark Royal*, which departed on 25 April for the launching position under escort of elements of Vice Admiral Sir James Somerville's Force 'H'. On 27 April, the first formation of eight Hurricanes was despatched at 0515 hours, after bad weather had prevented take-off on the 26th. Two further formations followed, all three guided towards Malta by a Fulmar of the Fleet Air Arm. They were met by a Sunderland on 228 Squadron flown by Pilot Officer L.G.M. Rees and two Marylands to guide them safely to within sight of Malta.

Rees launched at last light the evening before the sortie since it was dangerous at that time to leave the flying boat on moorings in daylight where it could be easily attacked by enemy aircraft. 'I took off at first light,' said Rees later, 'and made the rendezvous with the first seven Hurricanes as planned, and found the fighters had just become airborne. They formated on me and I led the formation back to the Island. The Hurricanes were to land at Hal Far and I circled that aerodrome until I had seen them all land safely. I then took my aircraft to Kalafrana, landed and moored onto the slipway buoy. Almost before the mooring was completed the beaching party were towing out the beaching legs in order to get the aircraft into the hangar as soon as possible. I left the aircraft in order to go for debriefing but I got only as far as the jetty when an attack was made on the Sunderland by three 109Es [of 7/JG 26]. They dived down from out of the sun to the south.' Flying Officer Norman Patrick Watkins Hancock, the

Hurricane flight leader, who had thought that they were about to bounce his Hurricanes, watched the 109s strafe the flying boat as it taxied to its moorings, setting it on fire and sinking it.

As the other Hurricane formations neared the coast a Ju 88 on reconnaissance with an escort of five Bf 109s flew over the Island. Twenty minutes later a dozen more 109s appeared, circling off the coast as the twenty-three Hurricanes were heading towards the Island but they all landed safely.

'Dunlop' was followed by other aircraft runs to Malta, Operation 'Splice' in May and 'Rocket', 'Tracer', and 'Railway I' and 'II' in June when, in all, 224 Hurricanes were delivered to the Island; 109 for local deployment and the balance for onward shipment to Egypt. On 6 June in Operation 'Rocket' nine pilots on 45 Squadron (which would be renumbered 126 Squadron) had embarked on *Argus* and then transferred to *Ark Royal* at Gibraltar. Escorted by Blenheims, they were mercifully spared the problems caused by the decrepit Fulmars and all of them landed unscathed.

In early June 1941, the new AOC, Air Vice Marshal Hugh Pughe Lloyd, had been introduced to some of the fighter pilots. Born on 12 December 1894, in 1915 he joined the Royal Engineers as a sapper and during the First World War he was wounded in action three times before enlisting as a cadet in the Royal Flying Corps in 1917 and joining 52 Squadron, flying the R.E.8 on army co-operation sorties. After the war, he remained with the recently formed Royal Air Force on a permanent commission. In January 1939 Lloyd was given command of 9 Squadron, equipped with Wellingtons. Later in 1939, he was promoted to group captain and given command of RAF Marham. His stay here was brief and in November he was appointed to the staff of 3 Group and, in May 1940, he became senior air staff officer at 2 Group. On 1 June 1941, Lloyd was appointed Air Officer Commanding in Malta.

Before arriving in Malta, Lloyd had met with Air Chief Marshal Sir Charles Portal, the Chief of the Air Staff, who told him: 'Your main task at Malta is to sink Axis shipping sailing from Europe to Africa. You will be on the island for six months as a minimum and nine months as a maximum, as by that time you will be worn out.'

Flight Lieutenant Thomas Francis Neil, a 20-year-old Battle of Britain Hurricane pilot who had arrived in Malta in Operation 'Splice', was one of eighteen Hurricane pilots on 249 Squadron commanded by Squadron Leader Robert Alexander 'Butch' Barton DFC. Born in Bootle on 14 July 1920, Tom Neil had a keen interest in aircraft as a child and also played cricket and football for local teams. His family moved to Manchester when he was 16, and he attended Eccles Secondary (grammar) School, where he was awarded an art prize for a drawing of an aeroplane. After taking the School Certificate in 1937 Tom had wanted to attend the RAF College Cranwell but his parents did not approve of his plan and in October 1938, while working at the District Bank in Gorton, he joined the Royal Air Force Volunteer Reserve (RAFVR) to fly at weekends. He was called up on 2 September 1939 and completed his training as a fighter pilot before joining 249 Squadron in May 1940, aged only 19.

His first scrambles in the Battle of Britain began that July and were followed by a three-week period in September, when he claimed five and two shared victories, which resulted in the award of a DFC on 8 October. Nicknamed 'Ginger', because of the colour of his hair, Tom's film star persona attracted the attention of Cecil Beaton, the famous photographer, who photographed him between scrambles (141 times in all) at North Weald. Tom would admit that luck and a lot of time spent ducking and weaving played a big part in his incredible survival. And he soon realised how important it was in aerial combat to have the sensitivity to know instinctively what was going on around him. However, on 7 November a Hurricane piloted by Wing Commander Victor Beamish collided with his aircraft, cutting off the tail, though both pilots safely bailed out. On 26 November Tom received a Bar to his DFC and on 16 December he was promoted to flight commander.

Another 249 Squadron pilot who distinguished himself in the Battle of Britain was Flying Officer Patrick Hardy Vesey Wells, born on 16 March 1917 in Johannesburg, who had three victories and was shot down twice, the second time by the famous Luftwaffe ace Adolf Galland. A fellow South African, Flying Officer James Terence Crossey, or 'Ossie' as he was known because he habitually wore a black, roll-neck jersey beneath his flying overall in the manner of Sir Oswald Mosley, the British fascist and leader of the 'Black Shirts', had notched up a few shared victories. Flying Officer Antony Robert Fletcher 'Tommy' Thompson, born 14 October 1920, had joined the RAF Volunteer Reserve about July 1939 as an airman under pilot training. Called up on 1 September, he completed his training at 15 EFTS and 5 FTS Sealand, and arrived at 6 OTU on 10 September 1940. After converting to Hurricanes, he joined 85 (F) Squadron at Church Fenton on the 29th and moved to 249 (F) Squadron at

North Weald in Essex on 17 October 1940. Thompson shared in the destruction of a Junkers Ju 88 on 28 October and destroyed a Bf 109 on the 30th. On 5 August Tommy Thompson would join the Malta Night Fighting Defence Unit at Takali. He damaged a Fiat Br.20 Cicogna (Stork) low-wing, twin-engine medium bomber at night on 11 November.

Hugh John Sherard Beazley, born on 18 July 1916, the son of a judge, had, on 27 September 1940, while attacking a Bf 110, been badly wounded in the foot but managed to nurse his aircraft back to RAF North Weald. He was subsequently hospitalised and therefore it was his last action during the Battle of Britain. He spent five months in hospital before re-joining the squadron in March 1941 in time to sail for Malta. On 25 September Beazley damaged an Italian bomber, a Bf 109 and, on an intruder mission over Sicily, he destroyed a train. On 19 January 1942 his Hurricane was hit by ground fire during an attack on the Italian airfield at Comiso and he was forced to crash-land on his return to Malta. In February 1942 he probably destroyed a Junkers 88. In February 1942, after 10 months of continuous action and 215 combat sorties during the Battle of Britain and over Malta, he was rested.

Meanwhile, on 12 June 1941, Pilot Officer Roich Hamish Mckenzie Munro, 28, of Salisbury, Southern Rhodesia, became 249 Squadron's first casualty when he was listed as missing believed killed; shot down over the sea off Malta.

By 18 June Tom Neil had been on Malta three weeks and at best his squadron could muster on average about ten Hurricanes – eight Mk Is and two Mk IIs. Many of Lloyd's fighter pilots expressed their willingness to play their part, but most made it

known that they needed something more serviceable and with
a better performance than the Hurricanes that had been foisted
on them. Most of the Mk Is were tropicalised but the Mk IIs
were not. Their open air intakes, situated under the engine and
between the undercarriage legs, were ideally placed to suck
in every particle of dust and filth whipped up by the whirling
airscrews during take-off, landing, and even taxiing. Neil made
his displeasure known about their 'lame-duck' Hurricanes
at every opportunity. 'Mr Sidney Camm,' Tom said, 'in his
moments of inspiration when designing the Hurricane, clearly
did not have deserts in mind – nor Malta!'

On 27 June, in Operation 'Railway I', *Ark Royal* flew off
twenty-two tropicalised Hurricane IIcs (one crashing on
landing), which were armed with four cannons. Then, on 30
June, in Operation 'Railway II' *Ark Royal* flew off twenty-four
Hurricanes in two gaggles of twelve and *Furious* flew off sixteen.
In spite of Tom Neil's prejudice against the tropicalised version
of the Hurricane, he was in no doubt that the un-tropicalised
ones just didn't cut the mustard. His squadron was constantly
having engine problems on all its Hurricanes, but especially the
few Mk IIs, so that hardly a day passed when he didn't sit there
during take-off, stiff with apprehension, waiting for the loss of
power or stoppage that would pitch him into the hill ahead or
the endless rows of stone walls.

When the second group of Hurricanes appeared, Neil was in
the mess at Takali on leave at the time. He watched them touch
down. Unfortunately, landing north to south, several of them
overshot badly; two or three careering past and one finishing
up on its nose. Tom found it heart-breaking to watch brand

new Hurricanes that were so badly needed, broken by inept and inexperienced pilots and there were loud groans and unflattering remarks about the legitimacy of several of those involved.

Included in the new group were four American pilots who had arrived in England via the RCAF. Neil had never seen Americans in RAF blue before so the arrival of Pilot Officers Howard M. Coffin of Los Angeles; Donald Allen Tedford, from Windsor, Ohio; Edward Elmer Steele; and Edward Streets Jr, who was born on 28 November 1921 at Talbot, Maryland; was of some interest. Chatting in the mess later with 'Pete' Steele and 'Eddie' Streets, 'one being tall and thin and the other positively wee,' Neil learned that on reaching England, they had been invited to Buckingham Palace, during which Streets, had, as far as one knew, asked the Duke of Kent's wife, Princess Marina, for a 'date'! Neil could not suppress a grin. 'What next for heaven's sake? Were they not *aware*?'

In the afternoon of 2 September, Italian Ju 87 Stukas, nicknamed 'Picchiatello', were presented with their first baptism of fire in the Mediterranean when they attacked a naval formation just outside Maltese waters. Three days later, in their first direct attack on the Island, Italian Stukas bombed Delimara with 500kg bombs after they had failed to find a large vessel in Grand Harbour reported by an earlier Italian reconnaissance. On the 15th a dozen Stukas escorted by Macchi C.200 fighters carried out a dive-bombing attack on Hal Far before they were routed by Gladiators and Hurricanes. On the 17th 'Jock' Barber took off with two other Hurricanes and pressed home an attack on a Stuka of 236ª Squadriglia, which crashed into the Mediterranean near Filfla. Flying Officer William Joseph 'Timber' Woods, destroyed a Fiat CR.42 biplane fighter, whose pilot managed to bail out before it crashed.

On 9 September 1941 in Operation 'Status I' *Ark Royal* delivered fourteen Hurricanes, all of which landed on Malta. Four days later, in 'Status II', the *Ark* and *Furious* flew off a further forty-six Hurricanes, of which all except one of the fighters arrived safely. By the year end Malta's air strength consisted of only about sixteen Hurricanes and four Gladiator biplanes but the Regia Aeronautica was unable to halt the British convoys that supplied Malta during September to November. However, towards the end of December, X Fliegerkorps, which specialised in coastal operations, and was commanded by General der Flieger Hans Geisler, began operations against Malta from Sicily.

A serious attempt to make good the acute loss of Hurricanes was now of paramount importance and reinforcement became something of a priority. Operation 'Perpetual', the final 'Club Run' to deliver Hurricanes to Malta, took place on 12 November, when thirty-seven of them were flown off *Argus* and *Ark Royal* and were led to Malta by four Blenheims, which had taken off from Gibraltar. Two of the Hurricanes came down in North Africa and one crashed in Sicily. Another almost lost its tailwheel when it swung violently to port on take-off but Pilot Officer Peter W. Lowe on 605 Squadron managed to reach Malta safely, where the wheel collapsed on landing. Pilot Officer James Dismore Tew Jr, a Harvard graduate from Vero Beach, Florida, landed his Hurricane wheels-up at Hal Far. On 1 March 1942 the 28-year-old pilot was KIA when he was shot down into the sea.

'Perpetual' took the grand total of Hurricanes delivered by sea in 1940–41 to 333. But in the early months of 1942, the ever-diminishing numbers of Hurricanes were soon shown to be totally outperformed in the sky over Malta and the Axis rapidly gained dominance over the airfields and made them their own. Often, the Hurricanes had to be vectored away from the Island for their own safety, until by March 1942, so few remained that some of the spare pilots were deployed on the rooftops in Valletta to act as aircraft spotters!

Hugh Pughe Lloyd visited his pilots about the time of Tom Neil's 21st birthday on 14 July, treating him to his 'now-familiar stern, Cromwellian glare from a distance of about nine inches'. The conversation was pleasant enough, but Neil took the opportunity to speak for the Hurricane pilots en masse when he unashamedly pointed out that despite the substantial number of reinforcement Hurricanes, 249 Squadron could seldom put up more than eight aircraft. 'The serviceability state was deplorable,' he said, 'because the squadrons still retained a few "clapped-out" Mark Is and un-tropicalised Mark IIs, whose engines seemed only to function when the spirit moved them'.

Whilst the Hurricane pilots could cope with the Macchi C.200s, Savoias and other Italian aircraft, if the Luftwaffe returned with their 109s and 88s, or if the new Macchi MC.202s put in an appearance, they would be hard put to hold their own. 'Were there no Spitfires available? Or Tomahawks, even?' Neil asked of his AOC.

The prospect of once more being inundated with Ju 88s and Bf 109s was little more than a grim joke, the general response in the bars in Valletta being, 'So what?' Hadn't they 'clobbered them in England', and couldn't they do so again? But could they? Despite their bravado, fuelled by drink, they knew that the Hurricanes just did not have the performance to match the Messerschmitts (not Es this time but Fs!).

Pilots had been lobbying persistently for Spitfires for months past, but their clamour fell on deaf ears in England and in Malta 'Hugh Pughe' simply ignored their requests, while accusing the pilots, who he felt 'should all be more offensive minded and carry the fight to the enemy and bomb them out of their stride!' His final comment, that 'it wasn't the aircraft, it was the man' upset Tom Neil, and no doubt all Hurricane pilots on the Island, when they got to hear of the AOC's injudicious remarks later. Clearly rankled, Neil recalled 'the ugly silence' that had followed when 'Hugh Pughe' made them; a silence in which, for one wildly absurd moment, he actually thought that someone might strike the AOC.

'This unhappy situation,' Neil later added, 'had been predicted, the warnings had been ignored by those who, earlier, might have strengthened the fighter force in Malta with Spitfires. Eventually, when driven to it, they did, the first Spits arriving in March of that year, by which time, alas, for some it was too late! Needlessly so, in the opinion of many.'

Chapter 2

Spitfire Heaven

'Either, Sir, we get Spitfires here within days, not weeks, or we're done. That's it.'

Squadron Leader 'Stan' Turner DSO DFC and Bar speaking to the AOC, Air Vice Marshal Sir Hugh Pughe Lloyd. A visit by Group Captain Basil Embry to Malta in January 1942 led to Embry recommending Spitfire Vs for the Island, which would have the necessary climb, ceiling and firepower in order to deal with the enemy.

Turner, born in Ivybridge, Devon, on 3 September 1913, his family emigrating to Canada shortly afterwards and settling in Toronto, was a veteran of the Battle of Britain, with nine victories, two unconfirmed and one 'probable' flying Hurricanes. On 16 February 1942 he had been flown out to Malta in a Sunderland to take command of 249 Squadron.

An attempt to supply Malta with Spitfires had taken place in February (Operation 'Spotter') but defects had been discovered in the Mk Vbs' fuel tanks and the operation had to be aborted, the ships returning to Gibraltar on 28 February.

On 5 March Lloyd sent a signal urgently requesting Spitfires. On 7 March Turner welcomed the first Spitfires to be deployed outside of Britain to the island. The fifteen repaired Spitfire Vbs aboard *Eagle* were flown off and guided the 700 miles to Malta by seven Blenheims.

Only a few American fighter pilots were posted to Malta in 1941. Forty-two are known to have served there in Spitfire units in 1942. American Pilot Officer Donald Wilson 'Mac' McLeod, a 27-year-old native of Boston, Massachusetts, who was born in Blackstone, 33 miles to the north-east, on 21 April 1914, was a policeman before he took six weeks' basic training as a US naval air cadet in 1937 at Squantum air base. Then in 1941 he went to Canada to join the RAF Volunteer Reserve before completing service pilot training at the Curtiss-Wright Corporation, Polaris Flight Academy at War Eagle Field. It was here in the Mojave Desert in California that McLeod made a good friend in James 'Jimmie' Elvidge Peck from Berkeley, California, who had started flying lessons at age 15 and got his flying licence the day he graduated from high school. He had originally applied to join the US Army Air Corps but was considered unsuitable. Following his rejection, he crossed the border into Canada and was accepted by the RAF for pilot training.

Undergoing training at War Eagle Field at the same time was John Joseph Lynch Jr, of Alhambra, Alabama. Lynch, born on 3 February 1918, had joined the USAAC in the late 1930s and learned to fly. He lived in Oklahoma and was a pilot instructor there until he joined the RAF in Canada in 1941. He would serve on 121 and 71 'Eagle' Squadrons but when the Eagle squadrons were transferred to the USAAF on 29 September 1942, he elected not to transfer with them and was posted to Malta that

November. On 28 April 1943 he would score Malta's 1,000th victory of the war, shooting down a Ju 52/3m and winning an RAF sweepstake prize of £129.

On 22 July 1941, McLeod, 'Jimmie' Peck and Joe Lynch were among those who were shipped overseas on board a steamship from Montreal to Liverpool. On 11 August they began conversion to the Hurricane and Spitfire. In September 'Jimmie' Peck and Don McLeod were posted to the famous 121 'Eagle' Squadron, which had been re-formed on 14 May at Kirton in Lindsey, Lincolnshire, as the second Eagle squadron to be manned by American volunteers. It was commanded by Squadron Leader Robin Peter Reginald Powell, who had graduated from Cranwell in 1936. He had seen combat action on 111 Squadron over France and during the Battle of Britain.

In October 1941, 121 Squadron had begun defensive patrols with Hurricane IIs but in November it converted to Spitfires, moving to North Weald in December, and in February 1942, began to take part in fighter sweeps over northern France. That winter, 'Jimmie' Peck and Don McLeod were chafing at the bit for more action; the lack of which, and the lousy weather, combined to intensify their rapidly mounting disdain. McLeod has been described by Percy Belgrave Lucas, better known as 'Laddie' Lucas, as 'an American with no noticeable inhibitions [with a] flow of transatlantic conversation [and whose] coloured events brought individuals graphically to life. In speech he was the antithesis of the reserved Englishman.'

An avid diarist, McLeod, predictably, began his journal by describing the British weather. 'Fog! Fog! Fog! That seems to be all there is around this bloody country … Myself and the two "Jimmies" [James E. Peck and "Jimmie" Daley] and Roy [Pilot Officer Roy W. Evans, who later transferred to the 335th Fighter Squadron, 4th Fighter Group, 8th Air Force] were again planning maps, seeking targets for our "Rhubarbs" [a small number of aircraft – usually just a pair – that flew at low level into France or Belgium, normally in bad weather to avoid enemy fighters, to shoot up targets of opportunity on the ground]. Jim and I had decided on a target and were mapping our approaches (that is the quickest way in and the quickest way out). Tomorrow would be our turn. As "Jimmie" Daley and Roy had been in close to our appending target, we were getting a few tips on anti-aircraft fire in that vicinity. This was all that we had been doing and we were thoroughly disgruntled pilots.'

This discontent though was about to end, as Don McLeod was to recall: 'The CO's voice thundered through the fog: '"and 'Jim' come here." This was the start of one of the war's greatest adventures for "Jimmie" [Peck] and me. In his hand the CO held transports (Overseas Shipment Orders) for "Jimmie" and I. Proceed immediately to "PDC" (Personnel Dispatch Centre) in Northern England. Destination unknown!

'Upon our arrival in Glasgow, Scotland, on 25 February 1942, we learned that we were to sail immediately on the *Queen Victoria*. Having heard of several of the English ships of the "Queen" type, I visualised a tremendous transatlantic liner, which turned out to be nothing but a lowly, tiny tramp steamer.' SS *Queen Victoria* was a 4,937-ton cargo motor vessel built in 1936 by Barclay Curle & Company, Glasgow. She would be escorted overseas by the destroyer *Airedale* and *Petunia*, a corvette.

'Prior to embarking on the boat, we met our new companions of this never to be forgotten trip. Sixteen members made up 126 Squadron that embarked on this unknown story of Malta. Pilot Officer [Michael Adrian] Graves was an Irishman. The same kind of an Irishman as an Irishman would expect to meet. Tow-headed, pink-cheeked and who shaved about once each month. Fiery tempered, brusque in tone, but a hell of a flyer. He asked no quarter and gave none.

'Pilot Officer [John Henry Eric] "Bis" Bisley DFC RAAF, born 7 May 1920 in Molong, NSW, was a diehard, confirmed "Aussie" who would fight at the drop of a hat and who lived to the fullest extent. A hell-for-leather individual, typical of Aussie fighting men. "Bis" gave and took a lot of the load.' He had named his mother, Janet, as next of kin when he joined up on 14 October 1940, having worked as a clerk for the Commonwealth Bank at Bathurst before the war. He was posted to Britain in June 1941, where he underwent further training at 57 OTU Hawarden and was then posted to 122 Squadron at Catterick and Scorton flying Spitfires.

'Pilot Officer "Bill" Bailey – also known as "Old Bailey" – the type you would expect to find teaching school and carrying a piano lesson briefcase with him, was the unassuming kind of man. We often wondered if he ever got excited, but it was this level-headedness and his inborn courage that kept "Ba" alive through many battles.

'Flight Sergeant [later Flight Lieutenant, William Lister "Dusty"] Miller [a New Zealander, from Invercargill] was quite unassuming and a level-headed kid. Quiet until the reports of battle came in.' During the next four months he damaged five Bf 109s and one day flew the only operational Spitfire off the island to escape an incoming raid. Leaving at sea level, he climbed to 25,000ft but two Bf 109s flew around him in a wide circle before they left. 'Dusty' would leave Malta on 23 July 1942. Upon arrival in England, he discovered he had contracted jaundice.

'Flight Sergeant [Walter Harry Leonard] Milner was a Canadian. Small of stature and of the good-natured sort, he would fight only when cornered on the ground, but continuously while in the air. Flight Sergeants [Eric Ambrose] "Junior" Crist, who was from Wallaceburg, Ontario, and "Ricky" Ryckman from London, Ontario, must be mentioned together. Inseparable comrades from the birth of their training in Canada until "Rick's" tragic end on 20 April 1942, "Junior" avenged in a tangible way the loss of his bosom comrade in future air battles. Sergeants' Wilbert George "Turkey" Dodd; G.S. Bolton from New Zealand, and [Cyril F. "Joe"] Bush were inseparables; two of whom left us for different squadrons on the Island because of their fighter experience on Hurricanes.'

Dodd, described as 'a demure and gentle looking Winnipegger', was born on 8 December 1920 in Rennie, Manitoba. On 29 March 1942 he flew off HMS *Eagle* and was almost immediately assigned to 185 Squadron flying Hurricane IIs, changing to Spitfire Vs in May. By 8 July 1942 he had been awarded five enemy aircraft destroyed, a one third share in a Cant Z.506B Airone (Heron) trimotor floatplane, two 'probables' and four 'damaged'. He completed his tour on Malta that August. In 1943, flying Spitfire Vbs on 402 Squadron, he was awarded a Bf 109 destroyed, a half share in a Do 24 and a Fw 190 'probable'.

'We could have had no finer leader on our enterprise than Squadron Leader Gracie, a famous Battle of Britain pilot [who] had once broken his neck [on 30 August 1940 flying a Hurricane, when he was shot down after destroying a Heinkel He 111 and damaging another, to take his score to five destroyed, two 'probables', two 'damaged' and a share in two others. Fortunately, the fracture mended and he returned to fly and fight again]. Gracie, known as "Jumbo" to all of us amongst ourselves, but when in his presence, always a very definite "Sir", was as rough a character as you or I would ever care to meet.'

Edward John Gracie was born 21 September 1911 in Acton, west London. At the beginning of October 1940, he received a DFC. He was rested in January 1941 before taking command of 23 Squadron that March and then moving to 601 Squadron late in April. He had left that squadron in late December. On arrival in Malta, Gracie would take command of 126 Squadron, their Hurricanes being replaced by Spitfires. 'Laddie' Lucas wrote that 'Gracie, who smoked "V for Victory" and "Belle of the Orient" cigarettes through an extra-long holder [was] a thoroughly capable and experienced character, who offset surprisingly poor eyesight with the heart of two lions ... a blunt and thick-skinned officer – a "restless pirate" – whose methods bordered on the ruthless, but whose resource and ability were never in question. He was a compelling comrade to have on one's side.'

'One of his two flight lieutenants,' wrote Don McLeod, 'was Anthony Richard Henry Barton; known to all and especially to his enemies, as "Killer" Barton. One line would be sufficient to describe Tony Barton. He was shot down five times and ended up by destroying twice as many "Huns" as had knocked him down.

'Gracie's other flight lieutenant, "Tim" Johnston, was to become in the eyes of every pilot, the most intrepid, daring and courageous a man as one would hope to meet. Every flight he made became almost an epic.'

Hugh Anthony Stephen Johnston was born on 7 December 1913, the son of an Indian civil servant. In 1932 he arrived at Brasenose College, Oxford, a Domus Exhibitioner, from King's College, Canterbury. He soon proved himself to be an excellent example of a good all-rounder and graduated in 1935 with a very creditable second class degree in Modern Greats. In 1936 he entered the overseas civil service and went on to serve in the RAF from 1940 to 1945. It was at Oxford that he discovered he liked 'Americans and people from the Dominions and had as much in common with them, as with other Englishmen'.

On the long sea voyage to Malta, Johnston and his fellow pilots tried to pump their CO as to where they were headed, but to no purpose. 'All he would say was that they should soon know and that there would be no lack of action. All we knew was that the amount of luggage which we were allowed shrank at every stage of the journey until it reached a limit of 10lb.

'The pilots were faced with the pressing problem of where to store their belongings, including the two ridiculous pith helmets, which, though light, were extremely bulky. Each had 30lb of clothing and essentials to find a home for but the Hurricane, being a fighter, had room for little more than a couple of maps. In the event, their kit was crammed anywhere and everywhere – in the radio compartment behind the armour plate, tied to the "floor" in the rear of the fuselage, left and right of the pilot's seat, and in the ammunition boxes in the wings, the 3,000 rounds of .303 being removed for that purpose. This last arrangement had them chuckling; if the enemy were sighted en route, they would be able to give them a quick squirt of McLean's toothpaste from all eight guns, followed by a little of the hard stuff – a few bars of Lifebuoy soap!

'In the operations room in the island of the carrier, we drew lines on maps and wrote down courses. For reasons of security, we would be flying just above the water and maintaining R/T silence throughout, and each group of Hurricanes would be escorted by a Fulmar; as the naval fighter carried an observer-navigator in the back, this was felt to be a prudent measure. Which led to a rather odd discovery: besides whatever else the observer carried in his cockpit, the beneficent Navy provided him with a Thompson sub-machine gun, one of the Al Capone varieties. We discussed this choice of weapon with incredulous laughter. A Tommy-gun, for heaven's sake! With a range of about 20 yards! What on earth was that for? Then, on second thoughts, we decided it was probably for the observer to shoot the pilot, then himself, if things got out of hand.

'The route we were to take was anything but straightforward. After take-off, we would fly for about an hour before sighting Cap Bon on the northern tip of Africa, where, more than likely, we would be intercepted by the Vichy French with their Curtiss Hawk 75s, an aircraft they had recently bought from the Americans. That our ex-allies were hostile, we knew; whether or not they would attack us, remained to be seen.

'After Cap Bon, there would be a dog-leg to avoid the island of Pantelleria, inhabited by "Hun Me 110s" we were told, taking care thereafter to skirt both Lampedusa and Linosa, both enemy-held. Finally, with God's grace, we would hit Malta, whereupon we were to circle Filfla Rock, to the south of the island, in order to identify ourselves, before landing, one-third each, on the airfields of Takali, Luqa and Hal Far. In all, we would be flying about 450 miles over a period of two and a half hours, a journey well within their maximum range and endurance of just over 1,000 miles and six and a half hours, respectively.'

'On 27 February 1942,' began Don McLeod's log aboard SS *Queen Victoria*, 'we were travelling under sealed orders. We were allowed to carry one bag due to limitations on weight. We had brought important things such as candy bars, cigarettes, etc. And now it came to pass that we were aboard a dingy tramp steamer which had been converted slightly in the hold into our luxurious (?) quarters. There were nine of us in one small room and six in the other. Of course, the CO had himself a cabin, such as it was. On looking over the entire ship, we found that there were tons of sand aboard for ballast and the remainder consisted of 16 brand new Spitfires in crates.

'"This," we said, "must be something." Sixteen pilots and sixteen Spitfires. Nothing else on board. We had no idea at the moment of where we might be going. Some said Australia, some said India and some said Canada. "Jimmie" and I even hoped it might be the USA. It gave food for thought as we steamed slowly out of the Clyde, past the river towns of Greenock and Gourock, Scotland, into the misty, choppy Atlantic. With our meagre knowledge of celestial navigation, we tried to set our course in our minds.

'Were we going north, south, east or west? "Jimmie" with his very limited knowledge deduced that we were proceeding in a west, south-westerly direction. Immediately we, "Jimmie" and I, said, "West, south-west. That's the USA."

'The next evening, I deduced that we were sailing due west so the hopes of all our Canadian brothers arose as Canada was in that direction. But lo and behold on the third night we deduced that we were sailing south. Due South. We gave up wondering and our answer was given to us the next morning.

'Fifteen solemn pilots, their minds racing back and forth as to what we faced, listened intently to the CO, who finally said, "Gentlemen, you are in this war to fight. I think that I can offer you that fight." "Men", in words I will never forget, as he held a cigarette in his mouth with the aid of a cigarette holder, "We are going to Malta." The name itself vibrated around the room and there was a sudden hush. Because Malta was the apparent last stronghold of the British, but in a year to be an allied stronghold in the war. We knew that Malta was close to Africa. When the battle was going bad and with Africa would go the second supply route to Russia and after that – no one knew. Then a barrage of questions. How? When? Where? What? No one could conceive or possibly imagine what was being done to save that island. Just what would this next month take us through?

'We had been aboard 14 days and each day seemed to get worse and worse with monotonous regularity. After the first evening the only form of amusement we were to have was to see the same faces and do the same things time in and time out. The one redeeming feature of the entire trip was the wonderful food which we, for the first time since the entry into the war, were having.

'I might add that during the trip we were well protected insofar as surface vessels held present. Our escort was a destroyer and two corvettes. The only excitement we had was the approach of two submarines, which were driven off very comfortably as far as we were concerned by our escort. As a matter of fact, their stay was only brief. Depth charge explosions were heard and we learned later that our two subs had been driven off.

'On the fifteenth evening we steamed into Gibraltar harbour. At night, Gibraltar, through necessity, was desolately and completely blacked out. While a seemingly stone's throw away, Tangiers, a neutral section on the African coast, was lit up like a Christmas tree. It seemed so strange that war and peace, as far as lights were concerned, could be so close together. Of course, it had been our expected desire to dock at Gibraltar and run around into the town and partake of the goodness of life in its various forms, but we were to be sadly disappointed. As we steamed into the harbour in the black of night, we were informed that we were to remain in quarters aboard the ship during all daylight hours.'

Don McLeod could not think of no more sadly disappointed men than the fifteen were upon receiving those orders 'but it became very obvious to us after two days why these orders had to be carried out, for it was not just involving we sixteen, but thousands of other lives on Malta as well.'

'For a week at "Gib" the pilots lived on the *Eagle*, with nothing to do but amuse ourselves,' recalled 'Tim' Johnston, 'while the ground crews, under the direction of "Shorty" Hughes worked day and night, but mostly by night, in the sultry heat of the ship's hangar, to assemble and test our aircraft. We swam, ate and drank, and pottered about the town, while every day the papers told of increasingly heavy attacks on Malta. We all sensed it was the lull before the storm, and I think most of us, while making the most of the moment, were busy bracing ourselves in spirit for the ordeal which we knew to be just ahead.'

On the fateful Friday the 13th, seven Spitfire pilots who were needed to help fill the depleted ranks on Malta, had left London's Paddington station on the tedious journey on the Great Western's flyer for Plymouth, where they were to board a Sunderland for Gibraltar with a final destination at Kalafrana Bay. 'Laddie' Lucas and Pilot Officer Raoul Daddo-Langlois, (pronounced Longlay), a Channel Islander from Guernsey, who was known to his friends as 'Daddy Long-legs' or simply, 'Daddy-L', shared a carriage with Robert H. 'Bob' Sergeant, an experienced Spitfire pilot who had flown many of 11 Group's sweeps and 'circuses' over France. Reflecting on their chances of survival, Sergeant mused, 'I wonder how many of the first ten will come back?'

'Laddie' and 'Daddy-L's' five other companions for the flight in a Sunderland of 10 Squadron RAAF to Malta on Monday, 16 February were the usual mix of RAF and Dominion pilots. Flight Lieutenant Robert Wendell 'Buck' McNair, born in Springfield, Nova Scotia, on 15 May 1919, was the son of a railway engineer, who had worked for Canadian Airways as a radio operator and handyman before enlisting in 1940 and has been described as 'the most courageous fighter pilot Canada produced during the war'. Jeffery George West DFM RNZAF, a former civil servant, born in Palmerston North on 30 October 1912, had previously flown Spitfire IIas and Vbs on 616 Squadron, and had notched up two Bf 109 kills, a half share in two others, a Bf 109F 'probable' and another 'damaged'.

Sergeant Adrian Philip 'Tim' Goldsmith DFC DFM RAAF was born on 25 April 1921, to Sidney Goldsmith, a timber merchant, and his English wife Philippa in Waverley, NSW.

Flying Officer George Andrew Forsyth 'Buck' Buchanan, born in Dundee in South Africa on 28 November 1912, was employed at the outbreak of war by the Zambesi Saw Mills Co. at Livingstone in Northern Rhodesia. He had left Livingstone in April 1940 to join the RAF. Prior to his departure he was given a send-off by the then Mayor and Mayoress of Livingstone, Mr and Mrs Orr. Mrs Orr suggested he look up her niece in Scotland; this he duly did, and married her on 3 May 1941 in Glasgow.

Squadron Leader Percival Stanley 'Bull' Turner DFC*, the new CO of 249 Squadron, was a widely experienced squadron and wing leader, born in Ivybridge, Devon, on 3 September 1913, whose parents emigrated to Toronto, Ontario, when he was at a young age, and who, while studying engineering there, had joined the Royal Canadian Air Force Auxiliary. He was not, in the words of one of his pilots, 'precisely a man of refinement and he hardly ever used polite language when he uttered an opinion on something. It was not easy to discuss things with him or to contradict him. After drinking a few beers, "he would scare off a regiment of Polish infantry!"'

During the early hours of 21 February another Sunderland – from 95 Squadron this time – arrived from Gibraltar at the end of an eleven-hour flight carrying more fighter pilots. They included Pilot Officer 'Bob' Sergeant; Flight Lieutenant William Charles 'Bud' Connell of Nipawin, Saskatchewan; Squadron Leader Ronald Ivor Chaffe, who was to take command of 185 Squadron at Hal Far; 24-year-old Pilot Officer Gordon Russell Tweedale RAAF; Flight Lieutenant Keith Ashley Lawrence and Pilot Officer Richard E. 'Sandy' McHan, who had served on 121 Squadron RAF, the second Eagle squadron. 'Tweedles'

Tweedale was born in Brisbane on 18 April 1918 and had worked as a stockman in Queensland before enlisting in the RAAF.

Lawrence, a New Zealander, was born in Waitara on 25 November 1919. In 1940, when he flew Spitfire Is, he had destroyed or damaged seven and a half enemy aircraft and had a third share in a Ju 88. On 26 November 1940 he had been shot down by a Bf 109, bailing out with a broken leg and dislocated arm.

The Sunderland flew through a 'disturbed, electric night' from Gibraltar and along the length of the western Mediterranean to Malta. At about 0430 hours 'Tim' Goldsmith made his way to the flight deck to see what their position was. Standing in the cockpit behind the South African skipper, Squadron Leader Ian Maxwell Theodore de Kaap Bocock, Goldsmith could see several searchlights about 40 miles to the north.

'Where are the searchlights?' he asked.

'Malta,' the skipper replied.

'Well, why aren't we headed that way?'

'Because there's a bleeding air raid on, chum and we don't want the bleeding machine smashed around our bleeding ears.'

Feeling rather 'squashed', Goldsmith clambered back to the gunners' hatch to watch the proceedings. For two hours the Sunderland circled north of Malta until the all clear was given by wireless, just as dawn broke.

It was a sunny, late winter's morning at Kalafrana Bay when the Spitfire pilots stepped out of the Sunderland.

'We were fresh from flying well-maintained Spitfires in Fighter Command in England,' wrote Lucas 'and more than a little blasé about it.'

As they walked away from the jetty beside the lapping waters of Kalafrana Bay and made their way to the mess for breakfast, the air-raid sirens began wailing. In a few moments they looked heavenwards. 'There, clawing and clambering up through the early morning haze,' 'Laddie' Lucas espied 'four, clapped out, antiquated Hurricane IIs, struggling for height, in an old-fashioned Vic formation. They couldn't have been at more than three or four thousand feet as they passed overhead.'

The pilots discovered later that it was all the defence could muster out of the ten or twelve supposedly serviceable on the Island. The Spitfires had yet to arrive.

'Six or 8,000ft above our quartet,' Lucas noted, 'flying their beautifully loose, open formation, were three sections of four Messerschmitt 109Fs, sweeping in fast and confidently, well ahead of the incoming raid. The customary "blue note" of their Daimler Benz, fuel-injection engines, was transmitting its ominous message to the ground. It was a chilling spectacle.'

Lucas and the others would fly these elderly Hurricanes against the hordes of Bf 109Fs for a month before the first Spitfires began to filter through from the carriers. It was a daunting interlude Lucas would never forget. 'It taught us what the pilots had been enduring every day during the last, few, tortuous months. Visions of another Crete began to unsettle our sleep.'

Unfortunately, Ron Chaffe's sojourn on Malta was brief. Just twenty-four hours after landing on the Island he failed to return from his first Hurricane sortie. Intent on achieving his first kill, he chased a Bf 109 out to sea but failed to notice his attackers and he was forced to bail out. He was last seen in his dinghy a few miles south of Delimara Point, but a search proved fruitless. The 27-year-old pilot, who was from Bristol, where he had once worked for a firm of insurance brokers in the city, left a widow, Betty Joan Chaffe.

With Malta's force of Hurricanes reduced to just thirty-two operational aircraft, another 'Club Run' to bolster the Island's defence with more Spitfires was imperative. 'Spotter II' would go ahead after the Spitfires' defective fuel tanks were repaired and this time tested, with an expert being flown out from Britain and involving the cannibalisation of one other Spitfire for spares. On 6 March the fifteen Vbs were put aboard *Eagle*, which sailed from Gibraltar, with *Argus* and her embarked Fulmars for fleet protection, escorted by the battleship *Malaya*, the light anti-aircraft cruiser *Hermione* and nine destroyers.

Squadron Leader Stanley Bernard Grant, had joined 249 Squadron at Takali (where the squadron personnel were known as 'Takalites') as a supernumerary squadron leader and had taken command of the squadron. Born on 31 May 1919, and educated at Charterhouse, Grant had entered the RAF College Cranwell in January 1937 as a flight cadet and graduated in December 1938 with a permanent commission. At the outbreak of war, he was serving on 65 Squadron at Hornchurch. Off Calais on 26 May 1940, he had claimed a Bf 110 destroyed. Next day he was awarded a half share in a Do 17 'probable' and a Bf 110 'probably destroyed'. Grant claimed a Bf 109 on 9 July but it was unconfirmed.

Twenty-two-year-old Flight Lieutenant Norman Carter MacQueen, one of his flight commanders, had been flown to Gibraltar to lead the newly arrived pilots to Malta. Born in

Walsall, he had joined the RAF as an aircraftman 2nd class at Padgate on 10 September 1939.

The next few weeks would prove unlucky for some of the thirteen newly arrived pilots, who had made the voyage on the *Cape Hawke* and thence from Gibraltar to the flying off point for Malta. Pilot Officer Peter Alfred Nash, 20, who was born in Barnes three days before Christmas 1921, was from Beckenham in Kent and had worked on the staff of *The Times* before he joined the RAF in 1940. In January 1942 'Pete' had left 609 Squadron having shot down two Bf 109s, damaged a Fw 190 and three Bf 109s, and had 'probably destroyed' a Fw 190, during sweeps over France. On 10 March, now with 249 Squadron, he became the first Spitfire pilot to make a claim over Malta and was subsequently awarded a Bf 109F 'probable'.

Pilot Officer Ioannis Agorastos 'Johnny' Plagis had volunteered for the RAF in 1940 and was only accepted after Greece had joined the Allies late that same year. Born on 10 March 1919 at Gadzema, Southern Rhodesia, the son of Greek immigrants, he had been sent to England in 1941, where he was classed as 'Above Average' at the end of his pilot training. Sergeants Raymond Brown Hesselyn RNZAF and 23-year-old Virgil Paul 'Bren' Brennan DFM RAAF would begin a friendship that would result in their later collaboration on *Spitfires over Malta* with journalist Henry Bateson that would be published in London and Sydney in 1943.

Flying Officer Norman William Lee was born in Willesden in north-west London on 10 April 1919 to parents who would have four children. In 1937 Norman attended Clare College, the second oldest of Cambridge's thirty-one colleges. Leaving in 1938, he joined the RAF Volunteer Reserve, although it was not until 1940 that he was called up to commence his training. Awarded his 'wings' on 27 November 1940, he was promoted to pilot officer, followed, in December with promotion to flying officer. In 1941 he volunteered to fly Sea Hurricanes in the Merchant Ship Fighter Unit (MSFU) close by the River Mersey at RAF Speke in Liverpool. In November Norman began a brief period on 276 (Air Sea Rescue) Squadron.

This was soon followed by a posting to RAF Perranporth, Cornwall, to join 66 Squadron flying long-range Spitfire IIs, which were fitted with an extra 30-gallon fuel tank in their starboard wing. While on 66 Squadron Norman Lee got to know 'Laddie' Lucas, who was then a flight commander, and Daddo-Langlois. They would all meet again on 249 Squadron on Malta, and they would serve with distinction. Lucas, who in June 1942 was promoted to command the squadron, said that Lee's 'rather diffident approach cloaked more than his fair share of purpose and resolve'. In time Lucas would make Lee and 'Daddo-L' his flight commanders. 'It was to two Englishmen of solid worth and ability that I turned for my flight commanders,' he wrote. 'Norman Lee and Raoul Daddo-Langlois, two well-educated products of the British public school system, became the linchpins in the team on whom I could always depend. They quickly gained the respect of their overseas comrades. Authority came easily to them.'

Twenty-three-year-old Sergeant Robert James Sim RNZAF of Mairoa, Auckland, New Zealand, had been a costing clerk on the Cook Hospital Board at Gisborne before enlisting. He had already flown twenty-nine operations on 130 Squadron in 1941 and would fly nine sorties on 249 Squadron before joining

185 Squadron, flying a further forty-one ops (including an ASR mission), before joining 616 Squadron on 29 October 1942 and flying eighteen operations with them.

On 616 Squadron also came Flight Lieutenant Philip Whaley Ellis 'Nip' Heppell DFC. He had been one of 'the Flying Heppells', the name that the local press duly dubbed the family of aviators from Newcastle upon Tyne. 'Nip's father had been a reconnaissance pilot in the First World War. Between the wars, he was a founder member of Newcastle Aero Club, where he taught 'Nip' and sister Rhoda, who became a wartime ferry pilot in the Air Transport Auxiliary, how to fly.

In order to take off from *Eagle*'s short flight deck, the Spitfire needed take-off flaps. However, the Spitfire's pneumatically operated flaps had only one setting of 85 degrees (drag flap for landing). The solution was to wedge the flaps at a 25-degree setting with a wooden wedge. Once safely airborne, the flaps could be lowered to drop the wedges and then raised again. To counter the prevalent dusty conditions that they would encounter on the island, they had the large Vokes filter under the nose, which created more drag and lowered the aircraft performance.

On 7 March, after the fifteen Spitfires were flown off the carriers and met their escort they began their return to Gibraltar. With Squadron Leader Grant at the head of the formation in one of the Spitfires, they were guided to Malta by seven Blenheim bombers. All the Spitfires reached Malta safely but the enemy, aware of the Spitfires' long flight to the island, and their arrival, timed a raid on Takali to take place as they were on the ground refuelling.

'The Spitfires came waggling their wings as if to say "OK boys, we're here",' wrote an RAF sergeant manning a fire tender on one of the airfields that day. 'But that very same evening the gen went round that a big plot was building up over Sicily and within half an hour or so we were to see that "Jerry" really meant business. Standing at a vantage point in the village of Zurrieq, I saw the first waves of "88"s coming all the way over the island. They dived down on Takali, where the whole batch of Spits had landed. We tried to count them as they came in, but it was an utter impossibility. Straight down they went, belting rounds up like nothing on earth and the tracers filled the sky before it really got dark. If things weren't so serious, one could have called it a lovely sight. The din was terrific and Takali seemed to be ablaze from end to end. The lads would shout that some gun or other had stopped firing, and the crew had been knocked out. But no; they've started again, pushing up rounds harder than ever. This time "Jerry" seemed to be under orders to finish the place and, by hell, he tried his best.'

At 1020 hours on 10 March seven Spitfires of 249 Squadron were scrambled for their first combat sorties from Malta to meet an incoming raid by three Ju 88s escorted by Bf 109s. The Spitfires and a dozen Hurricanes made this the largest number of fighters the island had been able to put in the air for some weeks. At 1037 hours, eighteen enemy aircraft, including three Ju 88s, crossed the coast and dropped bombs on Luqa airfield. Between 1050 and 1115 hours four Spitfires jumped the escorting Bf 109s. 'Nip' Heppell of 249 Squadron claimed the Malta Spitfires' first kill. 'Nip's victim was Bf 109F 'Black II' of 8/JG 53, the 'Pik As'

('Ace of Spades') Jagdgeschwader, piloted by Feldwebel Heinz Rahlmeier, who was killed.

Adding to 249 Squadron's score during the late morning of Tuesday, 10 March, Pete Nash and 'Johnny' Plagis (on this, his 23rd birthday) each claimed a Bf 109F probably destroyed. Further enemy raids were made throughout the rest of that afternoon. At 1640 hours eight Hurricanes of 242 Squadron and four Spitfires on 249 Squadron were scrambled from Takali to intercept incoming Ju 88s and Bf 109s. Three of the Hurricanes scored hits on two of the Ju 88s but one Hurricane was shot down and the Australian pilot killed.

From 249 Squadron, Norman MacQueen damaged the wing of a Ju 88 and Flying Officer 'Buck' Buchanan damaged another Junkers; both bombers jettisoning their bomb loads into the sea off Filfla, an uninhabited islet south of Malta. Then when Bf 109s counter-attacked, 'Laddie' Lucas claimed one 'damaged'. Raoul Daddo-Langlois, too, claimed a 'damaged' having seen pieces fly off a 109 when he had fired at it. Daddo-Langlois would survive a head-on collision with a Bf 109 on 20 April. He crash-landed. Ten days later he and Lucas were flown to Gibraltar on a transport aircraft to lead back part of another new batch of Spitfires.

The Spitfire flown by 20-year-old Australian Pilot Officer Kenric Newton Lathrop Murray was hit by Kommandeur of II/JG 3, Hauptmann Karl-Heinz Krahl, who claimed a Spitfire at 1710 hours. Murray bailed out over Ta'Zuta, on the island's south coast, but his parachute failed to open fully. Badly injured on landing, he died later of multiple injuries in hospital. On a search for Murray, 'Buck' Buchanan was jumped by a Bf 109 and his Spitfire was badly shot up, forcing him to land at Takali with many small shrapnel wounds to his legs. He was hospitalised for four days, followed by nine days off flying.

Over Grand Harbour on Wednesday, 11 March, Stanley Grant probably destroyed a Bf 109. Norman Lee on 249 Squadron flew his first action this day without making any contact and he flew four times during the following days. On the 18th he made his first claim. In the early evening a large raid of twenty-four Ju 88s with a large fighter escort had begun bombing the airfields, and six Hurricanes and four Spitfires were scrambled to intercept. Lee fired at the Messerschmitts without success, but also shot at, and claimed a Ju 88 as 'damaged', using up all his ammunition in the process. A week later he made his second claim; this time for a Ju 87 as 'probably destroyed', noting excitedly in his logbook 'Hundreds of bloody Stukas'.

At 0935 hours on the morning of Saturday, 14 March, a Ju 88 shadowed by a pair of Bf 109s making a reconnaissance from east to west was fired on by anti-aircraft guns on the Island. The Ju 88 and one of the Bf 109s, piloted by Leutnant Walter Seiz, were damaged and the 109 collided with the other Messerschmitt piloted by Heinrich Blum of III/JG 3, who was killed. At 1115 hours Norman MacQueen scored his first victory flying from Malta, when, over Gozo, he saw strikes on the fuselage of a Bf 109F piloted by Unteroffizier Adolf Jennerich of 7/JG 53, who bailed out. Jennerich and Seiz were rescued later by a Dornier Do 24 flying boat escorted by twenty-nine Bf 109s.

Next day, Pilot Officer Jeffery West was awarded a half share in damaging a Ju 88. On 8 April West attacked a Ju 88 head-on and saw strikes on its cockpit. He then turned onto the tail of a Bf 109F and closed, firing all his ammunition and causing black smoke to appear; this may have been the 6/JG 53 aircraft flown by Leutnant Hans Müller, which crashed into the sea off Valletta. Müller was later picked up by ASR from Sicily.

On 18 March MacQueen shot down 22-year-old Leutnant Kurt Lauinger of Stab III/JG 53, who bailed out north of St Paul's Bay and broke his left leg. His second Bf 109 he shot down on 22 March. On 4 April MacQueen destroyed a Ju 88, another on the 10th and a third on 20 April near Takali. The following day he destroyed a Bf 109F and damaged a Ju 88 near Filfla south of Malta. Added to this impressive score were two half shares; for a Bf 109 destroyed and one damaged, on 14 April. On 1 May he was to claim a share in the destruction of another Bf 109 to take his tally to seven, two shared destroyed and four 'damaged'.

On 20 March, meanwhile, a five-hour raid began soon after 0800, involving about twenty Ju 88s, which arrived at intervals under fighter escort. At 0805 hours, at 10,000ft, four Spitfires on 249 Squadron led by 'Laddie' Lucas provided cover for twelve Hurricanes intercepting the fighter escort. Patrolling at 11,000ft, 249 Squadron observed six Bf 109s heading north over Filfla. The Spitfires, with a 2,000ft height advantage, peeled off and made for the enemy aircraft. One of the Spitfires was piloted by 'Buck' McNair. 'We got our scramble call and soared up to 10,000ft. We were just turning down into sun when "Daddy" called on the R/T that there were 109s at 6 o'clock – behind and above. We had time to turn around and break into them and I screamed round to the right and found I had turned too quickly and the Huns were still some distance away. I eased up a bit on my turn, for if I had continued it, I would have put my belly to a 109, so I straightened up and he would have to turn his belly to me. He did and I let off a great squirt at him. The 109 went into a spiral dive and looking round and finding no other Huns about, I went down after it, having no trouble in following. I waited my chance to fire again and got a good burst into it. I saw hits on the starboard wing, pieces came off but he still didn't take any evasive action. Just continued with the spiral dive.

'Down to 3,000ft I started clobbering the 109 all over. I emptied my cannon and continued with the machine guns. Oil and glycol from its cooling system poured out. The white glycol looked beautiful streaming out into the clear air; it was a really lovely day. Looking round there was still nobody behind me. The German now pulled up over the roofs of Valletta, reached the sea and crashed into it.' It was the Canadian's first victory flying from Malta. The body of Unteroffizier Josef Fankhauser of 7/JG 53 was recovered on the shores of Sicily seven weeks later.

'It was a matter of a few weeks before our 16 Spitfires were non-existent,' wrote 'Johnny' Plagis: 'We at all times fought the enemy with great odds against us. If four of us were airborne and we encountered twenty enemy fighters and bombers we considered it a reasonable fight. Most of our pilots had been killed in action and almost all the aircraft damaged or completely lost.'

Among the losses was his good friend, 21-year-old Pilot Officer Douglas Cecil Leggo, who was killed on 20 March, probably falling to the guns of Leutnant Ernst Klager or Leutnant Hermann Neuhoff, both of III/JG 53, who each claimed a Spitfire within three minutes of each other. Anti-aircraft guns also engaged, claiming one Ju 88 and a Bf 109 destroyed and four bombers 'damaged'.

Lance Bombardier Stan Fraser of the 4th Heavy Anti-Aircraft Regiment, who witnessed the demise of 'Dougie' Leggo at Hagar Qim, wrote in his diary: 'Before breakfast we witnessed a dog-fight above our site, which resulted in a rather sickening start to the day's activities. One of our Spitfires had one of its tail fins practically shot off and the pilot lost control of the plane. It fell like a falling leaf, describing small circles, with its nose downwards, and several times it seemed as though the pilot had managed to straighten out into a glide, but no – on it came until, just over 100ft from the ground, the pilot bailed out. He was too late; his parachute just billowed until the cords were taut, when he reached the ground about the same time as the plane.'

Leggo was born on 13 July 1919 at Western Cape, South Africa, and raised in Portuguese East Africa, where his father was employed on the Beira and Mashonaland Railway. As a boy, he became enthralled with Malta when he read a book about the Great Siege. Before enlistment he had been a gunsmith with a firm in Bulawayo. He and 'Johnny' Plagis were both fluent in Shona (a Bantu language) and would use it to communicate in the air, which of course completely baffled any German trying to listen in. Leggo's Spitfire was called *Eva IV* in honour of his wife in Salisbury, Rhodesia, and it carried a very rude message in Shona – *M'Boriako Hitler from Jay and Doug* ('Jay' being Plagis, whose Spitfire was also inscribed with the words: *My Darling Kay II* below each side of the cockpit – Kay being his sister).

Plagis blamed himself for the death of his friend, as he had tried to persuade him not to fly when he thought that he was not fit to do so. He swore that he would shoot down ten German aircraft to even the score.

'The enemy attacked in strength, never less than three times a day,' recalled 'Nip' Heppell. 'The pattern seldom varied. Stukas and Junkers 88s escorted by yellow-nosed 109s carrying out dive-bombing attacks on the airfields at Hal Far, Luqa and Takali, and, of course, Grand Harbour itself. The number of attacking aircraft varied from forty to over one hundred, and we seldom could oppose them with more than a handful of Spitfires. Because of the huge numbers of Luftwaffe raiders often the few Spitfires we had could enter the fray, fire a few bursts, and depart virtually unnoticed.

'On 8 April just two of us took off to intercept more than a hundred bombers escorted by a similar number of 109s. We were in as much danger from our own gunners as from the enemy because they met each incoming raid with a ferocious barrage of AA fire. Leading this pair of Spitfires into the fray, with our gunners banging away at the bombers, I collected a direct hit from ground fire and my Spitfire simply disintegrated. I fell about 7,000ft before regaining consciousness.'

'We were having a spot of luck with the bombers,' wrote Don McLeod 'until "Nip" Heppell was chasing an "88" in the barrage and we saw him open fire on the "88". Then suddenly the Spitfire was no more. "Nip" had received a direct hit from a heavy shell and it had blown his plane to bits. It was a very fortunate thing that he was blown out of the cockpit. "Nip" remembered nothing of pulling his ripcord. He came to while floating downward with bombs falling all around him. He landed in a shell hole and spent many, many hard minutes watching bombs fall all around as he lay unable to move. He was rescued by the gunners of nearby gun emplacements and spent many, many days in the hospital. It was one of the miracles of the island that he was able to live.'

'Nip' was awarded a Ju 88 destroyed and another 'damaged'. After some weeks in the hospital, he was evacuated to Egypt by air on 30 April. He then had a spell as both ferry and test pilot in the Middle East, before returning to Malta at the end of 1942. He found the situation much changed.

'The island was now secure and it was our turn to go on the offensive – fighter sweeps over Sicily and a fair amount of train bashing. Early in 1943 I bailed out, off Kalafrana, because of a bomb hang-up and landed in the sea, where I was soon picked up. I was promoted to Squadron Leader to command 229 Squadron and shortly afterwards was clobbered by the pilot of a Focke-Wulf 190 with a remarkable deflection shot. I was hit in the chest and the backside, but managed to stagger back to Malta, where I put my Spitfire down safely and was taken to hospital. After sick leave in England, I took the opportunity to fly as "Johnnie" Johnson's wingman on fighter sweeps over France. Then I was given command of 118 Squadron.'

On the afternoon of 10 April, six Spitfires and ten Hurricanes intercepted a large force of around eighty Ju 88s and Ju 87s attacking Malta's airfields and the Grand Harbour. Norman Lee on 249 Squadron claimed one Ju 88 damaged and another shot down while it was attacking Takali airfield, the bomber breaking up in the air with the gun turret breaking away from the aircraft and landing with the dead gunner still inside it onto the airfield. Although also claimed by the airfield gun battery,

Norman believed that this was his victory and he kept the dead gunner's cap as a souvenir. The following day, along with Pete Nash, Lee went to the military hospital at Imtarfa to visit some of their injured pilots on the squadron. Whilst there they saw several of the German aircrew who had been shot down and were also receiving medical attention.

On the afternoon of Monday, 20 April on the way to dispersal, pilots on 249 Squadron had to jump into a crater at Takali as bombs fell around them. Junkers Ju 88s screamed overhead and the pilots raced to get into their Spitfires before the next attack. Eleven Spitfires were scrambled from Takali and five from Luqa. 'Woody' Woodhall, ground control officer on Malta, called up Flight Lieutenant 'Mac' MacQueen, who was leading, and said that there was a big plot building up but it was taking time to come south. 'Keep your present angels and save your gravy. I will tell you when to come in.'

Group Captain Alfred Basil 'Woody' Woodhall was born in South Africa on 9 January 1897. In August 1914 he was a lance corporal in the Witwatersrand Rifles but was appointed to a commission in the Royal Marines on 8 January 1916. He went to HQ 20 Group on 28 December 1939 and was posted to RAF Duxford on 12 March 1940 as controller, with the rank of wing commander. On Malta he was senior controller. Pilots had a fanatical faith in his controlling. It was a faith that gave them a completely unreasonable confidence when, one day in April, he had controlled 3 Spitfires and 4 Hurricanes against an enemy plot of 130 plus. And, it was he who organised and conducted the fighter defence of the Island before as well as after the Spitfires arrived.

The Spitfires 'stooged around' until 'Woody' gave them the word. Then they sailed in. 'Bren' Brennan destroyed a 109 and a Ju 88. 'Buck' McNair destroyed a Bf 109 and was awarded a Ju 88 'probable' and another 109 probably destroyed. Pilot Officer 'Bob' Sergeant destroyed a Ju 88 and Norman MacQueen claimed a Ju 88. 'Laddie' Lucas was awarded a 109 'damaged'. Sergeant John Lovett 'Junior' Tayleur's cockpit canopy was shattered by cannon fire from a 109 that had attacked from head-on and he was badly cut about the face and bleeding freely. Despite this he soldiered on and probably destroyed a Stuka before landing with wheels and flaps down at Takali, where he was immediately whisked off to hospital. In another head-on attack, Raoul Daddo-Langlois observed a 109 coming straight at him, with guns blazing. 'Daddo-L' returned fire and held his bead on the enemy fighter. Neither pilot was willing to give way and with a closing speed approaching 600mph the two fighters collided, the tip of the Spitfire's starboard wing hitting the root of the 109's wing, severing it completely and sending the 109 spiralling earthwards. Only the outer section of the Spitfire's wing had been severed. Daddo-Langlois landed at speed until he retracted the undercarriage to prevent an overshoot and then leapt from the cockpit just as four 109s were beginning an attack across the airfield, their guns blazing, and threw himself into the nearest slit trench. He was covered in dust but otherwise unharmed.

At 1700 hours, alerted by the approach of another big raid, Sergeant Ray Hesselyn and Flying Officer 'Buck' Buchanan on 249 Squadron, who had watched the events of the late afternoon unfold from the ground, were scrambled to provide airfield defence for Takali, flying out to sea to provide cover for the returning Spitfires. As they climbed to 10,000ft, glancing behind, suddenly Hesselyn saw four 109s coming down on him. Three of them overshot. The fourth made his turn too wide and he got inside him. The New Zealander was slightly below when he attacked from 200 yards. He kept firing as he was determined to make certain of him. 'He caught fire, black smoke poured out, he rolled on his back and went into a vertical dive and straight into the drink,' he wrote later.

In his excitement Hesselyn had forgotten to look behind him but luckily none of the other 109s had dived on him. 'Woody' now reported that the 88s were diving on Takali, and Hesselyn pulled up to 10,000ft. The next instant the 88s were diving past the nose of his Spitfire and the other Spitfire pilots were coming down from above to attack them. Hesselyn picked out one and went for him. As he pressed his gun button, the rear gunner opened fire. Hesselyn had fired for about a second when his port cannon packed up but, concentrating on the 88's starboard engine and wing root, he could see his starboard cannon shells hitting and the Junkers was well ablaze when it crashed.

Two days later, on 22 April, Jeffery West, in another aircraft, courageously tried to save 21-year-old Pilot Officer Frank James Jemmett, who nonetheless was shot down by Bf 109s at the end of an aerodrome defence sortie with 'Junior' Crist. Jemmett, who was from Fortis Green, Middlesex, crash-landed near Rabat, slithered into a stone wall and the engine caught fire. Although after a great deal of difficulty he was pulled from the burning plane by some army personnel, he died later in hospital. At the end of the month, West was evacuated to Egypt after falling ill. On 24 August, after the fall of Sicily, now a squadron leader on

103 MU and flying a Spitfire IX, he shot down a long-range Bf 109G into the sea off the North African coast.

Seventeen crated Spitfires intended for Malta had arrived in Gibraltar harbour in SS *Queen Victoria* on 13 March. The plan was for *Eagle* and *Argus* to sail in company for Operation 'Picket I' to ferry them to Malta. Don McLeod and his fellow Spitfire pilots waited for their movement orders, which could only take place once their precious Spitfires were assembled from their crates on board *Eagle*, while *Argus* embarked Sea Hurricanes for protection.

'Due to the close proximity of Spanish territory and the tremendous amount and number of Spanish workers,' McLeod noted in his diary 'one might well have been immediately aware of what might have happened had not we all been cautious and all activity as to future endeavours aboard ship and otherwise been kept secret. At night, during dismal, dark hours, when all else was still, special crews of men lifted from the hold of the ship the crates which carried our trusty Spitfires and deposited them on the docks of Gibraltar. In the dark of night these crates from the *Queen Victoria*, but relentlessly, were put aboard the *Eagle* and stowed below deck.

'During and after this operation a special crew of mechanics, aircraftsmen, projector specialists, engine-men, hydraulic men, all carefully selected from combat crews in England, were flown to Gibraltar for the special purpose of assembling these aircraft within the confines of the innards of the carrier. In other words, in a very confined space, those now had the sole responsibility of putting sixteen aircraft together from the crates, adapting long-range tanks to the same and making sure that when a pilot flew their particular aircraft for the first time from the 430ft deck of the carrier, of which only 400ft could be used, no minor detail would be incorrect, as one slip meant death for the pilot. Never in the history of aviation have men been entrusted with such a job and never have pilots depended so much on ground men for the success of their individual accomplishments. It is hard for individuals not connected with sea or land fighting to realize just what this meant. An average fighter plane, not equipped for sea flying, but built especially for land defence as our Spitfires were, would require a minimum of 800ft for take-off. They would at any time during the operation of their flight try to land at an airfield so designated if any minor trouble would occur.

'We were to take off at high dawn in the Mediterranean, approximately 700 miles from the island of Malta and close to 400 miles from Gibraltar. Had there been any mechanical failure such as oil pressure, failure of long-range gas tanks to work, or propeller trouble, no matter how minor, or had even one wheel failed to retract entirely, it would have meant failure for the aircraft to reach its destination. The pilot, therefore, had he been airborne, had three choices, the first to try to land on the carrier, which would have been utterly impossible, due to the fact that we had no restraining hooks to catch the landing wire. The second was to bail out into the sea and hope to be picked up by an approaching warship, and the third was to fly into neutral territory and be interned for the duration. None of the three offered much consolation for the pilot.

'On the evening of 19 March, we left our chubby little home on the *Queen Victoria* and boarded *Eagle*. The crews of the aircraft carrier knew nothing of our enterprise. The exact plan was known only by 16 men. I imagine many rumours and thoughts flew through the ship, but I know from their remarks that they didn't realize just what was going on. We were assigned two pilots to a stateroom, sharing then with Royal Navy pilots, who were already aboard the *Eagle*. Needless to say, they did not entirely agree with our pushing in on their homes and we were relegated to the top bunks. As the navy would say – "top side".

'Just before dawn, we steamed majestically into the Mediterranean and when I looked out in the morning, I saw a sight which made my heart sink. There we were, 16 pilots and 16 Spitfires, being escorted by the entire British Mediterranean fleet, right out into enemy territory. It was a sight and feeling that can be felt only upon being present. The huge battleship *Malaya*, which was in the very near future to write history as one of the six leading battleships, was therefore our protection. Cruisers by the numbers, destroyers by the many, corvettes and every type ship imaginable including two other carriers lay all along our route. A truly great naval armada. I remember remarking to "Jimmie", "they sure must want to save that island."

'At dusk the fleet loud speaker system went into operation and as we stood by, every ship in the fleet received the same message. The Admiral of the fleet aboard the *Malaya* called attention and told every man in the fleet this story: "We are glad in a small way to play our part in one of the most daring episodes in aviation history. We are carrying aboard the *Eagle* sixteen fighter pilots and sixteen Spitfires, who tomorrow, at a designated time will fly from that carrier to the island of Malta. That word Malta is a symbol in our age. I wish to give those men Godspeed and good luck." I think I have never heard a more effective speech.

'Out of sight of land, going over the pouncing waves of the Mediterranean, wherever we looked, our eyes met those brave navy men and yet they considered themselves but a minor part of our operation. They were carrying us much farther into enemy territory than safety could actually afford them to, but they had to or we could not have reached Malta. (You should have been there and have seen the patience and courage on the part of the naval personnel.)

'I arrived back in my stateroom with "Jimmie" to find my naval friend resting on the top bunk. There was nothing they wouldn't do for us. Then, the wondering as to when events would start unfolding themselves started.

'Just prior to retiring on the night of 20 March, "Jimmie" and I were called up to the captain's quarters. As we had just left the Eagle Squadron, he wondered if we had ever seen the plaque that had been sent by him to the Eagles from Singapore. Naturally we had, which made him very happy. Then he added a little humorous touch to what proved to be a very enjoyable evening. After we had a short talk with him, we retired to normal life. We were not used to hanging around too much "braid" and we retired at a fairly early hour. Although we had no idea of the time we would take off, we imagined that it would be at dawn. Without closing our eyes and smoking as many cigarettes as the time limit would allow, we awaited the knock on the door which would start us getting into the state of readiness.

'Four a.m., Saturday, 21st March, the knock, light as it was, sounded like the pounding of a hammer on a brass bell. It brought us out one and all from our sleepy dreaming as to what might happen and put us into a tumult of reality. A quick shave, up to the mess room for a hot cup of tea and a biscuit, then off to the ready room.

'It was dark and dismal. The sun hadn't yet come over the line of clouds on the horizon. The wind was howling and the carrier tossed to-and-fro like a match box. Then began the process of bringing the Spitfires from below deck to the top. And while we went through the carefully laid plans for the last time, the "Spits" were deposited on the upper deck of the carrier. We had been told over and over again, and once more it was repeated: "Don't panic!" This can be done. If you get lost, fly a set course and you will strike land and then fly a set course and you will hit Malta. So easily said but … "Do not fire unless you have to, obey all signals from the carrier, and look on take-off."

'We were given our maps and were just ready to depart when the radio operator rushed into the room and handed a message to "Jumbo" which he decoded and read to us. "The airfield on Malta has been bombed to shambles. Land at the only other one. If that is gone when you arrive, make the best of your situation." We couldn't have had anything more to build our morale. This was the crowning glory. Even if we got there, what then?

'Carefully depositing our toothbrushes, a couple of spare packs of cigarettes, and other small incidentals we knew we would need, in the empty gun compartments of our plane (only cannon were loaded, machine guns empty to save weight), we stowed small amounts of candy in the cockpits and we in "A" Flight took our parachutes, stowing them in the cockpits and went back to the ready room and awaited further orders.

'By now the sun had risen above the clouds, putting a more cheerful aspect on the scene. The chopping of the waves seemed to have subsided and the wind was blowing as we desired. For our operation to be a success it was necessary to have a wind of 30mph. This, coupled with the forward speed of the carrier, approximately 27mph, allowed us to make the remaining 35 to 40mph on the 400ft deck run of the carrier. If we did not obtain flying speed in the short run, obviously the aircraft would tumble into the waves and be run over by the carrier. If a pilot could possibly have gotten out, which was a very remote possibility, a destroyer was assigned to follow the carrier for such happenings. At 7 am the wind was considered correct and we were told to stand by our own aircraft.

'At 0715 we were still standing by. At 0730 we started engines, getting more nervous by the minute. At 0731 we were told to cut engines. Valuable gas was being wasted. At 0745 we started engines again.'

'A' Flight's Blenheim escort was late and that for 'B' Flight did not arrive so only the eight pilots of 'A' Flight and a ninth flown by Flight Sergeant John William 'Jack' Yarra RAAF (also known as 'Slim'), who had some experience flying Hurricanes on 232 Squadron, were flown off. The 20-year-old Queenslander was a volunteer for anywhere out of England – not because of the lack of activity against the enemy but he simply did not like the cold weather and the pebbled expanses that supposedly were beaches. Yarra was packed to leave in two hours, anticipating more activity over Malta. He would not be disappointed. But in February, when he had been despatched to Gibraltar aboard the *Cape Hawke* hoping to leave on 'Spotter', the operation was aborted and he had returned to Gibraltar.

The Spitfires were to form the nucleus of a re-formed 126 Squadron alongside 249 Squadron, which was equipped with the Spitfires that had arrived on 7 March. However, 249 Squadron had lost a number of aircraft over the previous few days and so the two units had to share the newly arrived Spitfires.

'"Jumbo" was pushed into starting position,' wrote Don McLeod. 'I saw the man with the flag. I could see the aircraft shaking as if it were wanting to jump. The flag descended and his plane jumped from the start and then seemed to slow down. Actually, it was just the lull of the start and the after effect. Our CO rolled down the deck slowly. To me he seemed to have no speed at all. As he reached the end of the deck, I saw his plane hover for a second in the air and then disappear downward from view.'

'"Tim" Johnston, who would be going off second from last, couldn't see anything from where he was either so he watched the expressions of the airmen, and after what seemed a long interval, he saw them break into smiles. Next instant a very small Spitfire staggered into view about half a mile in front of the ship. Johnston heard afterwards that Gracie very nearly "hit the drink"; not surprising, he'd only flown a Spit once before. Bolton went to the other extreme and almost stall turned into the sea as he crossed the bows but he managed to regain control. All the rest were normal.'

It had been a hollow feeling for 'Mac' McLeod to know that he was the second from Gracie to go. 'As I watched him the second plane had been pushed into the starting position. The same roar; the same movements. I still looked once more for "Jumbo" and no sight of him. The flag went down and the same way, before the weather over Malta deteriorated and *Eagle* had to return to Gibraltar with eight Spitfires still on board. slowly, slowly he got to the end, but instead of doing the same as "Jumbo", he pulled the stick back hard and his plane shot into the air on one wing and disappeared from my view as I was being pushed into the starting line. He appeared to be in a very embarrassing position. No sight of "Jumbo" as yet. I remember, out of the corner of my eye, seeing the deck controller jump on my wing and shout meaningless words. He smiled, patted me on the back. I know he was trying to reassure me, but I was beyond that stage. I again saw that same flag.

'My engine was wide open, brakes full set. I was getting every ounce of power; every possible bit of full momentum was being gathered that was within my means of getting. Down came the flag, off came my brakes and down that same deck I went. Halfway down I passed the main section. It looked to me like I was slowing down. I didn't see how it was possible that I could fly. I could not quit now. Had I tried to stop I would have gone into the drink. I had no alternative left. I must go on. I must get off that deck or I was a gone pigeon. I passed off the deck and seemed to hover. I felt that feeling of emptiness. I know that I was in the air. One-fifth of a second would decide whether I would fly or swim. I hung in the air, seemed to settle momentarily and then received that wonderful feeling of being airborne. I had made it. With a deep sigh I said, "it's over."

'I had no time to look for anyone else. I picked my wheels up. They worked. I checked my propeller. It worked; I climbed to 1,000ft and tried my extra tank. It worked and was I happy! My oil pressure was good. My plane felt fine. I was as happy as I have ever been in my life, but not quite as happy as when I looked in front and there in the distance were two Spitfires.

'During the time that I was busily checking my instruments, etc and seemingly trying to keep my new-found buddies in front of me, five other Spitfires had winged and were safely off the carrier. Our plan had been to climb to 8,000ft in a slow circle to form up and fly a set course for Malta. By the time we had reached our altitude, all eight aircraft which composed "A" Flight were in fairly close formation. "Jumbo" set course for Malta and the rest of us tagged along in our own positions. My last look at the fleet made me feel like a chicken just leaving its mother. It had been a haven of safety and a refuge until now. And now I felt pitifully small and weak without it. There was nothing it could do for me, or anything I could do for it. Having been previously warned that there would be no radio communications interplane, quietness reigned supreme in that Mediterranean blue sky.

'Just after we had set course, a plane slid upside of me, waggled its wings and then it slipped off to my right and once again "Jimmie" and I were together. It did not seem so far back, not more than a year ago, that "Jimmie" and I met when we joined the Royal Air Force. "Jimmie" Peck was a 19-year-old kid, as American a boy as any boy could be. Outstandingly brave and afraid of nothing. He was small where I was large, slight where I was heavy, dark where I was fair and quiet where I was boisterous. "Jimmie" and I had been through the war up until now together, side by side. We had joined the Royal Air Force together, had flown in England together and went to the same training school for three long weeks of gruelling training. We had shared our first leave together and joined the Second American Eagle Squadron together.

'After flying for a little over an hour we were able to pick up in the distance, Galite Island off the north coast of Africa near the Tunisian border. As we approached that island, the flight leader gave a pre-arranged signal and we closed into a tighter, but more defensive, battle formation for just beyond Galite Island, just past the beautiful cities of Tunis and Bizerte, lay the island of Pantelleria. Intelligence had informed us that we would have to be aware of Me 109s, as well as Italian fighters based there. As we flew over Tunis and Bizerte and looked down into the beautiful Tunisian cities, it was hard to realize or visualize, had we any way of knowing, that in just one short year all hell would be raging; in one of the greatest battles of World War II. For it was through this tiny, beautiful-looking section of Africa that the Allied armies routed the trapped army of Rommel. Standing past Tunis, a small majestic island came into view on our left. It was Pantelleria. It looked so beautiful with its green grass stretching out into the blue water with many houses that dotted the island. We could easily distinguish the airfield and kept a close eye on it, but no aircraft took off to intercept us.

'Shortly before sighting the island, I had run out of gas in my long-range tank and had spent an anxious moment transferring to my main tank. A gasp in the engine let me know that gas was being fed to the engine immediately upon transfer to my main tank and which now purred like a kitten.'

When 'Tim' Johnston had taxied out, he had waited for all the temperatures to reach the right marks, made sure the airscrew was in fine pitch, held the brakes for a moment as he opened up and then had let her go. He pushed the stick hard forward and the tail had come up at once. Then, now seeing where he was going, he had no difficulty in keeping the Spitfire straight. He aimed at the marker flag in the forward ack-ack position, or just to the right of it, and felt himself airborne a few yards before he ran out of deck. There was a violent eddy, like hitting a slipstream, as the Spitfire crossed the bows, but then it had settled down into normal though sluggish flight. He raised the undercart and watched nervously to see whether it would function properly, heard it click home and was relieved to see the red light showing that it had locked; that was one problem fewer. At 1,000ft the change over to the auxiliary tank had to be faced; he did it very carefully, thinking how silly he'd look if he jettisoned it by mistake – the two levers were adjacent – and he waited to see whether it was going to function. He knew nothing about the mechanism so he sat and called on his reserves of faith in things he didn't understand, and after half a minute he reckoned the danger period was over and he could relax; that was another problem fewer.

Glancing down at the fleet; even from 1,500ft, the ships seemed very widely spaced and astonishingly small; no wonder bombs miss he thought. As for landing on the *Eagle*, it was out of the question – like trying to land on a matchbox. The ships that before had seemed safe and friendly had suddenly become remote and inaccessible and he felt it was useless to look to them for help; they were in a different element and there was no more they could do for the Spitfire pilots. But 'Tim' and all the other pilots made it to the Island safely.

As they headed for Malta many thoughts had passed through 'Mac' McLeod's mind. 'How big was it? Would we be able to find it? Would the "Hun" be waiting for us? Just what awaited us at Malta?

'Presently in front of us there were bilious cumulus clouds which were a tip-off as to what lay underneath. We had previously been told that those clouds usually formed over the island during the day. We first sighted the island of Gozo, which lay directly beside Malta. A strange twist of fate made Gozo a neutral island; neutrality which was respected by both the Germans and the Italians at this time. The two islands jutted out of the water into small cliffs and locked seemingly like the trunks of two trees. Gozo is very small and Malta very large. The brownish look the islands gave against the blue Mediterranean and blue sky made a very pretty picture to the eye.

'We gradually lost altitude so that we were coming in practically on the deck. At this moment we could hear the CO calling Malta to let them know of our approach. We no sooner heard his voice than a smooth, even quiet voice came back on the radio warning us that Messerschmitt 109s and 110 twin-engine fighters were bombing the island and to beware. You could easily see smoke and dust rising from the bomb blasts as we came in.

'This was almost too good to be true. Were we to get a fight before we even landed? This truly was a fighter pilot's paradise. But no. We were immediately directed to Luqa airfield where we landed. It had been a long flight. I had been airborne four hours, which was unusually long for a Spitfire in those days. As we rolled to a stop on the bomb-battered runway we were flagged quickly to the end and then taxied off into a small wooded section about a quarter of a mile from the runway and the aircraft were parked. Jumping out I noticed how really stiff I was. My head ached from the tension and my back ached from the position. We immediately started spreading camouflage over our aircraft and took our few precious amounts of gear from the panels in which we had hidden them. The all-clear signal sounded from the raid and we were picked up in a truly dilapidated bus, which was lacking in practically everything except a motor. It was a dusty, dirty ride of about a half a mile to the so-called Mess, where a hot meal consisting of stew, hot tea and biscuits awaited us. Many of us complained about this meal. Little did we dream that in a few weeks hence we would be so glad to get one like it.

'In due time we had completed our "meal" and our good old rattletrap bus with worn-out tyres, few windows and a broken exhaust, which inside was adorned with many ecclesiastical prints and postcards of the Virgin Mary and Child, was waiting to transport us to the other airfield at Takali on the other side of the island. We wound our way from Luqa through the tiny Maltese streets and out into the open country as we made for the airfield, which was about eight miles away, never once failing to be amazingly impressed by the damage that had been done to the civilian homes and other non-military objects as we passed them. We also noticed that the one movie we passed in the town featured, when last opened, the new picture named *Ben Hur* of 1926 vintage.

'About halfway to our new field we saw a motorcycle, the rider lying prone across the street, apparently injured. We stopped the bus to administer what aid we could and had been there only five minutes when from out of the sky all hell seemed to break loose.

We were parked directly beside an artillery battery consisting of heavy guns and I don't think I ever heard anything make more noise than those babies. Looking in the direction of the onrushing procession in the sky we could see Ju 88s dropping bombs and diving on Takali, our new field destination, with monotonous regularity.'

'Tim' Johnston saw that there were eighteen in the wave and to him they looked like children sliding down a banister as they came down in a regularly spaced string. After the first waves there was a brief lull before another eighteen followed and repeated the same attack. He found it humiliating that there were no friendly fighters anywhere to be seen.

'In amongst the heavy bombers, you could see tiny specks shooting in and out', noted Don McLeod. 'These were Messerschmitt 109s. It was a sickening sight to see one and then another until 60 or 70 "88s" had dropped their bombs and headed for home. It was with pleasure that we saw two, hit by anti-aircraft fire, go spinning to the ground in flames. No matter how hard we looked we saw not one of our own planes airborne. The reason being that they had none. The ones we had just brought in were the only aircraft on the island.'

As soon as the all-clear signal rang, Don McLeod and his fellow pilots jumped into the bus and started roaring at 20mph to their new post. 'As we rolled along the so-called highway, dodging bomb holes, being very careful that we did not drive into any holes made by duds (unexploded bombs) we wended our way to the town of Rabat, overlooking Takali airfield. As we pulled up, we noticed a large crowd of people and smelled that burning powder and flesh smell which is so hard to misunderstand once you have smelled it. Getting out of the bus we noticed that the crowd was gathered in one spot.'

As the bus passed through a heavy stone gateway and pulled up before an imposing mansion, a wing commander met them, introduced himself as the station commander, apologised that he couldn't wait. Turning to his companion, said, 'Well Doc, are you feeling brave?' Both of them rode away on a motorbike.

'We soon discovered the reason for this,' said 'Tim' Johnston. 'They were going to recover and try to identify the bodies of the officers who had just been killed in the raid we'd been watching.'

The Point de Vue Hotel at Saqqajja, a popular venue for RAF personnel, had been hit by a 1,000kg bomb dropped short by a Ju 88 during the attack on Takali airfield.

'There was one chap I had known in California almost one and a half years before, who had gone to Malta and flown Hurricanes,' wrote Don McLeod sadly. 'Eddie Streets had finished his tour and was awaiting passage home. I was just hoping that I would get to see him before he left. But fate had been cruel because Eddie had been standing with four other pilots watching this raid when an "88" apparently jettisoned his bombs after being hit by anti-aircraft fire and one of them fell directly on where the boys were standing. The boys had received their passage early. Six officers had been blown to bits. We heard that one of the victims was Baker, formerly of 257.'

On that sickening Saturday afternoon, 21 March, Eddie Streets, who had once asked Princess Marina for a date, lost a leg and was blinded. He succumbed to his injuries in hospital. Two fellow officers on 126 Squadron, 26-year-old Flight

Lieutenant Cecil Harman Baker and 21-year-old Pilot Officer William Cardy Hollis Hallett, both suffered horrific deaths. So too did 26-year-old Flying Officer John Charles Mortimer-Booth and 28-year-old Flying Officer James Guerin RAAF of Wollongong, NSW, on 249 Squadron. Flight Lieutenant Arthur Amyand Victor Waterfield, a 32-year-old intelligence officer, and Dominic Ceci, an 84-year-old civilian, were killed outright. Five hundred airmen had to be evacuated and housed in Rabat and St Edwards College.

Flight Lieutenant 'Buck' McNair on 249 Squadron had a miraculous escape, having been thrown 20 or 30ft up a floor by the blast either through a door or through an opening at the turn of the staircase. 'When I came to, I didn't know where I was. I didn't feel I was dead, but I didn't feel whole. My eyes were open, but my jaws and chest didn't seem to be there ... I felt for my tin hat, then I started to be able to see just as if the sun was coming up after a great darkness. I rested myself. I felt carefully with my fingers and found that I had a face and a chest, so I felt better ... Heavy dust covered the bodies. I looked at them – studied them. One was headless, the head had been cut cleanly away from the top of the shoulders. I didn't see the head, but I could recognise the man by his very broad shoulders.

'I heard a moan, so I put my hand gently on the bodies to feel which of them was alive. One of them I noticed had a hole, more than a foot wide, right through the abdomen. Another's head was split wide open into two halves, from back to front, by a piece of shrapnel. The face had expanded to twice its size. I thought of shooting him with my revolver. As I felt for it, I heard "Bud" Connell's voice behind me. "Look at this mess!" I put my hand against the wall, but it slithered down it. It had seemed dry with all the dust, but when I took my hand away, I found it was covered with blood with bits of meat stuck to it – like at the butcher's when they're chopping up meat and cleaning up a joint. I turned to Bud. "For God's sake," I said, "don't come in here." Then I noticed that my battledress and trousers were torn and ripped ...'

'It brought home the meaning of war so close to us in this particular moment,' wrote Eddie Streets' buddy, Don McLeod. 'It let us know again, as war does, that this was not a plaything. We were not finished fighting this war until the war itself was over. One could never relax or take it easy at a place like this. But this would not stop us from fighting. It did nothing but encourage our appetites and it had taken a large toll in the morale of the boys that had been on the island prior to our arrival. It had not been so bad watching boys shot down in the air or get killed in measures that had involved their own skill against the other fellow, but to see six strapping young boys who had done their jobs, and done them well, be blown to eternity in one short second had hit everybody about the same.'

Pilot Officer Howard Coffin, who had been flying Hawker Hurricanes on 126 Squadron in defence of Malta for six months, and had suffered some head injuries on 9 March when he was forced to crash-land near Gudja after an attack by a 109, sat down to record the events of Malta's 'Day in Hell' in his diary. 'This day will never be forgotten ... Four ships sunk in the harbour. Hospitals bombed, churches and town after town cleaned out. What a slaughter of human lives. Unless help comes soon, God save us. No food, cigarettes, fuel. They are doing a lot of evacuating of English wives.'

'Our arrival was in a way a blessing to those on the island,' wrote Don McLeod. 'Many boys had come down months and months before flying Hurricanes and we found out that a few had flown in two weeks before us in Spitfires. This was a surprise to us and we were glad to hear that they had all made it. But since their arrival, all the Spitfires had been torn asunder.'

Chapter 3

Angels One Five

Information began to come up to us. Fifty-plus bandits approaching from the north; climb to Angels One Five – the usual stuff. Fifty-plus and eight of us! But, what the heck? We had heard it all before.

'We had found, in daylight, that the mansion made a good Mess,' wrote 'Tim' Johnston. 'Lack of a proper ante-room compensated for by a spacious flat-roof, which made a delightful place in which to sit in the sun. Looking out from it you could see, laid out below, the whole eastern part of the Island: straight ahead were Grand Harbour and the Sliema Creek, with Valletta between them and the towns of Vittoriosa, Senglea, Cospicua, Floriana and Sliema grouped round in a semi-circle; to one side of these Luqa aerodrome, could be picked out clearly by its runways; beyond it lay Hal Far aerodrome and the naval base of Kalafrana; in the foreground was Takali aerodrome. In sunshine this view, in its colouring, detail and lucidity, reminded me of a painting by Canaletto.'

Don McLeod too turned his thoughts to describing his new habitat: 'We were properly bedded in the villa overlooking the island's sacred town of Rabat, where centuries before the Turks had catapulted rocks against the walls in an effort to break into the Holy City. Truly this was an historical island. Malta was known as the "Halfway House" or the "Naval Highway" going through the Mediterranean. It had suffered in the course of its history two major sieges, as well as this, the third. The first of the epic sieges of Malta was when the Knights of Saint John successfully defended their island against the Turkish invaders. The second was when the Maltese people in 1800 refused to be conquered by Napoleon. In history almost everyone in that section of the world at one time or another became involved on the island.

'Malta is made up of many little towns, the principal of which is Valletta. The towns of St. Julian, St. Paul's Bay, Luqa, Floriana and numerous other small villages make up the structure of the island. The island itself is made of soft stone, which the Maltese people cut up and make their homes out of. It is often said that in the ancient days Malta was a completely barren island and that all the dirt, etc., and other forms of growth covering the island was carried by boat or mud scow from Italy and Greece. It is made up of small fields and plots of land enclosed by rock fences which extend from one end of the island to the other.

'Rabat, which was where we were to stay, is known as the Holy City, famous for its many cathedrals of beautiful architecture. The island was honeycombed from one end to the other by underground passages. It was possible to walk from end to end of the island, branch out at various side channels and come forth in the free air at any given point you would desire. In fact, a school teacher and her 30 students going through the catacombs was never heard from and it is imagined that they walked into an endless cavern and perished before they could reach outside air.

'On 21st March it was decided that 249 Squadron and ourselves, known as 126 Squadron, would divide the aircraft serviceable on the Island and fly as a unit. This was to conserve aircraft and give us the most pilots available. We had waited and waited for our other eight pilots and planes to appear, but apparently, they had some trouble in taking off the carrier, or the fleet had been intercepted by enemy warships and they had to abandon their venture for the time, for "B" Flight had failed to make an appearance. It would probably be a week or so before they would be attempting such a feat again.

'At dawn [on Tuesday, 24 March] we wound our way to Luqa airfield to alert ourselves for readiness. The night before two ships from a convoy from the Middle East had been bombed. The Navy was trying to get supplies in from Cairo and Alexandria. A ship famous to all Maltese people, the *Breconshire*, [which had received a direct hit in the engine room] had limped into the shelter of the easterly side of the island [in Marsaxlokk Bay, bad weather having prevented the disabled supply ship from being towed into the safety of Grand Harbour since noon on Wednesday and bombs were dropped through the clouds as well as from a dive. For nearly 6 hours, 120 enemy bombers accompanied by massed fighters attacked in wave after wave, dropping over 350 HE bombs of 250kg and 500kg on ships, docks and gun positions in Grand Harbour and 40 more on *Breconshire* in Marsaxlokk Bay. At 1632 hours she was hit in an attack by ten Ju 88s and set on fire]. It was taking water fast and could not be moved into port. It was given as close a naval escort as was possible for it had valuable stores of oil, ammunition and food aboard.

'The first hop of the morning sent "Tim" Johnston and Mike Graves out to protect the *"Breck"* as far as was possible. We were to work in relays of twos because of the lack of planes, so that it would be covered at all times. It was one of those foggy days so typical of England. I remember saying to myself, "Does the sun ever shine in this vicinity of the continent?" Directly ahead of me I could see the *"Breck"* listing badly from a bomb hit and as "Jumbo" and I approached we could see the Navy destroyers firing. I saw an "88" trying to get back into the clouds. "Jumbo" followed him into the clouds. In the turn I had lost him, so I shot under the clouds hoping he would break out the other side. In what was no longer than ten or fifteen seconds I spotted another "88" making for the ship. I turned towards it as fast as possible, but he saw me just in time and pulled up into the clouds. I contacted "Jumbo" on the radio and he had lost his also. Things went along fairly smooth after that until we were relieved.

'"Jimmie" and I were on standby. At 10 o'clock the Very pistol fired our signal of a raid and we were scrambled after an unknown plot of enemy aircraft. As our two trusty Spitfires wheeled down the runway, we both wondered how many of them there were. As it was to our great advantage to get height, we strained our aircraft for every ounce of climbing speed possible, climbing higher and higher into the bright Mediterranean sun. As we approached the north part of the island, still in a climbing status, we were being directed by a quiet, relaxing voice from way down deep in the rocks of Malta. It was Group Captain Woodhall, known to us all and dear as just plain "Woody".

'Over my radio I heard "Woody" say: "'Mac' there should be two just below you. Keep a sharp lookout."

'"Okay, 'Woody'."

'"Jimmie" came on the radio and said, "'Mac', I've got oil all over my windscreen; you'll have to spot them." As well as looking down we had to keep looking up to make sure there were no aircraft above us.

'If it were true that there were only two, this would be the biggest opportunity of a man's lifetime. For in these days man never fought the "Hun" in even terms. It was always against big odds.

'Against the glare of the sun, I made out two small forms far below me at 8,000ft, which at first seemed so small and tiny, going in the direction of Kalafrana Bay. They turned out to be enemy planes. We then started diving: 20,000, 16,000, 13,000ft. By this time, we were both going at terrific speeds. We were probably going over 600mph in our dives and the closing speed on the enemy was very fast. I called "Jimmie" at the last minute and said, "Do you see yours, 'Jimmie'?" Just as McLeod opened fire with a 5-second burst from dead astern, he heard "Jimmie" Peck say, "the sons of bitches."

'The 109 was enveloped in white smoke (apparently glycol) and started a gliding turn to the left. I saw "Jimmie" turn wide and then I zoomed past him. "Jimmie's" Messerschmitt turned directly into me with "Jimmie" on his tail. I did a quick stall turn, made a three-quarter head-on pass and used the rest of my ammo on a beam attack. On breaking from this attack, I saw the first e/a attacked by me, now a flaming ball of fire, diving straight into the sea and I could see parts of flaming aircraft spinning, disintegrating in its rush to a watery grave.

'I called to "Jimmie" – "Have you got yours yet?"

'As Don McLeod headed in the last direction he had seen "Jimmie", he heard a scream over the radio, "I got him!"'

'"Jimmie" had finally got him on the deck and he went into the water.

'I called "Jimmie" and asked if he needed help. No, he was okay. We joined up and then we headed back for the island. I called "Woody" and said, "'Woody', two up and two down, coming home."'

'"Woody" came back; "Good Show, good show."'

'We came home and had no sooner landed than our crew chiefs were patting us on the back. And thus, the first two fighters had been met and destroyed.'

'Both delighted, it was right and proper that they should notch their first on the same day,' wrote 'Tim' Johnston, 'because they joined up together in the States, trained together, went to England together, to 121 together, and came here together. Complete contrast in every way: "Mac" fair, "Jimmie" dark; "Mac" tall, "Jimmie" short; "Mac" burly, "Jimmie" slight; "Mac" garrulous, "Jimmie" (for an American) reserved; "Mac" a New Englander, "Jimmie" a Californian. They were old friends but would argue incessantly; even doing their bitching differently, "Mac" noisily and profanely, "Jimmie" quietly and lovingly. Today, "Mac", who can never keep his mouth shut, had called up on R/T and said: "Hello Peck, 'Mac' here. I've knocked mine down; do I have to come and help you with yours?"'

'Jimmie's' answer gave joy to all in the Fighter Control Room who heard it, as 'Woody' Woodhall recalled later. 'In their first flight on Malta, I vectored them on to two 109s carrying bombs [presumably fighter-bombers of 10/JG 53] approaching the island

and they intercepted them just off the island and "bounced" the Huns beautifully. They were very excited. "Mac" said, "You take the left; I'll take the right Jimmy. Oh boy ain't this grand?" And "Mac" shot his down. 'Jimmie's was a bit more difficult to finish off so "Mac" shouted "I got mine, Jimmie, have you shot down yours or do you want me to come and show you how?"

'"Jimmie" replied: "You big …!" followed by a lot of unprintable things and shot down his Hun.'

'During the time that "Jimmie" and I had been coming back from our scrap,' 'Mac' McLeod wrote later, 'Mike Graves and "Tim" Johnston had taken off and were climbing to meet a fresh onslaught from the Huns. This was the beginning of the very unequal odds which we were to run up against. Whereas "Jimmie" and I had only a couple to combat, Mike and "Tim" ran into several fighters escorting many bombers. The two of them had combats with the fighters while attempting to get to the bombers. They made many fake attacks as they preyed on the fighters, saving their ammunition for the bombers. Their job in the air was primarily not to knock down enemy fighters, but to keep the bombers off any given target. "Tim" was able to knock down a Stuka, but Mike had been continuously kept busy by the 109s and had been unable to engage the bombers.'

'Mike had suddenly spun and lost half his angels,' wrote Johnston [who the previous Sunday had destroyed a Ju 88 for his second victory]. 'I suppose I must have been climbing too fast for him. Didn't know what to do now. Problem solved itself; found I had been so busy keeping my eye on two 109s that I had lost sight of Mike, so I dived towards land, gave my two shadowers the slip and began to climb again. Almost at once more 109s appeared and circled over me, four immediately above and two farther away; I think they suspected a trap, because for some minutes they watched and waited. At last, one of them decided to attack; he came down very fast and at the same time dropped his starboard wing as if he were going to do a roll to the right. As he flashed by within 50 yards, he was past vertical and was going so fast that as soon as he began to pull out of his dive vapour trails appeared behind his wing tips. As he opened fire, I had been able to watch the patterns of bluish smoke in front of him. They looked rather like paper streamers being thrown out and it was difficult to believe that there was anything lethal about them. The others followed his example, but came down individually so that I was able to turn in to each one and take the attack head-on or on the beam; some fired; some didn't; none stayed to fight, but there were enough of them to keep me busy as a one-armed paper-hanger. I gave one of them, which was doing its usual stall-turn after the attack, a short burst, it was foolish – he was right out of range – and decided to keep the rest of my ammunition.

'Continued to play with them a little longer, then realised original plan was no longer feasible. So much for theory; had tried to gain height south of the Island and had climbed into the thick of the 109s, as predicted. Did an aileron turn and found I'd managed to shake them off; felt very tired from throwing the aircraft about, and had no idea what was happening. Gondar had been giving instructions, but I'd been too occupied to pay attention.'

Johnston flew inland towards Grand Harbour and he opened up on a Stuka nearest to him but all that came were some vivid flashes from exploding cannon shells and a stream of white smoke from the enemy's belly. Instead of breaking away properly 'Tim' sat watching him. By this time, he was out over the sea and he knew the 109s would not be far so he quickly gave the Ju 87 another three-second burst before he broke off and flew back to Malta. A last look revealed that the Stuka was further behind the formation than before and still trailing its white plume of smoke.

Johnston returned to Luqa, entered the circuit, dropped his wheels and was able to lower flaps when he noticed light flak bursting above him, 'At same time an incoherent transmission came over the R/T,' he wrote.

'I thought there must be a 109 gunning somewhere, and that it would be a wise precaution to put my wheels up, but couldn't see him anywhere; didn't want to appear to panic, so tried to spot him first. Looked round again, and this time saw him at 500 yards on the port beam flying towards me; whipped my wheels up and stuffed my nose down at the same time; as I did so he opened fire, but I felt fairly certain he wouldn't hit me. He flashed past, did a stall turn and came back towards me, but didn't attack again. I followed him north-west; knew I couldn't catch him, and that I hadn't much ammunition left, but thought I might be able to jump him later if he decided to go ground-strafing; possibly I was feeling bloody-minded at being attacked over my own base.

'I was about 1,000ft below him and half a mile astern, heading for some cloud-cover from which to watch him, when he returned and started a diving head-on attack; seeing it coming, I pulled up hard, in something between a loop and a climbing turn, towards a cloud to port. I continued to watch him over the side of the cockpit and knew he'd opened fire when the sinister blue tendrils shot out of his wings towards me; saw him follow me round in my turn and the deflection looked about right. This time I didn't feel a bit confident of not being hit. The aircraft had lost so much speed that the evasive action I tried to take as I saw him firing was sluggish and ineffective; the cloud had failed me by coming no nearer, and I felt as if I'd been dangled at the end of a piece of string for him to shoot at. He had flashed past behind me before I reached the cloud and then I stalled almost at once. Didn't realise until afterwards that I then fulfilled all the conditions described by the legendary fighter pilot: *"There I was, on my back, in cloud, with nothing on the clock, still climbing …"* Resisted temptation to hold the stick back, and fell out very slowly; looked carefully everywhere, but the 109 had disappeared, so returned to Luqa and landed, a good one in spite of a flat tyre. Told I had been up 35 minutes, it seemed like an hour and a half. Found three strikes in the machines, all in the leading edge; one of these had punctured the tyre; was amused to think that the Stukas had probably inflicted these, not one of the many 109s. Mike was back safely, but had been so harried by 109s that he hadn't seen the bombers at all.

'This was my first experience of mixing it with enemy fighters, except for an inconclusive engagement with a 110 off Lowestoft last year; on the whole I'd found it encouraging: with all the advantages on their side they still hadn't shown outstanding resolution. Heard afterwards that there had been 25 Stukas and about fifteen 109s. Two Stukas had been confirmed from the ground as destroyed.'

While it was being refuelled, Don McLeod had jumped into 'Tim's' Spitfire and was preparing to make his trip when the crew chief called and said there would be no more flying that particular aircraft that day. '"Tim" had picked up two bullets, one in each main spar of his wing. I jumped out of that aircraft into the next and "Jumbo" and I headed for the *"Breck"*.

'Our total score that day was two 109s, two Stukas confirmed and six Stukas probably destroyed. We had no losses and only a few bullet holes. It was truly as good mathematics as our squadron was aiming for.

'The Hurricane squadron on the other end of the island had managed to put up two Hurricanes as their part of the defence. The Hurricanes made no claims and said afterwards that they had been harassed by the fighters also.

'This raid was the beginning of the contingent of heavy raids on the island which were to come to an end only after we received added support in the way of Spitfires much later on.'

On Wednesday, 25 March 'Tim' Johnston went to Valletta with Mike Graves to try to secure some tropical kit. 'Sirens sounded soon after lunch,' Johnston recalled, 'so we made our way to the Fighter Control Room, also one of the best air-raid shelters in Valletta. There was a big raid coming in, 80 plus, against which we had managed to put six Spits and six Hurricanes. The R/T conversation was being broadcast from a loud-speaker and the breathless, staccato voices were coming through very clearly; we heard "Mac" say: "There they are, five o'clock below". Squadron Leader Stan Grant, who was leading, came back after slight pause: "Can't see them, you lead, you lead"; another pause, longer this time, then Pete's voice, very excited: *"Look, Stukas, Stukas, shoals of 'em"*, followed by Grant's long-drawn-out, *"Geez"*; another longish interval, tense and expectant, before an army telephone reported cannon-fire; another pause, then a very loud excited voice said: "Okay, Woody, I'm out of ammo, think I got a couple." More chatter, then the reports from the ground began to come in: two 109s confirmed, two 87s confirmed, half a dozen other Stukas probable or badly damaged; no losses. Clearly a pretty successful day. On return to the mess found that "Mac" had got one of the 109s destroyed; he was jubilant about it, more especially because he'd stolen a march on "Jimmie", who only claimed a damaged Stuka.

'I was rather selfishly relieved to find that the Stukas destroyed today died hard after taking a lot of punishment; they are supposed to be such easy meat that I'd been feeling disappointed at not having done better when I'd met them, but the general opinion now is that these are the new ones – Mark D, I think – heavily armoured and with twin dorsal guns.'

At daybreak on Friday morning, 27 March, fires broke out again amidships on the *Breconshire* and the ammunition supplies on board began to explode. Moments after her captain and officers had abandoned an attempt to scuttle her, *Breconshire* rolled onto her side and capsized but she was stranded high enough out of the water that some of her vital cargo, which included tons of ammunition and bombs and 5,000 tons of petroleum, was later salvaged. In August, and for months afterward, divers were still managing to retrieve tins of milk and bottles of gin from the capsized ship. The 'Breck' exuded oil and when the wind blew from the south bathing in Kalafrana Bay was rather unpleasant, as the water all around became impregnated with thick black oil.

'The next day,' wrote Don McLeod, 'we drew up what we jokingly called the "Malta Wing", which actually had only six Spitfires and four Hurricanes airborne. This was the first time in which we combined pilots from any other squadron with our own. These battles continued in the air day after day and we were having the same phenomenal luck of getting a few each trip without any damage to ourselves. It got so even we began thinking and wondering how long this luck could hold out. We had a day off due to bad weather and we spent our time moving into new quarters in Rabat. "Johnny" Plagis and Pete Nash on 249 Squadron joined "Johnnie", "Jimmie", Mike and I, sharing a room. Beds were out of the question so we just rolled up on the floor.

'Our billet was right on the edge of the great wall that overlooked Takali airfield. We did not relish the thought of being so close to the bombing run of the Germans. We had three little Maltese batmen, namely, "Charlie", "Jimmie" and Manuel, who were supposed to take care of our rooms and clean the place generally. It seemed to us that they spent most of their time jabbering in the corridors and cooking food for themselves. We often wondered where they got all the food and later found out it came from our rations. We were all eating, or so-called eating, in a central mess which conserved food. Our meals by this time consisted of very little bully beef, Spam, bread with marmalade and the inevitable tea. There had cropped up what seemed to be an inexhaustible supply of eggs which we could get by paying a little more. In due time we discovered where the eggs came from and had chicken for dinner and then we had neither eggs nor chicken. We were able for a price to get fish and chips at a so-called black-market place. We went until such time as the supply was exhausted, to fill our stomachs, which were gradually getting very empty. Cassie Busuttil's pub was where we went to get these priceless morsels of food. In the usual time she ran out of "eggs and chips", "four fried eggs and sometimes a pork chop for good measure" and we went back on a rigid diet and never did find out how or where she got the stuff for our meals. She cooked the sweetest chips we'd ever had and when asked what her secret was, she said she cooked them in a mixture of olive-oil and lard; the more olive-oil the better.

'By this time, of course, there were no electric light facilities or any of the other comforts of home to be had. We used candles for lights and used them sparingly as there were not too many of them.

'We were all working on the airdromes, building pens for our aircraft, shovelling sand and dirt into bags and piling them up so as to protect our aircraft, which were becoming more and more dilapidated from flying splinters from bombs.

'Up to this time we had had a small supply of beer and liquor to pass away the quiet hours, but even this was failing, now that the brewery had closed down due to the lack of barley and to the lack of imports, plus bomb damage, and what liquor we had was that which we could borrow, beg or steal from hoarded stocks. The Germans were running their raids almost by clockwork. We were inevitably having a raid at dawn, one at ten in the morning, one at four in the afternoon and one at dusk. Daylight bombing, bad as it was, never seemed quite as bad as the continual night bombing which we were soon to receive.'

On the morning of Sunday, 29 March, 'Picket II' – the balance of the Spitfires from the *Cape Hawke* and *Queen Victoria* shipments – and seven pilots, flew off the *Eagle*, led to Malta by two Beaufort torpedo bombers and three Blenheims from Gibraltar.

'The first one off,' recalled 'Junior' Crist, 'was "Tony" Barton. He disappeared over the bow and finally staggered into view half a mile ahead. That didn't inspire any confidence!' Crist needed have worried. It was not the first time that Barton had taken off from a carrier, and in Malta, to boot!

Barton, who was born on 17 December 1913 and had grown up in Oakleigh Park in north London, had, from 1927 to 1940, served as a midshipman on *Warspite*, *Valiant* and *Dragon*. By early 1936, he had reached the rank of sub-lieutenant and in May that year he learned to fly. In August 1937 he joined 823 Squadron, Fleet Air Arm as a super-numerary Royal naval lieutenant. At Hal Far, on *Glorious* he learned to fly off an aircraft carrier's deck. 'Bart' wanted to continue flying so in July 1940 he resigned his commission and joined the RAFVR and was commissioned as a pilot officer. In August 1940, he was posted to 32 Squadron and claimed four victories in his first three weeks. When the squadron was posted north to rest, he joined 253 Squadron at Kenley but on 15 September Barton force-landed his Hurricane after losing a duel with a Bf 109. Five days later he was shot down and badly wounded. He returned to operations in February 1941 as a flight commander on 124 Squadron. Early in 1942 he received his DFC for his five victories during August–September 1940. Flying Hurricanes in the Battle of Britain he had shot down three Bf 109Es, a Ju 88 and a Dornier Do 17 and had damaged two other enemy aircraft.

After four days of intense raids, only five serviceable fighters were available for the air defence of Malta. Ground crews had been collecting every serviceable part from damaged aircraft to restore other machines to flying condition. Fighter Command had resorted to using fake radio transmissions to try and fool the enemy into believing there were extra fighters in the air to intercept incoming raids. On the Monday seven sergeants of the Royal Australian Air Force were lost in an air battle as they approached Malta while attempting to deliver aircraft to the beleaguered island. Four of them died aboard a Hudson aircraft, which stalled on landing and then went into a tight spin and crashed before catching fire.

'On Tuesday, 31st March,' wrote Don McLeod, 'we stayed in readiness all day and the raids that came in were too large for our small unit. At 7.30 we were released for the night and we walked from our planes to the dispersal hut. We had been there not more than five minutes when we were informed that there was a large raid coming in. We tried to get permission to take off, but were refused. It was one of those spectacular after-dusk raids when the enemy aircraft would be caught in the beams of twenty or thirty searchlights and the tracers would go up from the ground with their fiery red appearance, just missing and then hitting the aircraft. The sight gave a thrill to all that watched.

'So far in the story we have mentioned only aircraft. The real heroes on the island of Malta in the eyes of everyone, including the eyes of the pilots, were the anti-aircraft men. Men who had to sit by the guns under all circumstances. Men who would put up a terrific barrage, eclipsing the sun over a given target and who shot down many German aircraft during this long hard battle. These men were subject to many attacks aimed directly at them, as it was good German logic to realise that if they knocked out the anti-aircraft guns their path of flight would be much smoother over the island.

'Many times, when we all got together at night, the discussion of invasion would come up. We knew the situation that presented itself in Africa. At this time Rommel was making an all-out push in the direction of Cairo. He had been steadily making an advance in that direction and was now waiting on supplies to further his push. If Rommel was supplied before the British Eighth Army could get to their supply, it was obvious that nothing could stop the German conquest on the Nile canal and area beyond. It seemed that Malta was the thorn in the side of the German plans. Would they invade Malta, the last Allied stronghold in the Mediterranean, and thereby give themselves clear sailing in for the convoys? Or would they try to neutralise the island by saturation bombing? We could expect no help from the Navy in case of invasion. It would be purely an off-shore rebellion of the horde.

'All we could do in a Nazi offensive was an occasional photographic reconnaissance over Sicily over the runway being lengthened for large stores of supplies in the vicinity and an occasional Junkers 52, which was used for troop transport.

'Many of the prisoners of war which had been shot down over the island were of the belief that we would be invaded and that there would be no stopping the enemy. If he tried to invade us, he no doubt could have conquered the island, but at a tremendous cost to both.

'Due to the physical impediments which the island offered to the seaborne invaders and the fact that we had thousands of troops, we knew invasion would have been a fight to the death. With this thought in mind, we knew that with the number of men he had involved in his other fronts he would probably keep on bombing us. We were more than busily engaged in keeping up what aircraft we had and in holding this island. And too, if they were not bombing us, they most certainly would have been bombing our friends and allies on the various other fronts.'

Unsurprisingly, only a very few fighter pilots survived a six-month tour on Malta. Of sixteen pilots on 185 Squadron, only Flying Officer James Ian 'Skip' McKay and two others survived but 'Skip', who was born in Owen Sound, Ontario, on 1 April 1922, was nearly shot down on his 21st birthday when a bullet hit his Spitfire just above his shoulder. 'Skip' had grown up in Owen Sound and attended Dufferin School. During the summer, he worked for the Owen Sound Transportation Company as a watchman/wheelsman on the SS *Manitoulin*, a Great Lakes passenger steamship. After graduating in 1939, 'Skip' had worked for the Canadian Imperial Bank of Commerce until he enlisted in Toronto, at the age of 19, in August 1940.

'I was lucky,' 'Skip' wrote. 'A lot must depend on the way you feel in the air. Every time you got into a fighter it (death) was never going to happen to you. Chivalry in war might be on the wane (this was a very tough war), but it had yet to disappear altogether from aerial combat. Sitting in the mess, we all said we wouldn't shoot a man in a parachute but in the "Med" I saw one of my best friends "get it" while he was going down in his parachute so I guess everybody didn't think the same way. I'd seen the Jerries shooting up fellows in dinghies. Once I even saw them shooting up fellows in dinghies when we knew these targets were German airmen who had been shot down. What did we do then? Well, to tell the truth, we just laughed like hell and went along home.'

It was on the afternoon of 1 April that 'Johnny' Plagis had the distinction of shooting down four enemy aircraft in a single day on four separate flights. 'On the last flight of the day,' he wrote, 'there were four Spitfires and we intercepted and attacked 180 bombers escorted by 80 fighters; the total against us was over 250 aircraft. Despite the odds, we attacked. The ensuing battle would take a volume to describe. I managed to destroy one Ju 88 and damage a Messerschmitt 109, making my score for the day, 4 aircraft destroyed; one "damaged" and one probably destroyed. On landing at the base, my aircraft was badly damaged and I received superficial wounds.'

'On Thursday, 2 April,' wrote Don McLeod, 'our luck ran out. We had been having phenomenal luck in knocking the "Hun" down without getting hurt ourselves. At 0950 hours "Johnnie" Johnston, "Jimmie" Peck, "Canada" [26-year-old Pilot Officer Winston Francis "Mac" McCarthy] and I scrambled, climbed into a layer of clouds and kept climbing, up and up. When we reached 21,000ft, we were informed that there was a large formation of bombers coming in from the North. I called Ground Control and asked them where the "Little Boys" [Bf 109s] were and they said they were with the bombers [fifteen Ju 88s]. I spotted this large formation approaching about 9 or 10,000ft below. This was a fighter pilot's dream, which was soon to turn into a nightmare.

'As we turned down to dive on the bombers, the first thing I remember was that horrid clack of enemy fire hitting me and I knew instantly, but not soon enough, that we had been jumped from above. Just to my right was a sheet of flame, which turned out to be "Canada" going down. I tried to work my controls and found that my left leg was numb and my left arm hung limply by my side and there was again the shudder of cannon shells ripping into my aircraft. I had long since lost the desire to attack the bombers and my one thought now was to get away from the fighters that were attacking me. It so happened that there were 25 Messerschmitts above us and they attacked us out of the sun. The sun can be a pilot's best friend and his worst enemy. We had not been able to see them until they had struck.

'My ship was badly crippled and I knew it was hopeless to jump out so far away from the island. There was a possibility that had I been nearer I might be picked up by the Air/Sea Rescue unit. But then, too, they might be unable to go out after us because they were being strafed by German fighters. As a matter of fact, it had been two months since anyone had been picked up in the drink. I resolved that I would get back to the island if it was humanly possible.

'During my descent from 21,000ft to about 1,000ft I was continuously attacked and my aircraft was full of cannon holes. I had been hit several times in the cockpit, destroying my instrument panel, knocking off my throttle and primer. But luckily none had hit me personally save the first attack. I was about two or three miles off the island when I went into a small cloud formation, closely pursued by the "Hun". My aircraft was shot up badly. In fact, I could make practically no offensive or defensive movements; just barely skid. My controls and actuating gear were so badly gone that by holding full forward pressure in the stick I was just able to hold a slow dive angle. I put down to about 500ft. My engine burst into flame and the Spit did a sudden flip and I had no choice but to leave my trusty Spitfire.'

How McCleod, who weighed a strapping 16 stone, got out he could not remember. The first thing he knew he was falling head first toward the sea.

'I pulled the ripcord and received a sudden jolt upright and almost immediately I hit the water. I did not have time to release the parachute and I was being dragged along under the water, as the chute had a 30-mph wind to pull it along. The British-type chute I was wearing had instantaneously released, but my radio cord had jammed in the release. What was probably ten seconds, while I was releasing it, seemed more like two hours. I grabbed the dinghy with my one good arm, pulled off the covering and inflated as much of it as would be inflated by the CO_2 bottle, which automatically fills your life raft with air. I pulled myself into the dinghy by a half-conscious effort by one arm and just as I relaxed and took notice saw that I was drifting away from Malta. I remember saying, "Well, Cairo's only 1,000 miles away". A German fighter appeared, turned his nose towards me, and naturally I immediately rolled out of my dinghy and to underwater safety. Water deflects bullets. If he strafed me, I will never know because he did not hit the dinghy and my being underwater saved me.

'I watched for him to return, but he failed to do so and I began once again the effort of getting back in the dinghy. I sat there, helpless, as the Germans bombed the Air/Sea Rescue depot and I gave up all hope at that time of being picked up. From out of the corner of my eye I saw a Hurricane circle over me, waggle his wings to give me encouragement and suddenly dart off to the shore and then fly straight at me, circle again and repeat the performance. All of a sudden in the distance I saw the ASR launch coming out to get me. I was getting cold and weak as the launch pulled alongside of me and I remember them throwing over a large rope ladder. They climbed down and grabbed hold of me, pulled me onto the launch, wasting no time getting back to land. The same Hurricane boy who I never got to thank protected us on the way in. He was shot down the next day in an engagement with enemy fighters.'

There was no trace of any of the others so 'Tim' Johnston, who had claimed a Ju 88 'probable' and evaded a Bf 109 that had sat on his tail, before returning with his oil pressure down to zero and breaking cloud had found himself a mile or two south-east of Luqa, phoned Fighter Control. He was told that someone – they thought 'Mac' McLeod – was in a dinghy 3 miles east of Kalafrana; the rescue launch was already on its way, but would need an escort. 'Tim' arranged for 'Australia' ('Bis' Bisley) and 'Junior' Crist to go with it; a rumour had already come through that 109s were shooting up the dinghy, but this was unconfirmed. When they'd gone 'Jimmie' landed. He had seen the 109s at about the same time and had broken with 'Tim' Johnston; he reckoned there were fifteen of them, but hadn't been hit. He'd heard 'Mac' McLeod say that he was baling out east of Kalafrana and had gone there to search for him, but without success. Later 'Australia' and Crist returned and reported they had seen someone picked up by the rescue boat off Kalafrana, and this proved to be McLeod, who was slightly wounded. Nothing had been heard of 'Canada', so 'Australia' and Crist set off again to make a sea-search, but found no trace.

'One of the pleasant parts of this trip,' wrote Don McLeod 'was the tall glassful of bourbon; pre-war mind you, that was poured into me. It tasted so good and I was so cold that they gave me another. In the hospital, over the rocks of Kalafrana Bay, they put me under a heating lamp to take the chill out of me and picked the few pieces of shrapnel from my arm and leg. I could not understand until I remembered the two glasses of bourbon why I was getting tight. I call combining two glasses of bourbon and a heating lamp the simplest way I can over remember of getting a jag on.'

Sixteen-year-old Anne Pullicino, one of eleven members of Sir Philip and Lady Pullicino's very high-class family of six males and five girls, whose father was Malta's Attorney General and legal advisor to the forces, thought 'Mac' was 'a card' and a great line shooter! 'McLeod always had to have the last words,' recalled 'Tim' Johnston.

'In a few hours,' Don McLeod recalled, '"Jimmie" Peck, "Johnnie" Johnston, "Bis" and "Crisy" Crist came in to visit me. It was clearly a bad day as far as we were concerned. We had received the first of our many casualties and it was with a good bit of sorrow that I heard of "Canada's" going – "Mac" McCarthy never really had a chance. All through our climbing for altitude I had called him several times to open up his position and as this was his first combat mission over the island I felt more or less responsible for him. The great ball of flame that I had seen just as I was hit myself had been "Canada" going down in flames. "Jimmie" had looked for him, but without success. It was quite obvious that he had been killed in the initial attack. Johnnie had seen the enemy fighters approaching at the last instant and my radio had baulked and I did not hear him yell. "Mac" was a renowned and famous swimmer from Ottawa, hard-headed but with a good sense of humour which we didn't have time enough to appreciate. But I am sure if "Mac'" had had a chance, he would have gone on to unknown heights. The double fact of losing "Canada", plus two Spitfires was not so easy to take.'

On Sunday, 5 April 'Tim' Johnston went to Kalafrana at lunch time; the water was like a mirror. He found Don McLeod in the underground sick quarters with shrapnel in leg and arm, but 'astonishingly cheerful'.

'He said he had just sighted the bombers when he was hit, had never heard "Jimmie" or me say "break left", and had never seen what got him. His left leg had gone quite numb at once so that he had to use his right foot on both sides of the rudder; his arm was also hit but remained serviceable.

'The actuating gear seemed to have been shot away, because he had to hold the stick fully forward with all his strength to maintain a slight dive; his port aileron had been knocked almost upright, and the only evasive action he had dared to take was a gentle turn in one direction and a skid in the other. He had headed west and hoped to get the machine home, but had been followed by 109s all the way down, had counted six attacks in all; the starboard side of the instrument panel had been shot away, his R/T had been shot away, and he had had to cower behind his armour-plating and listen to the bullets rattling against it. The machine I'd seen flying west with its glycol streaming out had probably been his, but he didn't know about that and had thought his motor was all right.

'Before his R/T had been taken from him, he had apparently talked incessantly. I'd been too busy myself to notice, but "Jimmie" heard it all. First, he'd said: "Hullo, Gondar, Red Leader here, think I've been hit, but trying to make base"; later, "Hello, Wombat aircraft, go down after the big jobs, I've got all the Little Boys playing with me."

'Then: "Think I can make it, but if I don't, good huntin' fellers."

'Finally, "Hello 'Jimmie' – going down in the drink just east Kalafrana."'

At cloud level McLeod's Spitfire had begun to burn and he had prepared to jump out; then the elevator wires had snapped and the aircraft had flipped up on its back, making it rather difficult for him to get out, but he had got clear in his parachute and hit the water close behind his machine. At first, he'd been unable to get rid of his harness, because the R/T cable caught in the release buckle.

'By this time, he was almost exhausted and thought he would drown. He remembered saying to himself "Godammit, 'Mac', this is the hell of a way to get killed," but had then managed to free himself, inflate his dinghy and crawl into it. Soon afterwards a strange aircraft had flown low overhead; silver all over with a small black cross – neither 109 nor Macchi MC.202. It had begun to circle and he thought it was aiming to shoot him up, so he jumped out into the sea and hid behind the dinghy; it had come back, but hadn't fired. After what seemed like an hour to an hour and a half – actually twenty to twenty-five minutes – the rescue launch had arrived and picked him up.

'We took "Mac" back to the mess with us, somewhat bizarrely dressed,' 'Tim' Johnston recalled. 'This had been our first loss; the arithmetic suffered but was still quite good: seven destroyed and some probable, for the loss of one pilot killed and one slightly wounded. Poor "Canada"; he never even had a shot at them.

'I don't like the way the number of hits that I receive is increasing,' Johnston wrote later. 'The first time it was two strikes, the next time three, then five, now 20 something – there's no future in it.'

On 5 April, there had been raids on Grand Harbour and airfields on the island involving more than seventy-five bombers and fifty-plus 109s. At 0750 hours twenty-three Ju 88s and Stukas attacked the dockyard and Floriana, dropping high-explosive bombs, including rocket bombs, which caused heavy damage. Then, at 1122 hours fifty-three aircraft came in from the north and dropped more bombs on the dockyard area. The all clear was signalled shortly after noon but at 1410 hours large formations of Ju 88s, Stukas and Bf 109s were sighted and four Spitfires of 126 Squadron were scrambled to intercept the enemy raiders. Making individual attacks, 'Tim' Johnston probably destroyed a Bf 109; 'Bis' Bisley claimed his first two victories when he destroyed a Ju 87 and a Ju 88. He also attacked another Ju 88 and fought off eight Bf 109s before being wounded in the legs and hand by a cannon shell. With no ammunition left, he dived to sea level in an attempt to throw off his pursuers. After being chased back to the coast he managed a wheels-up crash-landing at Takali airfield. 'Bis' would spend two weeks in hospital at Imtarfa.

Pilot Officer Hiram Aldine 'Tex' Putnam RCAF claimed a Ju 88. 'Like many Eagle squadron volunteers, "Tex" had seen the curve coming,' wrote 'Laddie' Lucas, 'and wanted to be in there pitching, well ahead of the game.' 'Big Tex', who was born in Bobville, Texas, on 4 November 1913, was one of the new pilots on 126 Squadron. Fellow Texan, Bruce Charles Downs, born on 24 June 1916 in San Angelo, Tom Green County, had joined the RAFVR and served initially as a pilot officer on 121 'Eagle' Squadron but was posted to 126 Squadron in Malta in May 1942. 'Goldie' Goldsmith had been flying with a valiant Hurricane squadron on the Island; Flight Sergeant Patrick Alfred 'Paddy' Schade DFM was from Malaya. 'At this point we were truly an international squadron,' wrote Don McLeod.

By the evening of Tuesday, 21 April only seventeen of the original Spitfires that had flown in the day before were still in one piece following enemy air attacks. On 601 Squadron, 25-year-old Pilot Officer Stanley Frederick Brooker of Regina, Saskatchewan, who on Monday had marked his arrival on the Island by damaging a 109, was shot down into the sea and was killed. 'Tex' Putnam crashed into a steel wireless mast near the quarters of the 8th Battalion, King's Own Royal Regiment at Siġġiewi. At first it was thought that this was an accident, but cannon fire from an enemy fighter had spun his Spitfire out of control and the 28-year-old pilot died of his wounds in hospital the next day. Some of his friends had handkerchiefs made by a local Maltese seamstress from the silk of his damaged parachute. Putnam's effects went to his father, a restaurateur.

Meanwhile, the sense of feeling had returned to Don McLeod's leg and arm. 'Outside of a stiff neck received when my parachute had opened, I felt all right,' he wrote. However, on 11 April 'Mac' was found to have pulled a cartilage in his throat and he was grounded. 'Jimmie' Peck insisted that this was not the result of having to bail out, but of the inability to stop talking about it afterwards! 'In any case,' 'Tim' Johnston added, '"Jimmie" for one couldn't see what "Mac" was so proud about – if he'd been bloody careless and got himself shot down in a 25,000 dollar-ship he wouldn't go bragging all over the place about it. Mike Graves too had gone unserviceable, with a sprained ankle. "Australia" was still in hospital, so we were rather short of pilots, especially section leaders. Dare not admit it, though, in case we'd have to give up some of our readiness to 249.'

'Later as we lay in the hospital talking,' wrote 'Mac' McLeod, 'the air raid siren went and it turned out to be our old friend "Steamboat Charlie". This was a name we had tagged onto the German photographic plane. He would come over sometimes before a raid and sometimes after. It became the goal of all pilots to attempt to send "Mr. Steamboat Charlie" to his ancestors. He would come over at high altitude out of range of our anti-aircraft fire and leisurely fly around the island taking pictures. I had gone at him at one time, as had almost everyone else in the Squadron, but due to the terrific speed of his stripped-down plane, we were always unable to catch him. It fell to the lot, at a later date, of one of the most colourful pilots on the island, "Buck" McNair, to finally catch up with "Steamboat" and send him down into the sea right near his home base. Of course, we all missed "Steamboat", but as you can well imagine, he was replaced by "Steamboat Charlie the Second" in very short order.

'The next couple of days we had to repair the aircraft and spent most of our time looking around the battered wrecks trying to get them into flying condition. The ground crew were having a tremendous job trying to keep a striking force of aircraft in serviceable condition.

'We usually managed to get the reports from the Italian radio and some of their wide-staked claims brought joy to us all. Their claim was the usual "thirteen Spitfires destroyed for the loss of none of their aircraft." This was certainly news to us, as there would have been no Spitfires flying that day. As usual, many rumours flew around. Some said they had been given out by the Rome radio and probably a lot of them had been started by fifth columnists. Rumour had it that the holy city of Rabat was going to be bombed. At this time, we were living in Rabat and we as well as the civilians were becoming very jumpy, that is, a little more than usual. At that time the gun fire and the crash and exploding of dropping bombs not even near, sent everyone rushing to shelter. We often wondered what the Maltese people thought of seeing so many pilots on the ground. It was hard to make them understand why we could not have more planes and why we could not fly those we did have. We learned one very good lesson though while in a shelter. We could hear the people of Malta mumbling and it got so that it got on our nerves. I remember asking a small Maltese boy who spoke English, "What in the world are they jabbering about?" He said, "Oh, they are praying for the pilots that are in the air and for the gunners who are above the ground unable to get protection". It made all of us more than a little ashamed for having been annoyed at their jabbering.

'During the air raid I struck up an acquaintance, in shall we say an athletic way, with the Maltese priest whom I used to call "the Midnight Express". I found out that although I was very slow afoot ordinarily, my speed on foot when advancing in the direction of a shelter increased tremendously when bombs were falling. I took off my hat to no–one except "The Midnight Express". I could not for the life of me beat my dark-robed friend to a shelter and believe me I was trying. With one hand on his head, holding his ancient-type hat and the other hand pulling up his skirt to allow freedom to his legs, he soundly trounced me in every one of our many sprints.

'It was this same afternoon, while we still were jittery at having passed the first raid, that we decided it wasn't all rumours. For in about two hours there was a gang of us on the roof, when suddenly, from out of nowhere there appeared about 25 Stukas. They were flying in crocodile straggle fashion. When directly above us, they started diving directly at our building. There was a dilapidated pool table on the floor below where we were standing, and inside of split seconds there were about thirty individuals under that pool table. Why I don't know, as it didn't offer much protection from the crash of the falling bombs. The bomb crash came, but luckily, they had aimed them at the airfield which lay directly underneath us. We were truly on edge and needed a good rest.

'During some of our off times we would wander through the catacombs and the ruffian of a guide told some good stories about the various skeletons seen. Primarily he was more interested in venting his displeasure at catacomb keepers in other sections of the island. He gave us his worthy knowledge for the price of ten shillings, which we afterwards found he had taken word for word from a booklet which could be bought for six shillings.

'We dropped up to the hospital to see "Australia", who had since been wounded and had another chat with Kurt Lauinger. Kurt was a young German, one of the quieter ones. He did not seem to be depressed and there was no doubt in his mind which was the better plane and who was going to win the war. The German pilots had tremendous faith in their aircraft and would not believe that they could be shot down by Spitfires or Hurricanes.'

'Kurt still thinks Germany will win,' wrote 'Tim' Johnston. 'Russia will be dealt with this summer and then they will turn on us; it may, however, take up to 18 months. He also says that Malta will be invaded and that within a month *he* will be bringing us cigarettes instead of vice versa.'

'Everywhere,' continues Don McLeod's diary 'you would go you would see signs written by the Maltese people, "Bomb Rome", "Bomb Rome". This was quite easy to write, but not so easy to do as we had no bombers. They could not understand that.

'It had been the idea of all the pilots that the only way we could get the German bombers was to go into the anti-aircraft fire after them as the German fighters did not do this. They would escort their bombers to the barrage and wait for them outside, very sensible, I'll admit.

'Mike Graves had a queer thing happen to him. He had been shot up by an "88" one day while trying to get home. His engine became overheated and at the last minute he discovered he could not make the field, so he rolled the plane over and bailed out at 400ft, pulled his ripcord and his chute opened just as he hit the ground in such a fashion that he did not even fall down. This is truly remarkable at such a low altitude.

'Oddities were common on the island – so many that space does not permit mentioning. George Beurling, a Canadian, who by his very accurate shooting and skilful piloting, managed to roll up one of the most fantastic scores of this war practically on his own. But George ran out of luck in the end and although he lived, was badly wounded on his last day on the island.'

'Wednesday the 8th of April was a day of raids,' noted 'Tim' Johnston. 'Four Spits and some Hurricanes took off against the afternoon wave and we congregated on the roof of the mess to watch. We saw the 88s diving through the barrage over Grand Harbour and right on the tail of one of them a Spit; saw the Spit checked in its tracks as if it had been hit, and then dive straight on into the ground without ever looking as if it could pull out. No one had seen the pilot get out and we wondered rather gloomily who it was, but later the news came through that it was "Nip" Heppell and that he had bailed out safely. All sorts of theories about what hit him, ack-ack, a canister thrown by the 88, but it was established later that it was a direct hit from a Bofors firing at the 88 ahead of him.'

Heppell suffered nothing more serious than gashes to his head and legs, and severe bruising. The Spitfire crashed into a cemetery at Sliema.

On 14 April Harry Kelly was shot down by Bf 109s, claiming one damaged before being shot down. He was forced to bail out at just 800ft, over the sea 3 miles west of Hal Far. His parachute failed to open properly and he hit the water, becoming entangled in the parachute lines and losing his dinghy but the streaming 'chute had kept him erect and he had hit the water at a peculiar angle, receiving nary a scratch. A pair of Spitfires went out to find him until the rescue launch could rescue him. HSL 128 picked him up at 1140 hours a couple of miles off-shore swimming quite strongly without his trousers, but making no apparent progress; Kelly even put up two fingers at them and blew through his moustache – or so it was said.

Meanwhile, on the evening of Friday, 10 April, soon after 1800 hours, another ace ran out of luck. Leutnant Hermann Neuhoff, with forty victories, who the day before had been appointed acting Staffelkapitän of 6/JG 53 – the 'Ace of Spades' Geschwader, was leading his new Staffel in his Bf 109F-4 'Yellow 1' in an attack on three Spitfires when he was shot down. He bailed out to become a prisoner of war. There is some doubt, however, as to his attacker was; either 'Buck' Buchanan on 249 Squadron, with a single fifteen-second burst, or 20-year-old Canadian Sergeant Garth Edwards Horricks of 185 Squadron. Born on 23 June 1921 in Pembroke, Ontario, Horricks had enlisted in the RCAF immediately upon the outbreak of war. He had flown off *Furious* to Malta on 13 September 1941 and in 1942 had become one of the best Hurricane pilots on the Island.

'Neuhoff would not believe he had been shot down by a fighter,' recalled Don McLeod 'and we all laughed when he said to "Buck", "and you, how many victories do you have?" And "Buck", with a little grin, pointed his finger at Neuhoff and said, "You are it!" The German could hardly contain himself.'

Kurt Lauinger too, could not believe that Neuhoff had been shot down. 'Never,' he said. It was only after Lauinger was persuaded to write a note to his Staffelkapitän in hospital at St Patrick's Barracks near Fort Madalena and receiving confirmation, that he exclaimed: 'Neuhoff shot down! And the things he used to say to me about my flying! He is in good company!' Neuhoff, who was one day shy of his 24th birthday, was awarded the *Ritterkreuz des Eisernen Kreuzes* (the Knight's Cross of the Iron Cross) on 16 June.

In total, on 10 April, Malta was attacked by three waves of enemy bombers under heavy fighter escort. The first, at 1246 hours, witnessed about fifty Ju 88s and twenty-one Ju 87s approaching Malta when no defending fighters were airborne. At 1300 hours the first wave of eight Ju 88s turned south to bomb Luqa and the Safi strip that linked Luqa and Hal Far airfields. Five minutes later a second wave raided gun positions to the south of Grand Harbour and several were damaged. During a third wave, which attacked Valletta, bombs hit Floriana and parachute mines were dropped near the war memorial, the granaries and Capuchins' friary, while twenty-one Stukas attacked the dockyard and bombs hit the joiners, fitters and painters' shops, and the sawmills. Four Bf 109s that attacked Hal Far, causing craters on the aerodrome, came under return fire from a light ack-ack battery. Ten Ju 88s dropped bombs on the Safi strip, damaging a Wellington and badly damaging two Hurricanes.

At 1740 hours four Spitfires of 249 Squadron were scrambled and soon sighted a large formation of eighty-five enemy bombers with their fighter escort. Flying Officer Norman Lee claimed a Ju 88 probably destroyed and one 'damaged'. Pete Nash claimed a Ju 88 'probable' and a Bf 109F 'damaged'. Pilot Officer 'Buck' Buchanan destroyed a Bf 109.

Eight Hurricanes of 185 Squadron intercepted ten Ju 88s with an escort of Bf 109s, destroying one Bf 109, damaging another and also damaging a Stuka. Pilot Officer Oliver Ogle 'Sonny'

Ormrod, who was from Wrexham in Denbighshire, crash-landed at Luqa and escaped from the aircraft before it burst into flames. Phillip Wigley and Sergeant Charles Ernest Broad on 185 Squadron were forced to bail out. Born in Easingwold, York on 11 April 1920, Ernie Broad had been a solicitor's clerk before the war. He had arrived in Malta aboard a Sunderland flying boat in March 1942. It is believed that Leutnant 'Tutti' Müller of I/JG 53 shot him down. Broad bailed out with shrapnel wounds to his left leg but he would return to action in May, now flying Spitfire Vs, and by the end of June he had claimed a total of two and one shared destroyed, two 'probables' and five 'damaged'. He was flown back to England at the end of July and was awarded the DFC.

Chapter 4

No Place for Beginners

Two new squadrons – 601 and 603 – had, this time, been brought out as squadrons, not assembled a number of pilots who had never seen each other before and given them a designation. Provided they had plenty of experienced people it should work out better.

Flight Lieutenant Hugh Anthony Stephen 'Tim' Johnston, 126 Squadron

On 25 April AVM Sir Hugh Pughe Lloyd GBE KCB MC DFC sent a very strongly worded signal to the Air Ministry in London. 'Regret that the quality of the pilots from Operation "Calendar" is not up to that of previous operations. Seven pilots out of 23 on 601 Squadron have had no operational experience and a further four have less than 25 hours flying on Spitfires; 12 pilots of the 23 have never fired their guns in action. The 601 Squadron CO also reports that seven of his experienced pilots were posted away from the squadron just before they left. Only fully-experienced operational pilots must come here. It is no place for beginners. Casualties up till now have been the beginners.'

On 1 April just eight Spitfires and nineteen Hurricanes had been serviceable but by the middle of April, the total fighters available had fallen to minute numbers – on five separate days there was just one Spitfire that was flyable and on two days there were none at all. Malta was staring defeat in the face. The governor knew that if the Island was to hold out, drastic action was needed – immediately. With capitulation just ten days away it was a question of survival. Reinforcement was essential if the Island, which Winston Churchill called: 'the peg on which all else hung' was not to fall. 'If we could get out of this jam by giving up Malta and Gibraltar and some African colonies, I would jump at it,' the Prime Minister said. 'But the only safe way is to convince Hitler that he cannot beat us.'

But miracles could happen and sometimes did. The town of Mosta was prone to aerial bombardment due to its proximity to Takali airfield. At about 1640 on 9 April the Luftwaffe dropped three bombs on the church, and two of them deflected without exploding. However, one 50kg high-explosive bomb pierced the dome and entered the church, where a congregation of more than 300 people was awaiting early evening Mass. The bomb did not explode, and a Royal Engineers Bomb Disposal unit defused it and dumped it into the sea off the west coast of Malta. This event was interpreted as a miracle. And, if the population of the Island did but know it, another miracle was imminent.

'In Malta the rumours were that help was on the way,' wrote Don McLeod. 'We began to hear fantastic rumours; rumours which we would have loved to believe, but which we were prone to take as just rumours. The Maltese civilians somehow managed to hear all the news first, especially the news of military importance long before we got it. It was really fantastic. No matter what it was they knew it first. They would tell us and we would later put confirmation on it. The rumour spread about the island that the *Wasp* was going to bring many, many Spitfires to the island. This was truly great news but though we tried hard to believe it, we still doubted it. We needed Spitfires badly.'

The rumour mill was rife on Malta. In early April 'Tim' Johnston had written in his diary about various doubtful truths. 'One that was everywhere was that the mess was going to be blitzed; said to have been given out on the Rome radio and no doubt disseminated by the local Fifth Column. Civilians more jumpy than usual, pilots too, for that matter.' On Wednesday, 15 April 'Tim' wrote that: 'There are all sorts of rumours flying about: the most common one is that the Hun is leaving Sicily today, next week, in the middle of May; it was to have been at Easter, but he didn't go. Another, that he has announced his intention of bombing Mosta and Mdina cathedrals. A third, that he knows where we are quartered and has issued a warning that he intends to wipe out the place; the fact that to do so would be more in his tradition than the present concentration on legitimate objectives adds to its force.

'The latest Maltese story is that a convoy of three American aircraft-carriers is bringing not less than 150 Spits to the island; that's the silliest one we've yet heard. These rumours play on alarm and despondency on one hand, and unfounded hopes on the other; they're probably the work of Fifth Columnists; there are said to be a certain number of these about and, as in France, it is not a case of the higher the fewer.'

On Tuesday, 7 April, 'Tim' Johnston got up early for dawn readiness, only to discover that there were no Spitfires serviceable so he and Mike Graves walked to the Bastion to watch the dawn. Later they went to Valletta to do some shopping and have a good lunch. They had barely finished when the sirens sounded. They decided to go to Fighter Control. As they arrived the first anti-aircraft guns opened up. They chose to make for a gun-site that overlooked the whole of Grand Harbour. In what was the Island's 2,000th, alert 273 enemy bombers attacked in 17 raid alerts in 24 hours; the heaviest raid of the war to date. During 0905 to 1039 hours a large formation of eighty-five Ju 88s and Stukas attacked in eight waves. In the first wave the Ju 88s dropped their bombs across the harbour in the dockyard area. A heavy barrage returned fire and Johnston and Graves could hear the shrapnel falling. After a slight pause Stukas in the second wave appeared. They flew almost directly overhead before starting to dive and then came down much more steeply than the Ju 88s and pulled out at a lower altitude. The target appeared to be the light cruiser HMS *Penelope,* which had been in dry dock on the opposite side of the harbour since 27 March for essential repairs.

The two pilots crouched behind sandbags and saw bombs fall all around her but she shot back at her attackers with every gun. It was a most inspiring sight. The huge pall of dust and smoke gradually drifted over until the sky was hidden from view. Then came the third wave and this time the target was Valletta. Johnston found it 'really frightening' because they could not see anything and there was nothing they could do. Above the noise of the barrage, they could hear 'the scream of a diving engine, the whistle of bombs and the thud and concussion of the explosion'. Sometimes the whistle was long and they'd know the bomb would fall some distance away; sometimes it was short and very sudden and they'd know it was near. The shortest of all ended in a 'stupendous' explosion about 6ft behind them and just 800 yards from the front of the public library, making an immense crater.

Johnston and Graves lay on the ground. 'Tim's' thoughts were of the graveyard passage in *All Quiet on the Western Front*. He wondered if this was as bad as the shelling of the First World War. He was definitely frightened and could feel his heart thudding, while at the same time shrinking at each whistle; something he'd never experienced in the air. He told himself that he would not be killed in an air-raid but he wished heartily that it would end. Eventually it did.

He heard afterwards that it was the largest raid that Malta had suffered until then. The all-clear finally sounded at about 1900 hours. Berlin radio would claim that many 1-ton bombs were dropped in the raid. Targets included the governor's palace and several residential districts in the capital. The Opera House was demolished.

The rumours about an imminent arrival of Spitfires had gained momentum, and generally, they were true. On 1 April Winston Churchill had cabled President Roosevelt, explaining in no fewer than four paragraphs the grim situation unfolding in Malta, and ending with an appeal for urgent assistance. 'Air attack on Malta is very heavy. There are now in Sicily about 400 German and 200 Italian fighters and bombers. Malta can now muster only 20 or 30 serviceable fighters. We keep feeding Malta with Spitfires in packets of 16 loosed from *Eagle* carrier from about 600 miles west of Malta. This has worked a good many times quite well, but *Eagle* is now laid up for a month by defects to her steering gear. There are no Spitfires in Egypt. *Argus* is too small and too slow, and moreover she has to provide fighter cover for the carrier launching the Spitfires and for the escorting force. We would use *Victorious*, but unfortunately her lifts are too small for Spitfires. Therefore, there will be a whole month without any Spitfire reinforcements … Would you be willing to allow your carrier *Wasp* to do one of these trips? We estimate that *Wasp* could take 50 or more Spitfires … Thus, instead of not being able to give Malta any further Spitfires during April, a powerful Spitfire force could be flown into Malta at a stroke and give us a chance of inflicting a very severe and possibly decisive check on the enemy …'

If the President agreed to help, then 'a powerful Spitfire force could be flown into Malta at a stroke'.

Roosevelt replied in the affirmative two days later, on 3 April. *Wasp*, with its critical ability to house forty-eight Spitfires or more against *Eagle*'s sixteen, would be made available for Operation 'Calendar'.

'While walking down to readiness on the 20th,' wrote Don McLeod, 'we heard aircraft overhead and we looked up and saw the first twelve Spitfires, and then another bunch of twelve and two bunches of eleven, 46 in all. As our hearts gladdened and our hopes rose, it gave us all a feeling which is as hard to describe as that of the first Christmas morning look when we were all children looking at the many new and shiny presents which with anticipation and great enjoyment were expected.

'As we neared the airfield our steps quickened because we were all eager for news and sure that the pilots that had come in were sure to be some of our old buddies from England and we wanted to know of the things that happened to our old outfits and how many kills they had made. Running the first three aircraft which were dispersed as soon as could be expected we saw no familiar faces and it was only the tired faces of pilots who had made the gruelling flight.'

'Tim' Johnston, who had certainly not been alone in hearing on the jungle telegraph that Malta was about to be reinforced, always found the sight and sound of a large formation affecting, but this one was so welcome and unexpected that it made him absurdly excited. 'We couldn't think where they'd all come from; general opinion was that it must have been from the Middle East, because there were too many to have come off the *Eagle* or even the *Eagle* and *Argus* together.

'We asked which and how many carriers had brought out the Spitfires and were amazed to learn that it was all done by one, the USS *Wasp*, which had fetched them all the way from England. It was lucky they arrived half an hour after the morning raid and we were able to get them stowed away in their pens before another could develop.'

As Don McLeod and his fellow pilots ran across the small opening to the next group of two Spitfires, the anticipation and great elation that they felt at seeing the delivery of Spitfires had begun to evaporate.

'Our joy turned immediately to apprehension as we heard the wailing of the air raid siren once again,' he wrote. 'We knew that the planes that had just landed would be short of fuel. They would be handicapped by long-range flight tanks and therefore would be unable to combat the "Hun" immediately. It must be realized that to refuel those airplanes each one had to be refuelled out of five-gallon tin cans of which each plane took 35 or more. It was our one hope that the Germans would be spotted, by radar. We pinned our one small hope on the thought that this would be our old friend "Steam Boat Charlie" on a reconnaissance flight. We dared to hope that we might have at least one hour to prepare those planes for combat. But once again we underestimated the "Hun". Shortly we heard the bursting of heavy anti-aircraft batteries. We realized that they alone at this time could save our aircraft. Climbing madly into the sun were the remaining six Spitfires we had on the island in the hope that they might ward off any threat to our two prizes. Standing there we realized that there was nothing we could do to save the lives. What we classified as our new babies. We watched the Ju 88s starting their bomb run on our airfields. Needless to say, we immediately dove into slit trenches and cowered there during the crescendo of the falling bombs.

'Part of our airplanes had landed at Takali and part at Luqa and we could hear the distant bomb blasts between our own shambles at Takali. We knew, too, that Luqa was getting a going over the same as we were. Since it had started what seemed to be a really fantastic number of bombers heavily escorted by fighters had come to Malta at the right time for them and had caught our Spitfires on the ground and blasted practically each and every one into unserviceable condition.

'Gazing around my eyes met the horrible picture of burning aircraft and the smell of smoke and torn asunder aircraft. We began now to see the men appear one by one, some with still high hopes, though most all with a definite solemn tired look on their faces. This surely was the straw that was going to break the camel's back. Yes, they got the planes to us all right, but we did not get to use them. The morale, already low, descended to the depths. The fury and hate which was already present against the enemy rose to a new and even higher peak, but all to no avail. We could not fly without planes; the planes had life all right, what was left of them. I remember running into "Jumbo" during the shambles and I never have seen a man so mad in all my life. What could you say? What could you do? "Jerry" had beaten us to the punch.

'It must have been a bunch of pretty pleased German pilots that winged their way back to Sicily after they had destroyed more planes in five minutes than they had been able to knock out of the sky in two months.'

The newly arrived pilots had been unable to scramble quickly because their Spitfires had come straight from the factory. Guns had to be harmonised and radios retuned. At 1930 hours eleven Spitfires from Takali and five from Luqa were scrambled to intercept the incoming aircraft. Six of the Spitfires from Takali had a dogfight with Bf 109s.

'Watching a dog-fight from the ground you would think it the most leisurely affair,' wrote 'Tim' Johnston. 'And it's almost impossible to imagine that the pilots are not circling warily round each other, but are in fact yanking their aircraft round until the g pulls their eyeballs down on to their Adam's apples.'

At 1720 hours on Monday, 20 April, sirens could be heard all over Malta. 'Tim' Johnston was not alone in wondering why they hadn't already been scrambled, as the Spitfires normally took off long before an alert. He found out later that the telephone lines were down. The delay prevented the five pilots that managed to take off from gaining enough height before the enemy bombers appeared. They saw six Spitfires take off from Takali and four Hurricanes from Hal Far, which made fifteen Spits in total; the most Johnston had ever known! As he took off, he discovered that his radio was not working. Johnston and the other five Spitfires in his squadron climbed to 8,000ft over the Island, the Spitfires flying five abreast, which he disliked because it was so unwieldly. Without R/T Johnston did not know what was happening when Squadron Leader Barton appeared to spot something. The formation had climbed up to 8,000ft and it now dived towards the north-west. Johnston could see bomb smoke and dust at Takali – 'not very much, what you'd expect from a few fighter-bombers' – and they came down to 3,500ft without seeing anything hostile, so they re-formed and began climbing once more. They could see a heavy dogfight in progress over St Paul's Bay.

When his engine developed a leak, spraying his windshield with oil, Johnston must have thought that this was not going to be his day. He had to abandon his pursuit of a single Ju 88 over Takali because he could not see through the restricted view. Skirmishing with other enemy aircraft, he headed back towards Luqa, where he spotted a pair of Bf 109s carrying out a strafing attack but in managing to avoid them at low level, his Spitfire was brought down by the blast from a delayed-action bomb dropped by a Ju 88 which exploded on impact with the ground. 'Tim' was blown straight up another 1,500ft but at 150ft he was able to bail out and open his parachute only seconds before he hit the ground.

Suffering nothing worse than a bruised heel, Johnston was flying with the squadron the next day, when only ten serviceable Spitfires and five Hurricanes were all that could be mustered to meet an estimated thirty-seven Ju 88s and thirty-four Bf 109Fs in raids on Grand Harbour, the docks, Luqa and Takali. Pilots of four Spitfires on 601 Squadron airborne from Luqa claimed two Ju 88s and one Bf 109 destroyed and a Ju 88 'damaged'.

The blast from the explosion that accounted for Johnston's Spit also knocked over 'Junior' Crist, who was on the airfield taking pot shots at strafing Bf 109s with his rifle!

'We were busy as soon as we arrived on Malta and were constantly after the Nazis,' Crist wrote. 'At first, they tried to chase us around and attacked our aerodromes and the harbour with their bombs, but we kept fighting back at them all of the time. Then they just dropped their bombs anywhere and did plenty of damage.' Crist, was twice wounded in action flying from Malta; the first time, on 29 April in an aerial combat over the Island when he was hit and slightly wounded by splinters in both hands and his left hip. After he recovered, he went back to the fight and in November he was wounded a second time, this time over Italy. He survived the war, having claimed at least one kill and two 'probables'.

On 20 April also, Flight Sergeant George Albert 'Ricky' Ryckman failed to return. The 22-year-old Canadian pushed his Spitfire into a left turn towards Valletta as he tried to escape the attention of Bf 109s but Leutnant Walter Zellot of 1/JG 53 followed and blazed away at his victim. Shortly afterwards

Right: Flight Lieutenant Thomas Francis Neil, a 20-year-old Battle of Britain Hurricane pilot who was one of 18 pilots on 249 Squadron who arrived in Malta on Operation 'Splice' on 19 May 1941 when 48 Hurricane IIs were flown off *Furious* and *Ark Royal*.

Below: Line up of 185 Squadron Hurricanes on Malta. (Rogers)

HMS *Ark Royal,* a veteran of several 'Club Runs' to Malta, before she was sunk on 13 November 1941 by a torpedo fired from *U-81* within sight of Gibraltar. The 1,487 officers and crew were transported to Gibraltar before the carrier capsized and sank at 0619 hours on 14 November.

One of the carriers to be used on Club Runs to Malta, HMS *Furious* was a converted Courageous-class battle-cruiser for the Royal Navy during the First World War, with a 160 feet flight deck built along its roof.

Above: Hawker Sea Hurricane on Malta.

Right: Air Vice Marshal Hugh Pughe Lloyd, who on 1 June 1941, was appointed Air Officer Commanding Malta.

Above: Hurricane night fighters at Takali in 1941.

Below: Savoia Marchetti SM-79 Sparviero bombers of the Regia Aeronautica in formation.

Squadron Leader Edward John 'Jumbo' Gracie DFC, who on arrival in Malta, took command of 126 Squadron.

HMS *Eagle* and HMS *Malaya* in the Mediterranean during Operation 'Spotter' on 7 March 1942.

Above left: Pilot Officer Donald Wilson 'Mac' McLeod (right) a 27-year-old native of Boston, Massachusetts and American 'Eagle' Spitfire pilot, who together with fifteen other pilots made up 126 Squadron that embarked on the long sea journey to Malta in February 1942.

Above right: Flight Lieutenant Hugh Anthony Stephen ('Tim') Johnston on 126 Squadron, who according to 'Mac' McLeod "became in the eyes of every pilot, the most intrepid, daring and courageous a man as one would hope to meet. Every flight he made became almost an epic."

Spitfire pilots en route to Malta on 'Picket 1' aboard HMS *Eagle*.

Above left: Group Captain Alfred Basil 'Woody' Woodhall, the esteemed Ground Control Officer during the Battle of Britain and on Malta was posted to RAF Duxford on 12 March 1940 as Controller, with the rank of Wing Commander. On Malta he was Senior Controller. One day in April 1942, he had controlled three Spitfires and four Hurricanes against an enemy plot of 130 plus. It was he who organised and conducted the fighter defence of the Island before as well as after the Spitfires arrived.

Above right: Squadron Leader 'Stan' Turner DSO DFC and Bar who in the spring of 1942 warned that unless Spitfires were sent to beleaguered Malta "within days, not weeks," Malta was "done for". That's it." On 7 March Turner welcomed the first Spitfires to be deployed outside of Britain to arrive on the Island.

American fleet defence Grumman Wildcats and Spitfire VCs, the latter earmarked for Malta, aboard the USS *Wasp*.

Left: Generalfeldmarschall Albert Kesselring, the German C-in-C South and the Luftwaffe's commander in Sicily.

Below: 'Tony' Clive William Holland on 603 Squadron taxi-ing out on *Wasp* on 20 April 1942 during Operation 'Calendar'.

Above: Spitfires on the USS *Wasp* for delivery to Malta.

Below: USS *Wasp* entering Hampton Roads on 26 May 1942.

Pilot Officer Jerrold Alpine Smith after making an emergency landing in his Spitfire Mk.Vb aboard the *Wasp*.

Maltese children play among the debris of a Ju 87 Stuka shot down over the Island.

Mercanti Market Strada destroyed by Axis bombing in 1942.

Above: Oil tanker on fire after an Axis air attack on Grand Harbour.

Below: Bombed out Maltese civilians at Valletta being evacuated to the Maltese countryside.

Spitfire VC (T) of 603 Squadron at Takali.

Spitfires of 249 Squadron at Takali.

Above left: American pilot, Reade Franklin Tilley, born in Clearwater, Florida on 15 March 1918. By July 1942 Tilley had increased his score to 7 enemy aircraft destroyed, 3 'probables', 6 'damaged'.

Above right: Squadron Leader Robert Alexander 'Butch' Barton DFC, the 249 Squadron CO with 'Howard'. In Tom Neil's view he was 'one of the best RAF fighter pilots of WW2, which was surprising, as he did not look like a hero. He was brave and calculating in battle, and, like many Canadians, was an excellent shot, both with a 12-bore shotgun and a Hurricane's eight Browning machine guns. Halfway through his tour of duty in Malta, he survived an engine failure on take off and a nasty crash in which he was injured and also disfigured by battery acid.' His final score was 12 and 5 shared destroyed, 2 probables, 5 and 4 shared damaged.

Air Vice Marshal Sir Keith Park, AOC RAF Malta in the final stages of the war.

Above left: Canadian Flying Officer James Hamilton Ballantyne on 603 Squadron. His final wartime tally was 8 and 1 shared destroyed, 2 'probables', 5 'damaged. He was KIA on 8 March 1944 flying a Spitfire IX on 403 'Wolf' Squadron RCAF looking for 'targets of opportunity' across the Channel.

Above right: Arthur Hay Donaldson DSO DFC AFC, Group Captain Churchill's wing commander flying on Malta.

Spitfire pilots en route to Malta on 'Pedestal' on HMS *Eagle*.

Spitfires being readied aboard HMS *Eagle* during Operation 'Pedestal'.

Rearming a
Spitfire on
Operation
'Pedestal'.

Above: John Joseph Lynch Jr of 249 Squadron, in the Qrendi Wing (left) and James 'Jimmie' Elvidge Peck from Berkeley, California (right) (an ex-American Eagle pilot on 126 Squadron like his friend Don McLeod) pictured in February 1944 in the Maltese Club of San Francisco. Lynch, of Alhambra, Alabama, shot down the thousandth Axis aircraft lost over Malta.

Left: 'Happy ever after.' Tom Neil and Eileen Hampton on their wedding day in 1945. It was at Biggin Hill in 1942 that Tom first met Flight Officer Eileen Hampton, who reached the rank of Pilot Officer in the WAAF. They had promised each other that they would marry as soon as the war was over.

the German could see a small flame and a light trail of smoke coming from the right side of the Merlin engine and pieces of the fuselage flying off. Swinging vertically from left to right, the Spitfire lost height, fell sideways and crashed into the sea from a height of just under 1,000ft. An oil slick was all that could be seen. It was Zellot's twelfth victory.

The next day, Zellot claimed his thirteenth victim when he shot down Squadron Leader John Derek Bisdee DFC, who had been given command of 601 Squadron in March. Bisdee had destroyed one of the Ju 88s for his seventh victory before he was jumped by 109s. Bailing out, he discovered that his parachute harness had been damaged and he was being held by one leg strap. Once in the sea, after extricating himself, he managed to inflate his dinghy. A 6-mile paddle took him back to Malta, where he then unknowingly walked through a mined beach. He was sent to the rest camp, returning to duty in May.

During the evening of 20 April, Hugh Pughe Lloyd, with his usual air of an attractive buccaneer, had given a pep talk at the Xara Palace for his newly arrived pilots. The AOC tried to put a brave face on things but he had been rudely interrupted by another bombing raid on the airfield. His pilots generally remained unimpressed. By the end of the day, about 300 Axis bombers had been sent to bomb the Maltese airfields. Forty tons alone had been deposited on Luqa and within three days 500 tons of bombs were dropped on the airfields at Takali and Luqa.

'The next day,' wrote Don McLeod, 'we had our usual few planes, nothing but battered wrecks, from which the crews managed to salvage a piece here and there and in time even managed to put a few of them in the air. Everybody, servicemen, ground men and pilots, all manpower available in fact, continually and earnestly made sand bags and revetments that we might possibly get some more aircraft.'

But the only aircraft that arrived on Malta in the early hours of 21 April were six Wellington IC bombers of 148 Squadron (with six additional crews and seven specialist groundcrew) that were flown in from Kabrit in Egypt via LG104 at El Daba, led by Wing Commander John Dudley Rollinson, plus one other from Gibraltar, all of which Hugh Pughe Lloyd had ordered in so that airfields in Sicily could be bombed. The Wimpys were speedily dispersed on the Safi strip, from where it was proposed that each should carry out three sorties each night against Comiso airfield.

'After an uneventful flight of 6 hours 20 minutes,' wrote Sergeant Wallace 'Wally' Gaul, a rear gunner on one of the Wellingtons, 'we were in the circuit at Luqa. The runway was well lit. There were no air raids on but we were told "to get our fingers out" and get over to the dispersal by following the truck in front. When we reached the dispersal and engines were switched off, I was the first out and I asked the truck driver what all the panic was about. "You will see in a few hours' time," he said.

'After the debriefing at the ops room we were told that billets for 16 crews and 96 aircrew and a few ground crews had been found for us at the palace at Naxxar (or "Nasher" as the RAF called it). We were told to stay out of sight when the raids were on. "Jerry" would not bomb the towns unless they were occupied by troops. That is why we were housed at Naxxar.

'What a contrast to the hut in a Maltese quarry where I had stayed one night in October 1941. A lot of people had lost their homes and were living in caves at the quarry. I was lucky to be invited into one where a family of eight was living. Although there was a shortage of food, especially of grain, and bread was rationed to just a few slices a day, the people of Malta were bearing up. At the end of the cave was an altar. An oil lamp had been burning and at one side was a small bunch of flowers. On the other side was a picture cut from the *Maltese Times* of a fighter pilot who had been killed on the Island. It was here that they prayed. Not for themselves, but for the fighter pilots, the men on the guns and the sailors on the convoys at sea.

'About thirty wide stone steps led up to the entrance to the palace at Naxxar. (I was expecting a footman to open the doors for us)! Inside the large hall were paintings on the walls and a well-polished floor led into rooms on each side. Most of the furniture had been stacked at one end of a room and had been replaced by RAF beds. As soon as we got sorted out it was time for kip. We had been on the go for 22 hours and it didn't take any time to get to sleep.

'I woke up next morning to the sound of air raid sirens. Not one of us bothered to get up. Then we heard the guns opening up and, although the bombs were some distance from the palace, the building began to shake. Get the hell out of here. There were slit trenches at the rear of the building, so we made a dive for them. Naxxar is on high ground, so we had a good view of the bombing.

'The yellow scramble flare was fired from Luqa, warning that a raid was imminent and to get fighters airborne. Children were pointing out to sea. They had seen the first wave of bombers approaching the island. Then I could see them; about fifty in the first wave. As they got close the guns began to open up. Soon the sky was full with black puffs of smoke and I could recognise the aircraft as Ju 88s. From about 15,000ft they started to dive on their target. This time it was Grand Harbour. It was the turn of light anti-aircraft guns to open up. I could see the tracers snaking up at the bombers as they dived. "There go the bombs!" someone yelled. A huge pall of black smoke was hiding the harbour from our view.

'As the first wave pulled away another wave was coming in. This time it was the Ju 87s; the Stuka dive-bombers. Their target was the airfield. As they dived, almost vertical, I could see the bombs leaving the aircraft and at the same time they would pull out of the dive and head for the sea. A Stuka released one large bomb … Christ! Was he going to pull out? No, he didn't. I could hear the islanders cheering as he crashed into the deck with an almighty explosion. They did this each time they saw a "Jerry" shot down.

'Our fighters were in amongst the bombers and the ack-ack. They were outnumbered by six to one. At the time we had only half a dozen that were serviceable. I saw one fighter coming in to land, probably out of ammo or fuel. Near to touchdown two Bf 109s attacked him. The fighter burst into flames. The pilot had no chance of getting out.

'As more bombers came in the sky was full with shell bursts, the black smoke from each shell forming into one big cloud. The sound of the guns and bombs was deafening. Amid all the noise I could hear the islanders cheering as enemy aircraft were brought down. The last wave had finished bombing and were heading out to sea, on course for their airfields in Sicily; airfields that we would be bombing that night. Quietness reigned over Malta. Smoke and dust were still rising and fires were burning on the airfields. Way out to sea a seaplane was picking up the airmen who had bailed out or had ditched in the sea.

'Three more raids, including an Italian raid, were to follow on 21 April. Six Italian aircraft, flying in vic formation with one at the rear at 15,000ft, released their bombs simultaneously flying on a straight and level course, leaving a trail of flak puffs behind them. They would hold this course across the island and never did I see one shot down.

'After each raid the bomb craters had to be filled in, runways repaired and cleared of debris. This would occur several times a day. The Royal Navy, soldiers, civilians and even the Maltese Police, assisted the understaffed RAF ground crews and at the end of the day they had had a "gut full". Valletta was out of bounds. Two of the boys did break bounds and got killed in the raids.

'I thought about the bar we used to go in, the mother, and the daughter George our Canadian front gunner fancied, and the Under 20 Club. I wondered if they had survived the bombing. I thought of the good times we had; the six of us. Now there were only three. How many more were going to make the boat?

'The "all clear" was sounded. It was time to return to the palace for a meal and to get our gear ready for the night ahead.'

'The Germans continued to harass the Island daily and almost continuously at night,' wrote Don McLeod. 'We had to keep moving our outfits from one place to another and it seemed that no matter where we moved, we became the target of the Huns. They certainly must have had a Fifth Column on the island somewhere. The only good feature of the entire show was the fact that several of our buddies had arrived on the island with the new planes. Tilley (called "Florida") and "Tiger" Booth, two buddies of "Jimmie's" and mine in the Eagle Squadron, joined our outfit.'

On 21 April 'Jumbo' Gracie led his flight of four Spitfires on 126 Squadron to the north, where he awaited the departing bombers. Spotting a section of three Ju 88s below, he dived on them from above and astern, claiming two shot down into the sea. He also scored strikes on three more before they flew home and was awarded two bombers destroyed, one 'probable' and two damaged. 'Jimmie' Peck claimed strikes on another Ju 88 before the escorting 109s descended on the Spitfires from 18,000ft. 'Tim' Goldsmith, flying No. 2 to Peck, claimed one of the fighters shot down.

On 24 April 'Tim' Johnston came to readiness at dawn and at 0730 he and three other pilots on 126 Squadron were scrambled. They just missed the first raid of the day but ran head-long into the next wave diving on Grand Harbour. It was every man for himself and they made for the nearest of the Ju 88s but 'Tim' had to fight off four Bf 109s before he finally was able to single out a Ju 88, which obligingly flew within 100 yards of his him. He dived on him flat-out and waited until he had closed to 200 yards when he opened fire with a five- or six-second burst from dead astern. He could see the HE incendiary shells exploding as they hit and what looked like a mixture of black-and-white smoke began pouring from both engines. The Ju 88 then turned right-handed very sharply until it was almost standing on its starboard wing-tip. For a moment Johnston hoped that he was going to roll over on his back and dive to the ground; in any case Johnston felt certain that he was finished, so he pulled away and began to look for another victim. However, the other Ju 88s had come out of their dives higher than his and he could not get up to their height before they reached safety, so he turned back and landed without further incident. He was awarded a Ju 88 'probable'. Two days later he claimed a Ju 88 'damaged'. On 6 May he claimed a Bf 109 'damaged' but was shot down in flames, which resulted in him being hospitalised with wounds to his arms and legs and burns to his face. He was awarded a Bar to his DFC and was returned to England when he was fit to travel. His total score flying from Malta was six destroyed, three 'probables' and one shared 'probable', with nine 'damaged'.

After four days of continuous fighting the number of available Spitfires had been reduced to six. On 22 April 'Buck' McNair wrote that: 'The old hands could only look at each other. It was Malta's darkest hour.'

Fortunately, following another appeal by Churchill to Roosevelt, the American President had come to England's rescue once more and Operation 'Bowery' could proceed. The PM sent a note to the Chief of the Air Staff. It consisted of one sentence: 'Now that the President has agreed about *Wasp* let me know the programme for feeding Malta with Spitfires, week by week, during the next eight weeks.'

Having arrived at Scapa Flow on 26 April, *Wasp* returned to the Clyde on the 29th for loading forty-seven Spitfire Vcs from lighters but the condition of the Spitfires' essential 90-gallon long-range fuel tanks was no better than it had been for 'Calendar'. They still fitted badly and consequently leaked. John

W. Reeves Jr, *Wasp*'s captain, stopped the loading and it only went ahead after the tanks were fixed by his own personnel. On 3 May *Wasp* and her two escorts, a pair of American destroyers, USS *Lang* and USS *Skerrett*, sailed for Gibraltar with the RN escort to join *Eagle* (now repaired after being laid up for a month with defects in her steering gear). 'Stan' Turner, who on 14 March had been promoted to wing commander flying at Takali, had left on 30 April for Gibraltar to organise the reinforcement flight from *Eagle*, which prior to joining Force 'W' on 7–8 May, loaded seventeen Spitfires delayed from previous 'Club Runs'.

'It wasn't until the night of May 8th,' wrote Don McLeod, 'that we finally got the story. "Jumbo" had disappeared from the island about a week or ten days previous and we all figured that he had gone to another theatre. But such was not the case. Wing Commander Gracie had flown to London in accord with the plan formulated in his mind to beat the "Hun" to the punch. As we waited, there was a group meeting of all·of the pilots on the island. "Woody" was in excellent humour, which was not the usual thing for "Woody" when things were going bad. There was no more important a man in the air battle of Malta. His quiet, calm, assuring, voice directed pilots time and time again on their prey, the German bombers and fighters. I think, without a question of a doubt, that one of the truly great men of the war was, in the eyes of the pilots, the saviour of the island of Malta. As "Woody" smiled, and sort of laughed to himself. "The AOC is coming up presently and he will give you the story."

'The AOC, commonly known as "Hugh Pughe", only of course, not in his presence, was a well-liked boss of the air battle of Malta. He was a man of indomitable courage and with a tremendous hate against the "Hun". It wasn't long before "Hugh Pughe" came in and gave a very short but effective talk. "… you all know what happened two weeks ago. To those of you who are now on the island that was only a taste of what the Hun has thrown at us here. It has not as yet been possible for us to strike back at them in the way we all want to. But by the grace of God, gentlemen, tomorrow we will turn the tide of the Battle of Malta. We will start the end of the destruction of the greatest enemy of mankind, the Nazi hordes … the fate of many lives will be born on your shoulders, the fate of the African armies, the fate of the Russian supply route and the fate of them as individuals depends upon the glorious success on the morrow.'"

Don McLeod found it inconceivable how Gracie had formulated his plans so quickly, but nevertheless the AOC, who that same evening addressed all squadron and flight commanders at the Xara Palace, revealed that 'tomorrow morning sixty Spitfires will arrive from the decks of the aircraft carrier *Wasp*. The *Wasp* being as large as she is will sail into the Mediterranean approximately the same distance as most of you did when you came in here. The pilots from the carrier will be just as tired when they arrive here as you were. The aircraft have been assembled in England and come directly here aboard the *Wasp* … each squadron on the island; namely 126, 249, 601 and 603, have definite plans in the air battle. That I will leave to your respective squadron leaders.'

'As he began to utter his final words,' recalled Don McLeod, 'the whistle of bombs, not so far away, caused most of us to duck into corners, but without breaking a word in his sentence, and almost drowned out by the crash of bombs, he said, "We must not fail." There was a tremendous uplift of the morale of all the pilots. Hopes rose as we all got into our different groups to get the final words.

"'Tony" Barton, now acting as CO, said, "Fellows, this is it. One half of the aircraft will land at Takali and one half at Luqa. As you all know there are many pens built. Each of these pens will house an aircraft. At each pen there will be a number of men of whom one will be an experienced Malta pilot. The minute the aircraft touches the ground he will be flagged immediately into a pen in the dispersal area. Ground crewmen will instantly tear off the long-range gas tanks; another crewman will begin pouring gas from already handy five-gallon tins. Each squadron will have a definite purpose. Our purpose will be to intercept combat enemy fighters. The positions of the other three squadrons will be varied. We will then attempt the diversion of the bombers from the targets. The other aircraft from the island will be used in defending you and other squadrons in their efforts. In other words, the success of the entire operation depends upon you becoming immediately airborne. With units cooperating as usual and with good luck gentlemen, we can turn the tide of this, our little war. The minute that our radar picks up a bomber strength building up over Sicily every aircraft will become airborne.

"'Immediately upon arrival at your pen you will get the pilot out of the aircraft who flew it in, put him to work in some handy way, get yourself into the aircraft, strapped in and ready for instant take-off. When your flare is given from the dispersal hut, each section of aircraft will give it the gun and take off. When your flare is given, you will have a clear field. If you should have only a half tank of gas take off anyway.".

'Needless to say, we all like a bunch of kids that night. Whether or not we could beat the Hun to the punch we were soon to know.'

In April the CO of 603 (City of Edinburgh) Squadron, Lord David Douglas-Hamilton had received a call at the officers' mess at Dyce Airport, Aberdeen, from Flying Officer John Walter Buckstone. The message was so secret that it could not be passed over the telephone, so Buckstone hurried to see him to deliver the news that the squadron was being posted to the Middle East. He added that he had seen reports from Malta of the numbers of aircraft shattered by bombs, and it looked as if Malta had had it.

Douglas-Hamilton and William Anderson Douglas, his second in command, born in Edinburgh in 1920, were Scots. On 14 June 1941 Bill Douglas had damaged a Bf 109. He destroyed another on the 21st and was wounded on the 23rd by cannon shell splinters on a patrol near Calais and was off operations until November 1941, becoming one of Archibald McIndoe's guinea pigs after being treated in the Queen Victoria Hospital, East Grinstead. The other pilots came from the USA, Canada, New Zealand, South Africa, Belgium, Ireland and England. Many of them had never fired their guns in anger. Only Bill Douglas, Buckstone and Lester Vincent 'Sandy' Sanders had flown on sweeps over northern Europe. The nine other pilots had never flown on offensive sorties.

On Easter Sunday, 12 April, 603 Squadron was taken by bus to from Shieldhall on the River Clyde, where before them lay the huge American aircraft carrier, the USS *Wasp*, with Spitfires being hoisted on to the flight deck. At 2030 hours, along with the pilots of 601 (County of London) Squadron, the pilots of 603 Squadron began to board, while in Malta the enemy had apparently abandoned the assault on morale following Tuesday's raid on Valletta. One RAF airman even had time to compose this ditty in between air raids aimed at the airfields:

Tis Holy Thursday, let us snooker
All the bloody Spits at Luqa,
Forward Messerschmitt and Stuka –
Hallelujah!

Good Friday, it is Hal Far's turn.
Prang the crews, the aircraft burn,
Will the blighters ever learn?

Now Kampfgeschwaders, rise and shine,
Mix Takali's medicine
'Satan' works like No. 9
Hallelujah!

Kesselring's Easter Hymn. (The Generalfeldmarschall was
   C-in-C South and the Luftwaffe's commander in Sicily)

In Malta, on 12 April, a Hudson of 267 Squadron from Egypt carrying Air Marshal Sir Arthur Tedder had touched down at Luqa a few minutes after a heavy air raid, to enable the AOC Middle East to obtain first-hand knowledge of the situation on the Island. As soon as Tedder arrived at Takali there was a raid on the airfield and from the veranda of the officers' mess he was able to get an excellent view of the Luftwaffe making diving attacks and to watch the encircling patrol of Bf 109s. Tedder's visit to Hal Far also coincided with attacks on the airfield by ground-strafing Bf 109s. Gefreiter Horst Gisy of 4/JG 53 was killed when his Messerschmitt was shot down by machine gun fire from Flight Sergeant H.T. Gibbs, 830 Squadron's senior ground NCO. One pilot officer recalled that Tedder gave them a pep talk and he lauded them for the 'magnificent job' they were doing but everyone wished he would go up in one of the Hurricanes and take on the 109s that outnumbered them at least ten to one!

LAC Metcalf at Takali confided in his diary that he 'would remember this Easter' (should he be one of the lucky ones that got away with it!). 'From dawn to dusk wave after wave of 88s, 87s and other "gash kites" to make weight bombed and better bombed.'

During one lull Metcalf bobbed his head above the slit trench and suddenly spotted a fresh wave of 88s coming in over St Paul's. He counted twenty-seven but when the leader put his nose down and began a power dive straight for him, he could neither speak nor move! Luckily for Metcalf the enemy aircraft came over a few feet too low and the bombs went over the top of him.

'What a Hell-hole,' he wrote. That night he heard the BBC report that *enemy activity over Malta was on a reduced scale.* He wished that 'the bloke who read it out' had been in the slit trench with him at 6pm!

By 13 April *Wasp* had collected fifty-two Spitfire Vbs from the two fighter squadrons with pilots. The Spitfires to be conveyed were fitted with 90-gallon long-range external fuel tanks to extend their range but the tanks leaked badly, a fault that recurred on 'Club Runs' and in addition, many of the guns were faulty and most of their radios did not work. By 1000 hours the *Wasp*, carrying forty-seven Spitfires, left Port Glasgow, slightly damaging its screw on the mudbank. At 0600 hours on the 14th, she was moving slowly down the Irish Sea, escorted by the Royal Navy's battlecruiser HMS *Renown* and six Royal Navy destroyers.

Finally, forty-seven Spitfire Vbs were embarked and *Wasp*, minus its torpedo bombers and dive bombers, which were landed at Hatston in Orkney, left the Clyde on 14 April. On Sunday the 19th, *Wasp* and her heavy British and American escorts went through the Straits without pause at Gibraltar. At 0415 hours on Monday, 20 April the Spitfire pilots had breakfast on the *Wasp*, which lay about 35 miles north of Algiers. At 0445 they received a final briefing from Wing Commander MacLean. *Wasp* spotted eleven Grumman F4F Wildcat fighters on her deck and quickly launched them to form a combat air patrol (CAP) over Force 'W'. Meanwhile, the Spitfires were warming up their engines in the hangar deck spaces below. With the Wildcats patrolling overhead, the Spitfires were brought up singly on the after elevator, spotted for launch, and then given the go-ahead to take off from their flying off position at 0530 hours. An RAF mechanic who inadvertently backed into the spinning propeller of one of the Spitfires was killed.

One by one, the Spitfires took off and roared down the deck and over the forward round down before winging their way toward Malta. 'Jumbo' Gracie was first away at 0545, followed by forty-six more Spitfires, the second group being led by Squadron

Leader John Bisdee and his twelve Spitfires. Gracie almost made a mistake by flying towards Gibraltar instead of Malta, but he was called up on the radio and he quickly corrected his course.

David Douglas-Hamilton's Spitfire was pushed on to the left of the flight deck and he started up the engine of his Spitfire. He let the brakes off with a snap and the aircraft slowly gathered speed, becoming airborne just before the end of the deck. After reaching the rendezvous height the other Spitfires formed up behind him and Bill Douglas. Everything seemed to be going like clockwork but Sergeant Salvatore 'Bud' Walcott RCAF, one of three Americans on the squadron, was 'missing'. Walcott, who had grown up in Lenox, in Berkshire County, Massachusetts, shared a cabin on the *Wasp* with Canadian Flight Sergeant Morton Haist Buckley. It is thought that Walcott had told him that he had no intention of going to Malta. The errant Walcott had once survived an horrific crash in a P-47 Thunderbolt at Raleigh-Durham, North Carolina. Later, while serving on an American Eagle squadron in England he had made an emergency landing in a Hurricane at Dublin Airport in the Irish Republic because he was almost out of fuel after getting lost. Rather than being interned he had been allowed to leave the next day. Walcott was not seen again after take-off from the *Wasp*. Stories abounded that he had crash-landed his Spitfire on the south side of the Atlas Mountains in Vichy-controlled North Africa and then made his way to a US consulate in Algeria, claiming to be a lost civilian pilot.

The rest of the Spitfire formations gained height, flying onwards at under 200mph to save fuel, towards the sun, still low on the horizon. Through the early morning haze the French

African coast could be seen to starboard. The blue sky against the grey Mediterranean made perfect flying weather and the pilots never lost sight of the African coast. Near Tunis the Italian island of Pantelleria, 100 miles from Malta, which was a base for Messerschmitts, came into view and if 109s were around, they were not seen. Sicily and Mount Etna could also be seen; the distant islands of Malta and Gozo tiny by comparison. Pilots gave Pantelleria a wide berth and began their descent towards Takali, a section of Spitfires from Malta covering 'Jumbo' Gracie's approach to the Island. The London squadron headed for Luqa while the Edinburgh formation circled Takali before making a formation landing into the wind in sections of four across the runway.

David Douglas-Hamilton taxied his Spitfire into one of the blast pens and jumped out. A pilot on 249 Squadron was coming to fly it once it had been refuelled. Douglas-Hamilton could see Malta's tiny, yellow-painted, square houses and fields honeycombed with stone walls, surrounding fig bushes, green crops and prickly pear. On closer inspection, however, this outwardly peaceful scene blended in menacingly with bomb damage all around.

Wing Commander Jack Satchell DFC arrived in his car and drove David Douglas-Hamilton around the airfield, showing the new arrival a bomb crater 'that could have swallowed a house'. There were parts of burnt-out aircraft of all descriptions that had been shot down nearby. Everywhere there were bomb craters, wreckage and battered buildings. Satchell had been bombed out of no fewer than three buildings and had moved into a tented HQ; his staff being quartered underground. Satchell drove up to the officers' mess in Mdina on a small hill overlooking Takali, a mile from the airfield. It was almost lunch time when the air raid siren began sounding, warning of the second raid of the day. Satchell told his passenger that it would take fifteen minutes for the enemy bombers to appear. They put on their tin helmets and went onto the mess veranda to watch the horrific series of events unfold. Anti-aircraft guns opened up with a crescendo of explosions from the 'pointer rounds', which if they burst near the raiders' aircraft would indicate the positions to the half dozen Spitfires and six Hurricanes that had been scrambled to intercept the Luftwaffe bombers.

'We saw the Me 109s clearly,' wrote Douglas-Hamilton later. 'They were weaving in and out of the shell-bursts. Suddenly, gun after gun burst into life, until a first-class barrage was in full swing. The bombers were arriving. The sky rapidly became dotted with shell-bursts, and then we saw them: three, five, ten about twenty Ju88s in straggling formation, all making for Takali – our aerodrome. One after another they dived down towards the aerodrome and dispersal areas. We could clearly see them releasing their bombs, and followed the bombs in their flight to earth.

'The 88s dived down to about a thousand feet above the ground, and we saw the great explosions of the bombs on their target. Seconds later we heard the noise of the explosions following on the sinister whistle of the falling bombs, and felt the blast. Meanwhile, the Bofors guns joined in the din as the 88s came low, shooting up streams of glowing red "cricket balls" at them. Huge fountains of dust rose up from the aerodrome where the bombs had burst, and in two places there was a thick column of black smoke billowing up. These were obviously petrol fires – they had got two of our nice new Spitfires.

'Someone shouted, "The Spits are getting into them!" We looked, and saw three or four Spitfires chasing the 88s. One of them opened fire, and we saw the puffs of smoke from its cannon. Almost at once one of the 88's engines streamed smoke. We lost sight of it, but heard afterwards that it came down in the sea. Then the Me 109s got mixed up with the Spitfires, and a general dog-fight ensued.

'We were all shouting as if at a football match: "Good show; now you've got him! Look out Spit, 109 coming down on you; turn, man, for God's sake, turn!" Then, "Thank God for that!" as the Spitfire turned and avoided the 109's fire.

'The Huns had no sooner finished with Takali than we saw a similar bunch of bombers going for Luqa aerodrome, another for Hal Far aerodrome, and yet another for the Grand Harbour. The harbour party was reinforced with a good sprinkling of Ju 87s, which amazed us by the steepness of their diving angle. We saw with horror many of the bombs going wide of their mark and bursting among civilian houses and villages.

'All this time the entire air over the island was filled with whirling aircraft and anti-aircraft bursts, and the noise of guns, shells and bombs was intermingled with the rattle of aircraft cannon-fire and the whine of diving aeroplanes. Here and there we saw an 88, streaming smoke, but we never actually saw one crash that day, though it is known to us that several were destroyed.

'For us new arrivals the sight of a first-class bombing raid from a ringside seat was the most staggering thing we had ever experienced. Many of us, including myself, had never even heard the whistle of a bomb before. Some of us had not till now even seen any enemy aircraft, and few of us had seen them in such large numbers, or been able, unmolested, to watch aerial combats from the ground.

'It all seemed an incredible spectacle to us coming from comparatively peaceful Britain, and we could hardly believe we were really there. It was more like being at a cinema show, for in many ways one felt quite detached. But now we rapidly learnt to distinguish between the sharp "bang" of an AA gun and the reverberating "woomph" of a bomb. The same performance was repeated again at tea-time, and at dusk we had a fourth raid on Takali.'

Air Vice Marshal Sir Hugh Pughe Lloyd and Group Captain Woodhall, the sector commander, one of the most exceptional fighter controllers of the war who masterminded countless aerial battles from the ground, had been delayed while trying to reach Takali to welcome the newly arrived pilots on *Wasp* when a bomb splinter punctured a tyre on their car. Usually, Lloyd made a point of arriving just when a heavy blitz was about to begin, much to the anxiety of his headquarters' staff. Dismissing shelters, he would tour the dispersal areas with bombs bursting all around his car.

Lloyd watched the bombing raids carefully, and counted about twenty-five Stukas and sixty-four Junkers 88s in wave after wave, dive-bombing Takali. By the end of the day about 300 Axis bombers had been sent to Malta, mainly to destroy the new Spitfires, many of which were still being serviced before being put back into the air. Forty tons of bombs had been dropped on

Luqa immediately, and within three days, 500 tons of bombs were dropped on the Takali and Luqa aerodromes.

That evening Lloyd and Woodhall addressed the new pilots, putting them in the picture about what had happened, and what would be expected of them. Woodhall urged the pilots to strike back as hard as possible at the Luftwaffe: Air Marshal Lloyd noticed the reaction to the new pilots to all of this, and wrote: 'Then had never been such an exhibition of concentrated bombing. The newly arrived pilots were speechless. They had never seen anything like it.'

Lloyd's, and Woodhall's pep talks, in which 'Woody' urged the pilots to strike back as hard as they could at the Luftwaffe, made a vivid impression on David Douglas-Hamilton: 'There is no doubt that those two men, who with dogged tenacity ran the aerial defence of the island during its most difficult period, have earned the undying gratitude of Malta,' he wrote.

But this proved to be the heaviest day of bombing Malta sustained during the war. The Luftwaffe pilots had been fortunate to score direct hits and the heavier bombs dropped had caused much damage. Their impact had blown the protective walls of the blast pens on to the Spitfires, putting most of them out of action. It was suspected that the raid had been so severe, not only because of the arrival of Spitfires, but also in honour of Hitler's birthday. It was evident that Takali was in a state of chaos, though thanks to the soldiers of the Inniskillings and the Manchesters, who worked throughout the night with arc lamps, the bomb craters were filled with hundreds of tons of stones, which they flattened and rolled flat. They also cleared the airfield of debris and it was operational again by first light.

And the AOC too, remained defiant, finishing his evening talk with the words: 'In the future, after this war, when the name of Malta is mentioned, you will be able to say with pride, "I was there!"' At that moment the whole building shook with the crash of the bombs of the dusk raid.

Ever after that, whenever anyone went through some particularly trying experience, such as a near miss by a bomb or being shot up in the air, he would be chaffed with the words: 'Never mind, you'll be able to say "I was there!"'

Chapter 5

Who Said a Wasp Couldn't Sting Twice?

*The primary need is Spitfires and more Spitfires. They must
not arrive in dribbles, but in really big quantities ... At all
costs we cannot avoid the danger of our fighter force being
worn down before the convoys arrive so that it will not be
strong enough to protect it on arrival ... If Malta is to be
held, drastic action is needed now. It is a question of survival.*
General Sir William Dobbie, the Governor of
Malta, 20 April 1942

On Monday, 4 May, at 5,000ft near Naxxar, Flight
Lieutenant Norman MacQueen on 249 Squadron
was bounced by Bf 109s of III/JG 53, one of which
piloted by Unteroffizier Walter Manz managed to dive through
the Spitfires, pull up under him, unseen from dead astern and
fire a quick snap shot in the underside of MacQueen's Spitfire.
Flying No. 2, Fred Elbert Almos had called him over the radio
to warn of the approach of the 109 and to break. There had been
no reaction. MacQueen faltered, and in the event, continued to
fly almost all the way back to Takali before watchers on the mess
veranda at Naxxar saw him nose diving into the ground just
short of the runway pouring white glycol smoke.

'Norman was flying with another Spitfire and about to attack
some 109s, when we saw a 109 sweep across the sky behind him,'

David Douglas-Hamilton said. 'Vainly, we shouted, "Turn Spit!" as if there was some hope that he might hear us. But evidently neither of them saw the 109 and just kept straight on. We saw the 109's tracer going right into Norman's machine. His Spitfire lurched and gave up a thin smoke trail. For some time, it seemed to be under control and circled downwards as if he hoped to land. Then suddenly, the nose went forward and the machine dived like a stone into the ground, bursting into flames as it hit. I felt a lump come into my throat.'

'It was believed that the tracer fire in the attack had wounded him and as a result, he had lost consciousness on the way back to his airfield. Poor "Mac",' wrote 'Tim' Johnston. 'He was the most likeable and modest person – also, one of the most successful, with seven confirmed plus "probables" in the two months he'd been here. When someone is shot down you shut your mind to it and carry on as if he was away on leave. It was only when I saw that MacQueen's bed, which stood opposite the door, and all his personal kit, including a photograph of a girl, had been taken way, that it came home to me what had happened.

'Heard Douglas-Hamilton of 603 describe how he'd attacked a Stuka and shot the whole glass-house off it. As he'd overrun it, he'd passed within a few feet and had been able to see the gunner sprawling over the back of the cockpit, one arm over the side, headless. They wouldn't give him more than a damaged.'

It is most probable that in letters home to Lady Prunella Douglas-Hamilton, her husband spared her the agonies of war. Save to say, he still painted a vivid picture of life on Malta. 'We are certainly in the thick of things here and every day has its excitements, but we have the feeling that it is a great job of work and will help greatly towards winning the war. The Germans have lost all chance of capturing Malta, I believe, and I am more convinced than ever that it will hold out. They may try and give it hell by bombing, but we are well used to that by now, and it will avail them nothing. Further, every day we hit back at them and give them not inconsiderable losses to think about.

'We console ourselves by saying that every bomb here is one less at home or against Russia: and I gather they say at home that every bomb there is one less upon Malta!'

Following on from the relative success on 'Calendar', Winston Churchill was growing deeply anxious about Malta under the unceasing bombardment of 450 first-line German aircraft. He cabled President Roosevelt once more: 'If the Island fortress is to hold out till the June convoy which is the earliest possible, it must have a continued flow of Spitfires. The last flying from *Wasp* was the most successful although unhappily the enemy's attack broke up many after they had landed.

'We are using *Eagle* to send in 15 or so at a time. I shall be grateful if you will allow *Wasp* to do a second trip ... Without this I fear Malta will be pounded to bits. Meanwhile, its defence is wearing out the enemy's Air Force and effectively aiding Russia.'

Once again, the American President agreed and on 30 April *Wasp* returned to Glasgow to take on board more Spitfires for Malta in Operation 'Bowery'. Early on Saturday, 9 May *Wasp* and *Eagle* reached their flying-off points to begin releasing their sixty-four Spitfires at first light. Squadron Leader Stanley Grant, who had led the first reinforcement flight in early March, had flown to Gibraltar on 30 April with several others to lead in this further group of reinforcements. At 0630 *Wasp* began flying off the eleven Wildcats of VF-71 to take up their defensive positions over the task force. *Eagle* prepared to fly off her seventeen Spitfires in two waves from the take-off point just north of Algiers; a flying time to Malta of three hours and thirty minutes at a height of 10,000ft. Her flight-deck was 667ft 7in, overall, perceptibly shorter than the *Wasp* with 720ft. Instructions from Wing Commander John Stirling McLean DFC, a New Zealander, born 19 February 1912 at Hawera, Taranaki, were clear cut and direct. 'After take-off climb to 2,000ft; switch on to the 90-gallon overload tank and switch off the main tanks. If, by chance, your overload tank doesn't work you either gain height and bail out, in which case the Navy ought to be able to pick you up, or, if you don't fancy that, then fly south to North Africa, destroy the aircraft and get off back home. In no circumstances try to land back on the carrier.'

Squadron Leader Grant took off from *Wasp* at 0643 hours but the flying off of one of the forty-seven Spitfires that was piloted by Flight Sergeant Robert Donald Sherrington RCAF, ended in tragedy. The 20-year-old Canadian from Toronto, Ontario, took off with his airscrew in coarse pitch and dropped off the bows of the carrier. He was cut in half as the *Wasp* knifed through his Spitfire.

'Laddie' Lucas, who that May would twice fly to Gibraltar to lead flights of reinforcement Spitfires from the decks of aircraft carriers, was just setting course from *Eagle* with his flight of Spitfires when down below he spotted a Spitfire circling *Wasp*, now steaming flat out in a twinkling, sunlit sea, with a wind speed of perhaps 45 or 50 knots over the deck. 'One pass over the ship and now the pilot was turning in tight towards the flight deck on his final approach.' Lucas could not believe it; he wondered who it could be with that sort of nerve. 'No hooks, no arresting gear … The Spitfire seemed almost to be hanging in the air having little more speed than the ship.'

Pilot Officer Jerrold Alpine Smith, a 21-year-old Canadian, born on 26 March 1921 in Regina, Saskatchewan, had discovered after take-off that his long-range fuel tank was u/s (failed to draw). Now incapable of reaching Malta, 'Jerry' jettisoned the tank and circled until the deck was clear before landing back on the *Wasp* without a tailhook with full authorisation of Captain Reeves.

The Landing Signal Officer, Lieutenant (later Captain) David McCampbell, who was to become one of the US Navy's most gifted and successful pilots in the Pacific theatre in 1944 with thirty-four victories, recalled the hair-raising incident with the returning Spitfire. 'Fortunately, I had given all the Spitfire pilots a briefing to acquaint them with operations aboard ship. I told them that if anyone saw me jump into the net alongside my platform, he would know the plane coming in was in trouble and must take a new approach. On his first approach, the pilot was much too high and too fast … so I simply jumped into the net. He got the news real fast. Next time I got him to slow down and make his approach a little lower. I then decided to give him the "cut" signal [to land] … He landed with his wheels a few feet short of the forward part of the flight-deck. That night in the wardroom, the Air Officer, Commander Michael H. Kernodle presented him with a pair of navy wings!'

'Jerry' Smith's landing on the carrier was the first ever for a Spitfire and was called 'a feat unparalleled' by Sir Hugh Pughe

Lloyd. Next day at Gibraltar, 'Jerry' Smith was taken to the wardroom on *Wasp*, where it was said Douglas Fairbanks Jr, the liaison officer, pressed the largest Scotch and soda you ever did see into his hand. 'Here', he said, 'drink this quick!'

Sergeant William John Johnson, who at the start of 1941, had been commissioned and had claimed his first victory on 26 June 1941, must have thought that a posting to 611 Squadron on Malta, on 1 April 1942, was an April Fool's joke! Johnson, born in Brandon, Suffolk, on 15 July 1919, had ambitions to become a professional cricketer and had joined the ground staff at Lord's Cricket Ground on leaving school but his mother had other ideas and she persuaded him to work for the Midland Bank in Wellingborough, Northants, where he remained for three years. He joined the RAFVR in in May 1939 and on 1 September that year he was called up. Within a month he was attending Aston Down OTU before joining 85 Squadron. A month later he was posted to 145 Squadron and his first victory followed on 26 June when, piloting a Spitfire IIb, he shot down a Bf 109 over Dunkirk. After flying off *Eagle* to Malta on 'Bowery' on 9 May, he took post on 126 Squadron. On 14 May he damaged a Bf 109 and on the 30th, he was awarded a quarter share in a Savoia-Marchetti SM.84 three-engine torpedo bomber, which returned badly damaged to Catania. At the end of June, he would return to Gibraltar in a Hudson to help lead in another reinforcement flight to Malta on 15 July in Operation 'Pinpoint'.

Another 611 Squadron pilot, Pilot Officer Joseph Aldard Walter 'Al' Gunn RCAF, would be returned to his former squadron in England on 1 July with a comment that 'his operational experience is not considered sufficient to permit of his fighting Me 109s at Malta, although he was expected to fight Fw 190s over France!'

Riversdale Robert 'Barney' Barnfather on 603 Squadron, who had seen action in the offensive sweeps over France, flew his Spitfire the three and a half hours off *Wasp* to Malta successfully. He recorded in his log book later: 'Good trip but lost a few en route!'

Two Canadian pilots, 23-year-old Flight Sergeant John Vaughan Rounsefell Jr, and 21-year-old Warrant Officer Charles Napoleon 'Nap' Valiquet of Montreal, were lost in a mid-air collision during an engagement with a Fiat floatplane near the island of Lampedusa 100 miles or so south-west of Malta. Rounsefell was born on 2 October 1918 in San Francisco, California. His father, who was from Vancouver, British Columbia, and his family, soon returned to Canada. In 1940 he had enlisted in the Royal Canadian Air Force. He later transferred to the Royal Air Force.

'Nap' had initially enlisted in the RCAF as a mechanic and gained his private pilot licence around the same time after being refused RCAF pilot training. After gaining his PPL he was accepted for pilot training in the RCAF and was later posted to England to continue his training.

Neither body was found and their names are remembered on the Runnymede Memorial.

Norman Ralph Fowlow, a fellow Canadian who flew off the *Wasp*, had, during the tense period of waiting in Gibraltar, met 'Buck' McNair, who would become a firm friend. 'Norm' was born on 9 August 1921, in Hodges Cove, Newfoundland, the son of Reverand Ralph Fowlow and his wife Annie. Later he called Windsor in Nova Scotia his home. He had enlisted in

Halifax on 22 August 1940 and, after the usual training, arrived in England in May 1941. 'Norm' had spent a couple of months at 55 OTU before being posted to 131 Squadron in July 1941, with whom he did most of his flying until he was sent to Malta. Within a few days he would be shot down but he bailed out, and he continued fighting over the Island until he was sent back to Britain in August. On his return from Malta, Norm's next squadron was 403 in August 1942. They were based at Kenley from 23 January 1943. Fowlow didn't find the fighter sorties and bomber escort operations any easier than Malta. 'If you ask me,' he wrote, 'compared with Malta when I was there, I'd say this was tougher because in Malta you did all your fighter work over your own territory. Here you leave England and do your fighting over strange country.'

In the spring of 1944, 'Buck' McNair asked Fowlow to be best man at his wedding, which gave 'Norm' the chance to get something off his chest that he'd been hiding from the wing commander – he had secretly married a nursing sister, Elsie Ogilvie, in April 1943, and he had a 4-month-old baby son, back in Nova Scotia, where mother and child were living with Norm's parents. 'Buck' apparently cursed, but was thrilled for his friend.

'Down on the field quite early [on 9 May] making sure that everything was in readiness we awaited the arrival of our aircraft,' wrote Don McLeod. 'Men were busily repairing bomb damage done to our field during the night and morning raids, after what seemed hours the first of the Spitfires arrived and landed. I could see the happy but grim face of "Jumbo" who had brought the outfit in. The system began working and aircraft began going immediately to pens. Special pilots were already strapped into cockpits and crewmen were busily tearing off gas' tanks. Men were pouring gas' faster than it seemed humanly possible to do it. There was a lull of maybe five minutes and then far into the field a Very pistol fired. It did not seem to me that the planes had time to even stop rolling. But a great deal had been accomplished and aircraft were no good on the ground when they could be flying. One column, then another and another until the last one.'

McLeod added: 'At about 0900 hours, the first batch of Spitfires flew over Malta. A few minutes later another arrived, then another and another, until the sky was filled with them. Malta had never seen so many at one time. As soon as one Spitfire touched down, a receiving ground crew member was out waving his white flag to attract the new pilot to the pen. No sooner had he swung the Spitfire around, tail pointing into the pen, than a swarm of men leapt on to the wings with screwdrivers, opening gun panels, throwing socks, shirts, cartons of cigarettes on to the ground. While two soldiers were removing the big empty belly auxiliary tank, and storing it behind the pen, others were chain handing tins of petrol to fill the tanks, armourers were rearming the guns and the Spitfire was back into the air in minutes. The same activity was taking place all over the island, it was as if each pen-crew was trying to out-do the other in getting their Spitfire into the air. A whole squadron of twelve Spitfires would land, re-fuel and re-arm, and be back into the air in seven minutes.

'Strangely enough the Ju 88s failed to appear for their usual early morning raid. In a few minutes the first of the new boys made their appearance over Imtarfa Hill. Between nine and ten, four Spitfires were scrambled to cover the arrival of the new Spitfires.

Everyone was happy and excited, keyed up with expectation. Ray Hesselyn led "Barney" Barnfather's Spitfire into his pen. The waiting ground crew pounced on it eagerly and began to rearm and refuel the fighter. "Barney" climbed out of the cockpit and Hesselyn handed him his written instructions. "More Spits were coming over the hill," recalled the New Zealander "and arrived in the circuit at the same time as a number of 109s". One of my erks, a big wild-looking fellow who had not shaven for three days, kept changing tools every few minutes. One minute he would have a rifle in his hands and be taking pot shots at the 109s and the next he would grab a tool and be undoing a panel or some screws on the Spit. Barnfather and I watched the Spits circling. "That one will get it in a minute," I remarked. It did. A Me 109 blew a large piece out of the Spit's port side near the cockpit. The Spit made hurriedly for the aerodrome and after three attempts successfully force landed. By his time there was a terrific din going on. The ground defences were engaging heavily and there was a lot of cannon fire between opposing aircraft. On the aerodrome, newly arrived Spits were being shepherded to their places. They were refuelled and rearmed quickly, and pilots clambered into their cockpits ready to take off immediately the order came. Within ten minutes of landing, many new Spits were going up again. It was a triumph of organisation. The dust was as thick as if we had been bombed. Pilots were making practically blind take-offs and going on the assumption that the system was working.'

Flying Officer Richard 'Mitch' Mitchell had taken off from *Wasp* at 0645 hours, two minutes after Squadron Leader Stanley Grant. Twenty miles west of Bizerte 'Mitch' had jettisoned the Spitfire's long-range tank before setting course for the Island, avoiding Pantelleria and Bizerta owing to the presence of fighters and flak there and taking a different route, because, as he wrote later, 'the formation leader [Grant] flew too fast and got his navigation all to hell, so I left them 40 miles west of Bizerta, five miles off the N. African coast'.

'Mitch' landed at Takali at 1030 hours with 20 gallons to spare in the main tank. 'I immediately removed my kit and the machine was re-armed and refuelled, landing during an air raid. Four 109s tried to shoot me up. Soon after the airfield was bombed but without much damage being done. I was scrambled in a section of four soon after this raid, but we failed to intercept the next one, though we chased several 109s down on the deck.

'Ate lunch in the aircraft, as I was at the ready till dusk. After lunch we were heavily bombed again by eight Ju 88s. Scrambled again in the same section after tea – no luck again. One Spit was shot down coming in to land and another one at the edge of the airfield. Score for the day, seven confirmed, seven "probables" and fourteen "damaged" for the loss of three Spits.'

After four hours of flight, 20-year-old Flight Lieutenant Raymond Harold Charles Sly RAAF landed safely at Hal Far, where the ground crews were ready to turn the Spitfires around as quickly as possible so that there would not be a repeat of the previous fiasco. Born on 1 October 1921 in Sydney, Sly had enlisted in the RAAF on 22 July 1940. Each pilot had been briefed to taxi to a specific aircraft pen, which was marked with his individual aircraft's code.

In the pens, dedicated ground crew were waiting for each aircraft so that they could be immediately refuelled and have their long-range tanks removed. It was hoped that every Spitfire would be airborne again within fifteen minutes. But when Sly saw his fellow pilots being attacked and shot down in the circuit by about sixty Bf 109s, ranging from 50ft in the circuit up to around 20,000ft above, he decided to take-off when he was still slowing down during his taxi in. In order to get airborne as soon as possible, he turned around and took off downwind. He was just airborne when his undercarriage struck the top of an aircraft pen. Sly was badly injured in the resulting crash and he died in hospital later that day. A telegram informing his parents, Harold and Ivy Jane, of his death was received at Summer Hill in New South Wales. Their son is buried in the Capuccini Naval Cemetery in Malta.

'The tempo of life here is just indescribable,' reported one of the newly arrived pilots. 'The morale of all is magnificent – pilots, ground crews and Army, but it is certainly tough. The bombing is continuous on and off every day. One lives here only to destroy the Hun and hold him at bay; everything else, living conditions, sleep, food and all the ordinary standards of life have gone by the board. It all makes the Battle of Britain and fighter-sweeps seem child's play in comparison ...'

The AOC had been of the opinion that if the Spitfires arrived in reasonably serviceable condition and in good light, it should be possible to turn them round in ten minutes, thus the damage inflicted on Operation 'Calendar' could be avoided. Five men were assigned to each pen with an experienced pilot ready to take over the aircraft. Long-range tanks were removed first, and each pen contained all that was necessary to rearm and refuel the Spitfires, the petrol being kept in four-gallon cans protected by sandbags.

'So magnificently did the ground staffs work,' reported 'Jumbo' Gracie, 'that our half hour service became an absolutely outside limit and the official records show that six Spitfires of one squadron took off to engage the enemy within nine minutes of landing on the Island. What a change in 36 hours! Within half an hour every serviceable Spitfire was in the air. I shall never forget the remark of one airman who, coming out of a slit trench, and seeing two or three squadrons in the air, said: "Heavens, look at the fog!"

'Aircraft quickly started for their rendezvous with the "Hun", said Don McLeod. 'As the aircraft were climbing the feeling of complete willingness and domination to fight was present among all the pilots. Now, could the Spitfires get high enough? Would they have time before the Germans on flight would arrive? And would the anti-aircraft guns aimed at the sky know the approximate vicinity of the enemy aircraft? Forward onto the island flew the 88s and Stukas and every available "Spit" waiting for them. Did the Nazi with his wild imagination feel that this would be another picnic? Before these bombers ever made their bomb run all Hell broke loose. Sixty Spitfires had gone into the air and the plan was working perfectly except for one thing. The Germans made a mistake. They sent very few fighters to escort their bombers. They figured, "We'll catch the boys on the ground again. It will be that easy."

'Shooting in among the German bombers, the Spitfires were like fleas on a stray dog,' wrote McLeod. 'What few fighters there were, were quickly put out of commission. They were sent hurtling and spinning in flames to the ground and the warm Mediterranean. One by one the bombers fell as panic broke out among them, jettisoning their bombs, turning and twisting and running, diving, and turning, but there was no escape and no denying the power of the Spitfires. It was a very solemn and scared bunch of Huns that made their way back to Sicily that memorable morning. The Spitfire losses were negligible, but the German losses were terrific.' The Spitfires landed, were serviced and ready to go once more.

'We hadn't been asleep this time and there were many Germans sleeping their final sleep because of that. The battle continued throughout the day as more and more German fighters appeared, but the back of the German Air Force in Sicily had been broken. The battle diminished in intensity during the next few days and this was followed by a lull. No air force in the world could stand the terrific battering that they had received. The island of Malta now had fighter superiority and would start to dictate its own terms. In many minds, one of the turning points of the war was this achievement of aerial success over the island of Malta.'

Churchill sent a personal message to Captain Reeves and crew: 'Many thanks to you all for the timely help. Who said a wasp couldn't sting twice?'

The RAF had flown 125 Spitfire sorties and 9 Hurricane sorties on 9 May. Pilot Officer Pete Nash on 249 Squadron was credited with the destruction of a Bf 109F, a Ju 87 and Bf 109F 'probables' and a Bf 109F 'damaged'. Six Spitfires on 603 Squadron that were scrambled from Takali to give high cover were attacked by four Bf 109s over Luqa. 'Sandy' Sanders destroyed one of the Messerschmitts. Flying Officer Anthony Clive William

'Tony' Holland and 25-year-old Pilot Officer Herbert Robert Mitchell RNZAF shared another. 'Sandy's' former colleagues at the Westminster Bank in Plaistow in London remembered him as having a 'sunny nature and cheerful outlook, which made him extremely popular with customers and staff alike'. Outside work he was a member of the Civil Air Guild and had gained his pilot's certificate in June 1939. He had left the bank to go on active service with the RAFVR in May 1940 and after a period of training in Rhodesia was posted to a squadron as a flight sergeant. Mitchell, born at Havelock, Marlborough, New Zealand, on 13 March 1917, had worked in the Public Works Department there and afterwards as a stonemason in Greymouth. After completing his training, he sailed for England on 12 July 1940 in the RMS *Rangitane*.

For just two Spitfires destroyed the enemy lost thirteen aircraft, one 'probably destroyed' and fourteen 'damaged' from fifty-six aircraft dispatched. At 1315 hours, eleven Spitfires on 126 Squadron, eight Spitfires on 249 Squadron and five more on 185 Squadron (who had begun a handover of its Hurricanes to 229 Squadron that no one was sorry to see go) were scrambled to intercept enemy aircraft. Pilot Officer Eric Lawson Hetherington, one of the 249 Squadron pilots who had taken off from the *Wasp*, shot down a Bf 109 for his first victory of the war. Born in early 1918 in Hartlepool, he was employed by the Midland Bank in Newcastle when he joined the RAFVR in about July 1939 as an airman u/t pilot. After converting to Hurricanes, 'Hether' was posted to 601 Squadron at Exeter on 11 September and served with them for the remainder of the Battle of Britain before flying Airacobras for a time. On Malta in the summer of 1942, he was promoted to flying officer and was made a flight commander. Twice he was obliged to crash-land; once on 7 July and again on 14 July. By 17 October, he had racked up a score of three and one shared destroyed, one 'probable' and five 'damaged'. On 24 October Hetherington was awarded a DFC.

Another of the newly arrived Spitfires that had been taken up by Gordon Tweedale on 185 Squadron on Malta was shot down by, it is believed, Leutnant Erich Beckmann of III/JG 53, while trying to fly from Grand Harbour to Takali. 'Tweedle's' aircraft crashed at Saviour Street in Lija, killing Gunner Seraphim Cauchi of the Royal Malta Artillery on his bicycle. The Australian died of his injuries in the cockpit. It was his first, and last, flight in a Spitfire. Flying Officer John Buckstone, the 'B' Flight commander on 603 Squadron too, was killed after ditching in the sea. He had married his fiancée Leonie just before leaving England.

At sunrise at 0545 hours on Sunday, 10 May, the *Welshman* moored up in Grand Harbour after her arrival from Gibraltar with food and general stores, 100 spare Merlin aircraft engines and RAF ground crews trained on Spitfires. The Luftwaffe probably thought she was easy prey and from 0545 hours they carried out a series of raids to try to sink the vessel but miraculously her most valuable cargo was unloaded under a smokescreen by noon. The Luftwaffe too had not bargained for such a determined defence from the ground gunners and a whole host of RAF fighters.

The heaviest raid of the day began at 1056 hours with twenty Stukas, ten Ju 88s and a heavy escort of Bf 109s. After trying to hit the *Welshman*, the German and Italian bombers were attacked by thirty-seven Spitfires and thirteen Hurricanes. 'Johnny' Plagis was one of five Spitfire pilots on 249 Squadron who were joined by five more on 249 Squadron that were scrambled at 1050 hours. 'We climbed to 4,000ft and then the barrage was put up by the harbour defences and the *Welshman*,' Plagis wrote later. 'The CO dived down into it and I followed close on him. We flew three times to-and-fro in the barrage, trusting to luck to avoid the flak. Then I spotted a Ju 87 climbing out at the fringe of the barrage and I turned and chased him. I gave him a one-second burst of cannon and he broke off sharply to the left. At that moment another Ju 87 came up in front of my nose and I turned into him and let him have it. His engine started to pour out black smoke and he started weaving. I kept the tit pushed hard, and after a further two or three-second burst with the one cannon I had left, the other having jammed, he keeled over at 1,500ft and went into the drink.

'I then spotted a 109 firing at me from behind and pulled the kite round to port, and after one and a half turns, got on his tail. Before I could fire, another 109 cut across my bows from the port side and I turned straight on his tail and fired until my cannon stopped through lack of ammo. He was hit and his engine poured out black smoke, but I had to beat it as I was now defenceless and two more 109s were attacking me. I spiralled straight down into the sea at full throttle and then weaved violently towards land with the two 109s still firing at me. I went under the fringe of the smoke screen to try to throw them off, but when I came out the other side, I found them both sitting on top waiting for me. I therefore kept right down at zero feet·and steep turned towards them, noticing the smoke from the gun ports as I did so. After about five minutes of this I managed to throw them off. I landed back at Takali and made out my report claiming one 87 destroyed and one Me 109 "damaged".'

Flying Officer Richard Angelo 'Mitch' Mitchell on 603 Squadron, a Londoner, born on 20 December 1910, who had flown off the *Wasp* the day before, destroyed a Ju 87 and damaged another. He also damaged a Bf 109. The crew of his first victim bailed out and were taken prisoner. 'Mitch' had obtained his pilot's licence in May 1935 and as he gained experience his score increased. He would make numerous claims throughout his time on Malta.

Pilot Officer George Maxwell 'Max' Briggs of 601 Squadron was shot down and killed. Sergeant Gerald Russell 'Reg' Dickson RNZAF on 601 Squadron also was hit by an anti-aircraft shell and his aircraft was blown in half. His seat straps snapped and he was thrown through the Perspex hood of the aircraft, causing him to sustain a badly gashed leg. With amazing luck, he managed to pull his ripcord and he fell into the sea a mile out from Marsamxett Harbour. He was later picked up and taken to an ambulance on top of a broken door being used as a makeshift stretcher.

That afternoon the Germans tried again to get the *Welshman*. Twenty-six Spitfires and six Hurricanes went aloft to deal with the seven Ju 88s and thirty Me 109s. At least one Me 109 was shot down.

The Italians attacked in the evening, with twenty Macchi MC.202s and ten Re.2001 Falco (Falcon II) Falco fighter-bombers, escorting five Cant Z.1007bis Alcione (Kingfisher) tri-motor bombers. They were followed by twenty Ju 87s and a swarm of Bf 109s, one of which was shot down in the ensuing dogfight.

There was a total of 110 Spitfire sorties and 14 Hurricane sorties that memorable Sunday, 10 May. Around fifteen enemy aircraft were shot down and the anti-aircraft gunners claimed another eight enemy aircraft.

The front page of the *Times of Malta* the next day was euphoric: 'BATTLE OF MALTA: AXIS HEAVY LOSSES' and 'SPITFIRES SLAUGHTER 'STUKAS' BRILLIANT TEAM WORK OF A.A. GUNNERS AND R.A.F.' 63 Enemy Aircraft Destroyed or DAMAGED OVER MALTA YESTERDAY.

'The last two days have seen a metamorphosis in the Battle of Malta. After two days of the fiercest aerial combat that has ever taken place over the island the Luftwaffe, with its Italian lackeys has taken the most formidable beating that has been known since the Battle of Britain two and a half years ago.

'Teamwork has been the watchword during all these weary months of taking a pounding, with very little else to do than grin and bear it.

'For months on end the gunners have hurled steel and defiance at the enemy. They have been subjected to probably the most diabolical bombing the gunners have ever known, they have been ceaselessly machine-gunned; they have suffered casualties, but others have taken their places. Never once have they faltered. The people of Malta owe them a debt which is incalculable.

'Since the beginning of April this Island has been pounded without ceasing. But yesterday the boot was on the other foot. The Hun set out to liquidate our aircraft on their aerodromes but he got a shattering shock. Instead of being on the ground our fighters were in the air, waiting for his blood. At the end of the day, he retired to lick gaping wounds which he had never anticipated.

'During the afternoon's raids, the sky looked like the outside of some fantastic wasp's nest, with aircraft milling about in a breathless, hectic rough house. The noise of cannon and machine gun was all the sweeter for the fact that half at least of them were for once on our side. That being so, nobody on the ground had the slightest qualms about the result.'

The 'Glorious Tenth of May' prompted Flying Officer 'Bert' Mitchell on 603 Squadron to write that 'it all makes the Battle of Britain and fighter sweeps seem like child's play in comparison but it is certainly history in the making and nowhere is there aerial warfare to compare with this'.

Later the War Diary, Air HQ Malta, announced that: 'The fighter strength was reinforced on the 20th by the arrival of 46 Spitfires from UK ... During the period when [they] were necessarily grounded for refuelling and re-arming and brought into a fully operational condition, many were damaged on the ground by enemy action. The inability to scramble our aircraft was due to unserviceability. Minor details such as cannon testing were not done and it would appear that the aircraft had come straight from the factory without being tested to see that they were fit to fly operationally ... It was very noticeable that with the arrival of the fighter reinforcements, the enemy preluded his bombing attacks with fighter sweeps and maintained fighters over the island even after the bombers had made their get-away.'

During the spring and early summer Malta would continue to see many new arrivals and departures. 'Jumbo' Gracie's days on the Island were coming to an end and he would be greatly missed. He was reputed to have set up a gibbet to warn off locals who were stealing aircraft supplies. His standing orders included: 'It is the duty of every airman to kill the Hun.' On 29 April he had replaced Wing Commander 'Jack' Satchell DSO as wing commander, Takali. In early 1940, Satchell had been sent to France as a fighter controller, based at Merville. During the retreat in May, he walked 40 miles to Boulogne, hiding during the day. He flew Hurricanes in the Battle of Britain, claiming three enemy aircraft shot down and three 'probables' leading 302 (Polish) Squadron. During his time on Malta, again flying Hurricanes, he added a further Ju 88 kill and two Bf 109Fs shot down and shared in a Ju 88 'damaged'. During the last two weeks of April, Satchell and Squadron Leader Innes Bentall Westmacott operated a pair of Vickers machine guns on Takali airfield and claimed a Bf 109F destroyed, another 109 and a Ju 87 'probable', and nine other enemy aircraft 'damaged'.

After taking up his new post, Gracie had thought nothing of walking around unhurriedly in the midst of air raids, becoming very popular and boosting morale.

On 16 May 'Tony' Barton, who had taken command of 126 Squadron, formed an all-American 'B' Flight. Led by 'Jimmie' Peck, it included Don McLeod, Bruce Downs, Reade Tilley, 'Tiger' Booth and Pilot Officers Fred Elbert Almos from 249 Squadron and 'Sandy' McHan of the 1435 Night Fighter Flight on Malta having flown Hurricanes on 185 Squadron. McHan scored four and two shared destroyed, and nine and one shared 'damaged'. Downs would transfer to the USAAF on 25 September 1942. Almos, born on 29 November 1921, in Long Beach, California, and who in 1940 was living in Sunnyvale, California, had undertaken service pilot training that year in Tulsa, Oklahoma. By 1941 he was assigned to 121 'Eagle' Squadron. On 20 April 1942 he flew one of the forty-seven Spitfires from the USS *Wasp* to Malta, where he was assigned to 603 Squadron.

On Sunday, 17 May shortly before noon, two Spitfires on 249 Squadron and six on 603 Squadron at Takali were ordered to climb up and bounce fifteen 109s and a Dornier Do 24 flying boat searching near the Island. Pete Nash and his No. 2, Flight Sergeant Lawrence Anthony 'Lawrie' Verrol RNZAF, attacked five Bf 109s, each of the two Spitfire pilots reporting one Messerschmitt shot down. Verrol also claimed a 109 'damaged'. Near Dingli one of the other Bf 109s then shot down and killed Nash. He had not yet turned 21 years old. Norman Lee noted in his logbook: 'That leaves only five left of the original "*Cape Hawke*" thirteen.' The award of the DFC – the citation recording twelve victories – was gazetted shortly afterwards.

That evening an Italian ASR Z.506B Airone (Heron) floatplane of 612 Squadriglia protected by nineteen Re.2001s of 2° Gruppo was attacked by seven Spitfires of 601 Squadron led by Argentinian-born Pilot Officer Mike 'Pancho' Le Bas. Over Takali two Spitfires were claimed shot down. Le Bas and Pilot Officer A.R. Boyle each claimed a Re.2001 probably destroyed, while the floatplane was damaged by fire from both a Spitfire and an exploding AA shell. Sergeant Frank Stanley Howard attacked the floatplane but he was then shot up by the Italian escort and his glycol tank was hit. His almost managed to make Luqa but he came in too low and hit a stone wall. The Spitfire cartwheeled across the airfield, losing its wings and the Rhodesian received serious injuries. He died three days later in hospital. Seven more Spitfires chased the Italian formation out to sea but only 'Johnny' Plagis, who fired at one of the fighters, and Sergeant Paul Brennan, who exchanged fire with some 109s to no effect, carried out their attacks. Plagis could not forgive himself for letting the enemy fighter get away and could only claim it as a 'damaged'.

During a morning raid on 3 July, 'Sandy' McHan's Spitfire dived headlong into a field near the town of Siġġiewi, crashing with such force that both of its 20mm Hispano cannons were firmly lodged in bedrock. McHan bailed out and landed close to his crashed Spitfire. He was taken to an army medical aid post and treated for his injuries, which included a broken ankle and concussion. 'Tiger' Booth would transfer to the US 4th Fighter Group in England in September 1942. Reade Tilley had claimed his first confirmed victory on 28 April when he shot down a Bf 109 and damaged another. He was one of the first two American pilots to be awarded the DFC during the defence of Malta. The citation reads in part: '… on three occasions by making feint attacks after having expended his ammunition he successfully drove off enemy fighters attempting to machine gun our aircraft as they landed'. By July 1942 Tilley had increased his score to seven enemy aircraft destroyed, three 'probables' and six 'damaged'. On 16 August, now promoted to flying officer, he returned to England. In October he transferred to 8th Fighter Command with the rank of captain. Early in 1944 he was promoted to the rank of major.

In June 'Jumbo' Gracie had been posted home to England, where he took command of 32 Squadron at West Malling briefly in September. On 1 October 1943 he was posted to Ayr to take command of 169 Squadron, which would operate Mosquitos on bomber support. He flew the squadron's first operational sortie on 20 January 1944, a night escort to Hamburg during a main force raid on Berlin. During a night intruder sortie on 14–15 February, he was flying a Mosquito II that was attacked by a night fighter near Hanover. When the starboard engine caught fire, Gracie held the aircraft for long enough for the navigator, Flight Lieutenant Wilton W. Todd, to bail out (he was taken prisoner) but Gracie was unable to leave the aircraft before it crashed. He left a wife, Patricia, and a daughter.

Flying Officer John Donald Rae RNZAF, a 22-year-old New Zealander on 249 Squadron, had arrived in Malta on 20 April on Operation 'Calendar' after flying off *Wasp*. 'Jack', his preferred name, was born on 15 January 1919, educated at Cornwall Park School and then at Auckland Grammar. When he finished his schooling, he took up employment as a stonemason. Sent to England to serve with the Royal Air Force in 1941, by early 1942 in combat with single-engine fighters he had claimed two victories, four 'probables' and two 'damaged' on 485 Squadron RNZAF over France. On 12 June he got off the mark over Malta, claiming a Bf 109 'damaged'. South-west of Sicily on 27 June he claimed a Macchi MC.202 Folgore (Thunderbolt) shot down and was also awarded an Re.2001 Falco (Falcon II) 'probable'.

On 4 July a Cant Z.1007bis fell to his guns near Takali. Three days later he shot down a Bf 109F. On 9 July he was awarded a Folgore 'probable' and a half share in a Ju 88A of Kampfgeschwader 77. On 13 July Rae claimed a Falco and two 'damaged', but to his amazement they proved to be extremely competent opponents. Highly manoeuvrable, in the right hands, the Falco could dogfight with more powerful opponents like the Spitfire. Twice Rae nearly 'spun off' as he stayed with one of them. Finally, the Italian fighter had started to smoke and Rae knew that his tail unit was damaged. As the Spitfires broke off, Rae was amazed to see the Italian turning with them to make 'one final and defiant attack' upon his section. Rae was impressed and hoped that he survived.

'After being badly shot up in the first ten days of July,' noted David Douglas-Hamilton, 'the 88s gave up dive-bombing and took to high-level bombing. Apparently, they found that dive-bombing while producing better results, had left them too vulnerable. They had certainly lost a packet! Moreover, we soon learnt how to deal with high-level raids, and they began to lose as heavily as the dive-bombers.

'Some days the Squadron had a great deal of bad luck about being sent off to intercept raids. One Squadron had to be kept on the ground to deal with any raids following rapidly on the first one. However, these latter seldom materialised and on two consecutive days (11 and 12 July) it led to our being bombed four times on the ground.

'One or two aircraft were damaged, but no one was badly injured in spite of some narrow shaves. One party of airmen were in a slit trench when a bomb landed on the dispersal hut about three yards from them.

'In another place a bomb landed close to a shelter in which there were some pilots; they were knocked over by the blast and had all the wind knocked out of them.

'The same routine of readiness and off-time was being kept up, but owing to the intensive activity we did not have any Squadron days-off for a few weeks at a time. This meant that everyone did about eight hours, or from lunch-time till dusk every day.'

By early July 603 Squadron had lost seven pilots, who had arrived from all over the world. Pilot Officer Gordon Murray RCAF, who was from the USA, had died in action on 22 April when he was last seen breaking away and was pursuing a Ju 88 when he is thought to have been shot down by Feldwebel Wilhelm Budke of 2/JG 53.

Pilot Officer 'Bert' Mitchell, who was from New Zealand and who had shared in the destruction of two Bf 109s on 9 May and damaged another, failed to return to Takali from an interception patrol on 12 May when he was shot down west of Ta-Venezia, possibly by Oberleutnant Ernst Klager of 7/JG 53. Mitchell's last words were to 'Woody' Woodhall over the R/T: '*Goodbye, Woody; I've had it.*' Mitchell was seen to crash at high speed into the sea. At Reefton, Nelson, New Zealand, 'Bert's' parents, William and Edith Mitchell, were notified by a telegram confirming his death in combat. Their son was 25 years old.

Pilot Officer Leslie George Barlow RAFVR, who was from Rhodesia, died in action on 8 June; Flight Lieutenant Buckstone, who had been KIA on 9 May, and Flight Sergeant John Hurst, who was KIA on 2 July, both came from England; Pilot Officer Neville S. King from Ireland was killed on 8 July when he broke off from the attack on a raider but made too steep a turn and his wing hit the sea and his Spitfire crashed, breaking up as it fell into the water. Pilot Officer Guy Andre Levy-Despas (aka Guy 'Carlet'), whose philosophy was that 'a life without the idea of sacrifice is not worth living', was the son of the wealthy owner of a French chain of department stores. He had been sent to the United States by his parents when war broke out and was studying at Amherst College, Massachusetts, when France fell in 1940. Guy had immediately volunteered for the Royal Canadian Air Force. On 9 July at around 1300 hours, he was shot down and killed. He had been awarded the French Legion d'Honneur and Croix de Guerre.

David Douglas-Hamilton made his own assessment of the psychological effect of the battle on his pilots on his squadron. 'We did not always get sent up even when a raid did come over, but whatever happened, most pilots were tired and generally felt like going to sleep after a spell of readiness. In the quieter days of June, it had been the rule that most pilots on readiness read books. Now it seemed harder to concentrate on reading: we just sat around in the Dispersal Hut and waited. Some would chat with others and argue, but conversation was generally very mundane. Everybody concentrated on doing the job in hand – none knew what the morrow would bring – consequently there was little thought about the future. Most tended to be fatalistic but at least we could console ourselves that the 88 crews must live in an even more profound atmosphere of fatalism!

'Some days a hot sirocco blew up from the south and nearly boiled us all. It made readiness periods very exhausting and on our "off" periods we would lie down naked under our beds and swelter.'

On 14 June Hugh Pughe Lloyd addressed his pilots, giving them the news that on the 14th or 15th two convoys would be arriving; a large westbound one from Alexandria (Operation 'Vigorous'), and a smaller, eastbound, one (Operation 'Harpoon') from Gibraltar. As part of the air cover, some Spitfires were to be fitted with extra tanks and would patrol over the convoy arriving from the west, more than 100 miles from Malta. Other Spitfires were to patrol the convoy when it came within 60 miles of the Island on 15 June. Sorties were continually flown by Spitfires, Beaufighters, torpedo-carrying and reconnaissance aircraft.

By dawn on the 15th the western convoy was already within range of the Malta-based aircraft. Towards dusk David Douglas-Hamilton flew over the convoy in the evening summer sunlight with Malta in the background. He looked down and saw many little ships 'rippling their way through the water'.

'There were Huns about,' he wrote later, 'and everything looked to be peaceful; it was hard to believe that those ships had been through the whole of the previous day. Only telltale streaks of oil on the water behind some of the ships indicated that all of their journey might not have been so uneventful as it then appeared. In fact, there was not a ship that had not had several near misses, and many had been damaged.'

Two of the six ships in the 'Harpoon' convoy completed the journey, at the cost of several Allied warships. The 'Vigorous' convoy was driven back by the Italian fleet after being badly damaged by Axis aircraft.

During the early morning of Saturday, 18 July, German raiders turned back halfway across the Malta Strait, although four

109s crossed the Island. In the afternoon more German raiders returned. Pilot Officer 'Chuck' McLean and seven other Spitfires pilots on 249 Squadron scrambled at 1405 hours. McLean was a former star lineman with Queen's University of Toronto and Toronto Argonaut football teams, and for five years holder of the intercollegiate middleweight boxing crown, who graduated from No. 2 SFTS Uplands along with two fellow Argonaut teammates, George Sprague and Doug Annan. He revealed that at the height of the siege of Malta, Allied pilots were seldom out of the cockpits of their planes. 'It wasn't much of a show until the Hun took over,' he once said.

Fifteen minutes after 249 Squadron's Spitfires had got airborne, eight more Spitfires on 126 Squadron climbed into the sky over Malta. One 249 Squadron Spit chased a single Ju 88 on a reconnaissance flight and fifteen escorting Bf 109s at sea level but 'Chuck' McLean dived after one of the enemy fighters so fast that his engine seized. He peeled off and decided that he would try to glide back to the Island. 'It was save the machines in those days. The fliers didn't count so much.' It didn't work out that way. Standing up, trying to loosen his cover in case he would have to jump, the stick between his knees, two slugs tore into the instrument panel, a couple more into one arm and then the petrol tank exploded. He was blown unconscious out of his Spitfire 23,000ft above the Mediterranean, his clothes on fire. In the minute it took him to escape from the inferno he was badly burned about his arms, thighs, groin, chest and face. He remembered being out on the starboard wing – didn't know why or how, and then he came to a way down, at 12,000ft, still fumbling for his parachute release ring and trying to beat out flames. And there he stuck. 'To hell with this,' said McLean. He was barely able to pull the ripcord on his parachute but he managed it and on landing in the sea about 4 miles off Gozo, too weak to inflate his dinghy, he floated in his Mae West in the Mediterranean for over two hours before he was rescued. Fortunately, another Spitfire pilot who had a ringside seat at the scene of carnage had circled 'Chuck' during his descent and alerted HSL 107, which soon arrived. McLean brought back one dragging leg and more than a liberal share of scar tissue (requiring 4,000 skin grafts). It is believed that the salt water saline solution had the proper effect on his near-fatal burns. One surgeon stated that 'only his splendid condition saved his life'.

On 27 July during an interception of another bombing raid on Luqa, 249 Squadron scrambled six Spitfires, joining sixteen others on 126 and 185 Squadrons. John Rae claimed a Bf 109 'probable' and a Macchi Folgore 'damaged'. A share in the probable destruction of a Junkers Ju 88 and one claimed 'damaged' was achieved the next day. Rae had long been troubled by a single bullet wound in his leg he had received on 1 May in a tussle with 6 Staffel II/JG 53. He had been shot down by a Bf 109 flown by 21-year-old Leutnant Herbert Soukop, who had five victories to his name, and the New Zealander was forced to bail out over the sea 7 miles from Malta. The prevailing breeze carried Rae to the Island, where he landed near Rabat and encountered a Maltese farmer, who, seeing the swastikas on his Mae West indicating his kills, became aggressive until he realised Rae was an RAF pilot. Rae was to remain in hospital for a month.

On 15 May Soukop was shot down by Douglas-Hamilton, who described his victory thus: 'I drew blood for the second time on one of those fighter sweeps. We were stooging around at 25,000ft for a considerable time: it was very cold and I even got frostbite in a finger. We were bounced once by a pair of 109s but avoided them successfully. Eventually we were told to go down. Suddenly, I saw a 109 sweeping down on my No. 2. It still came on, by this time at me, and we were approaching each other head-on at great speed. I resolved not to give way before he did and he evidently made the same resolution. We were going straight at each other and as soon as I got my sights on him, I opened fire and kept firing. He opened fire a second afterwards.

'It all happened in a flash, but when he seemed about 50 yards away, I gave a violent "yank" on the stick and broke away to the right. As I did so, his port wing broke off in the middle and he shot past under me. I turned and looked back: his aeroplane did about five flick rolls to the left and broke up. Then a parachute opened.'

Soukop had a broken left arm caused by one of Douglas-Hamilton's cannon shells and he was unable to properly control his descent. His parachute finally caught on the roof of a house in Zejtun, where he was left dangling in mid-air. This was fortunate because it prevented any risk of further injury or even death at the hands of the angry crowd that had gathered below. Eventually Soukop was apprehended by a guard from 'B' Company, 1st battalion, the Dorsetshire Regiment, who cut him down and he was taken to the hospital at Imtarfa. On the ward after surgery, Soukop was put in the bed next to 'Tim' Johnston of 126 Squadron, who had been shot down on 6 May.

Johnston had been firing at a 109 but failed to notice another Messerschmitt behind him until three cannon shells exploded in the bottom of the cockpit. The Spitfire plunged into a spin towards the ground, and with flames roaring from explosions of the cannon shells and the aircraft vibrating violently, he either blacked out or was knocked unconscious. When he recovered, he found himself still in his seat and squirming this way and that against the straps, but making no effort to undo the harness and get out, with a great flame rushing up from the bottom of the cockpit and being drawn past his face by the suction of the slipstream. His legs were peppered with shell splinters and he was temporarily blinded by burns to his face. His arms were severely burnt. 'Tim's' first thought was that this time it was certainly the end and that there must have been some mistake, because he wasn't supposed to die.

He corrected the spin, unlocked the locking pin of his harness, threw his stick forward and was shot forward into the air. Somehow his parachute opened and he landed at Siġġiewi, while his Spitfire crashed near Żebbuġ. As he lay smouldering on the ground, half conscious, his face covered in blood and sand, a crowd of sympathetic Maltese had gathered. He heard someone asking if the pilot was dead. He wanted to say 'no bloody fear' but shirked the effort; it was so much easier to keep absolutely still. He began to come round as the first soldiers arrived. They helped him to unbuckle the parachute and soon had him on a stretcher. He was taken to an aid station where a medical orderly put a dressing on his left knee, which was bleeding form a splinter wound. After what seemed a long wait, an ambulance arrived. By this time, he had begun to suffer from violent shivering fits and his face and arms were growing hotter and hotter and steadily more painful. He lay there wondering whether he would lose his eyesight and how much his face would be disfigured. After a long wait an ambulance took him to hospital at Imtarfa, where his arms and face were covered in bandages.

'In hospital my neighbour the 109 pilot,' wrote 'Tim' Johnston (who discovered that he was Soukop's thirteenth victim!), 'proved to be a Sudeten of Czech antecedents; he knew little English, but I learnt some of his history. He had previously been a Stuka pilot, had managed to get transferred on to fighters, and had made more than a hundred flights over Malta; he claimed five victories, one Blenheim, one Hurricane and three Spits. This was his first theatre of operations, although he'd been in the Luftwaffe more than two years. He seemed to have been assimilated by the Germans and, although he wasn't a party member, or noticeably a Hitler enthusiast, he identified himself with the Herrenvolk. His reasons for doing so were unconvincing and I thought he protested too much; it was probably self-interest. He said supposing we weren't English, but our country had been conquered by the English, wouldn't we fight for England? We said ask the Irish, but he didn't see the point.

'Douglas-Hamilton, who had shot Soukop down, visited him in hospital and couldn't help overhearing his and "Tim's" conversation. When asked why 109 pilots shot up dinghies and parachutes, Soukop denied that they ever did so and described it as *Schweinerei [a scandalous accusation]*. A case had just occurred in which one of our pilots had been picked up in his dinghy, either dead or at the point of death, with a cannon-shell through his neck; he was told of this but refused to believe it. The cases of 1940 were then quoted, but he still said obstinately: *"Das glaub'ich nicht"*. Nor would he admit that our rescue-launch had ever been attacked. I couldn't make up my mind whether he believed what he said or not.

'Later he asked me whether I found Italian fighters more or less formidable than 109s; I told him that, as far as I knew, I'd never been engaged with Italians; he laughed a lot, and, when I asked why, explained he was laughing at the Rome radio, which always claimed a heavy bag of Spitfires. He didn't care for Sicily; it was too dull and he seemed to hanker after bright lights. In spite of our denials, I am sure that he remained convinced that he'd been shot down by a Kittyhawk; he wouldn't have it that it was a Spit, because he'd never been out-climbed by one before.

'He was slight in build with fair hair brushed straight back, and I should say not more than twenty-two; he bore his pain bravely, but I never felt comfortable with him. I was glad to be moved to another ward soon after his arrival.'

In less than a month Johnston was fit to travel and he was driven down to Luqa to wait for a big Curtiss Wright CW-20. He had been on Malta only two months. At times it had been possible to contest the Axis aerial supremacy over the Island, but mastery had been stubbornly denied to him and his fellow pilots, and a steady loss of aircraft had been inflicted.

'The loss of the Hurricane pilots had been the hardest: they had taken part in all the bitter defensive battles, had suffered the casualties which the odds against them and the technical inferiority of their machines made inevitable, and yet had been robbed by the obsolescence of their aircraft of the prizes which they might have had. For the Spitfires the hard fighting was sweetened by substantial successes ... The dark days had been those of March and April. In May the situation had changed completely; with the decisive victory three weeks' earlier, aerial supremacy, lost when the Germans had returned to Sicily late in 1941, had been regained. Rommel's offensive had been launched a few days before; yet there, at Luqa, were Wellingtons already operating against his bases and lines of communication. The effort had not, perhaps, been entirely in vain.'

On Sunday, 10 May, when twenty Stukas and ten Ju 88s with a large escort of fighters bombed Grand Harbour, a formation of thirty-seven Spitfires and thirteen Hurricanes were dispatched to intercept them. During the battle, a total of fourteen German aircraft were shot down, for the loss of two Spitfires. Flight Sergeant 'Digger' Brennan on 249 Squadron, whose score stood at six kills, was piloting one of the Spitfires. Attacking one of the Ju 87 five bombers, Brennan later recorded that the Stuka 'disintegrated, with huge chunks flying off in every direction'. He was also credited with a Ju 87 'damaged'. Ray Hesselyn claimed a Bf 109 probably destroyed. In an engagement the next day, when he claimed a Bf 109 destroyed and another 'damaged', Brennan was wounded in his left arm. He was commissioned later that month.

On Tuesday, 12 May, six Spitfires were lost in combat, two collided on the runway during take-off and one 'damaged' in combat crashed on landing. Sergeant Charles Edward Graysmark, a 21-year-old pilot on 601 Squadron, who had flown off *Eagle* on Operation 'Bowery' on 9 May, was shot down and machine gunned in his dinghy when paddling ashore and he died of his wounds. Graysmark left a widow, Marjorie Vera, nee Turk, of Isleworth, Middlesex. The unfortunate pilot had been a member of 611 Squadron at Hornchurch, which, on 29 March, had been informed by HQ 13 Group, Fighter Command, that twenty pilots were to be posted overseas with no information about where or why, but they must go as a flight and all must be operational.

At 0915 hours on 14 May 22-year-old Sergeant John Livingstone Boyd DFM and two other Spitfires on 185 Squadron were scrambled from Hal Far to intercept enemy aircraft heading for an attack on Luqa aerodrome. Born in Byrnestown, Queensland, on 20 May 1919, 'Tony' Boyd as he was known, was educated at Gatton College in Queensland and worked as a jackaroo on a farm before enlisting in the Royal Australian Air Force in October 1940. He was sent to Canada to train as a fighter pilot and received his wings in June 1941. On 20 March he and the other squadron pilots had transferred to 185 Squadron and onto Spitfire Vcs.

While still a sergeant, on 1 May 1942 he was awarded the Distinguished Flying Medal 'for showing the greatest keenness to attack the enemy at all times regardless of the odds against him and had destroyed 3 and probably destroyed a further four enemy aircraft and 5 damaged'.

The Spitfires took on the enemy formation over the sea to the east of Grand Harbour. Boyd attacked the Bf 109F-4 piloted by Leutnant Alfred 'Martello' Hammer of II/JG 53, causing serious damage but the German ace survived and he nursed his aircraft back to Comiso in Sicily, where he crash-landed. Boyd had to watch fellow Spitfire pilot Sergeant Colin Vernon Finlay shot down by two Bf 109s that set his Spitfire on fire and he crashed into the sea 400 yards off Wied iż-Żurrieq. Finlay was seen to fall clear but his parachute failed to open. Two Maltese soldiers at once launched a small boat, reached the spot in ten minutes and pulled Finlay aboard but tragically he was found to be dead when they reached the shore.

Three hours later, at 1245, 'Tony' Boyd was airborne once more, as one of four Spitfires sent to intercept twelve Macchi MC.202s over Hal Far. This time, he was not so fortunate. Reade Tilley, watching from the ground, witnessed the events that followed.

'A dog fight started overhead. Three Ju 88s came in with 109 escort. Ack ack was going mad. There were bursts all over the sky. Then I saw a 109 sit on a Spitfire's tail and I heard the *brrrr* of cannon. The Spit rolled over and dived vertically in what appeared to be a controlled evasive manoeuvre, doing a series of aileron turns. There was no smoke trail and apparently the pilot was OK. But for some reason I felt he'd had it. Sure enough, he started to pull out too late at 100ft and then when it looked as if he would make it, the pilot either died or lost consciousness and ploughed into the deck on the far side of the airfield. At 300mph. So, at 1305 hours the career of Sergeant Pilot Tony Boyd came to an abrupt and spectacular end – just a terrific explosion and a long sheet of flame.'

Boyd crashed 200 yards from a defence post at the edge of the airfield and was killed. Tragically, he had been due to return to England for recuperation the day after this final scramble.

Chapter 6

Malta Dog

Jeffery George West DFM on 249 Squadron would regularly criticise the remotely sub-standard meat, but each time he succumbed to dysentery, more familiarly known as 'Malta Dog', he would bravely try to carry on as soon as he was over the worst of the attack.

But when, on the brink of being well enough to fly a trip of forty minutes, his CO, Squadron Leader Grant, after enquiring as to the popular New Zealander's health, asked before flying, 'But Jeff, can you fart without danger? That's always the test.'

West replied, 'Not yet sir, but I don't want to.'

Grant would reply, 'Right then, you're still stood down.'

Malta, The Thorn in Rommel's Side,

Laddie Lucas (Penguin, 1993)

After 14 May no more Junkers Ju 88s flew over Malta for several weeks. Bf 109s still flew fighter sweeps however, dropping bombs, and there were still night raids, but these were more of a nuisance value and in the main, ineffective. The new-found superiorly was further strengthened on 18 May when on Operation 'LB', all seventeen Spitfire pilots flew off *Eagle* to Malta. The carrier was accompanied by HMS *Argus* (which was carrying Fairey Fulmar naval fighters for fleet defence), and an escort of Gibraltar-based Force 'H' comprising the light anti-aircraft cruiser *Charybdis* and six destroyers. The seventeen Spitfires were led by Flight Lieutenant 'Laddie' Lucas and Flying Officer Raoul Daddo-Langlois. All the Spitfires safely arrived on Malta, although all six Albacores that were supposed to accompany them had to turn back with overheated engines.

The newly arrived pilots on *Eagle* included Kenneth William Samuels Evans on 126 Squadron and Arthur William Varey DFM. Evans was born in Blackheath, south London, on Christmas Eve, December 1919. He would leave Malta in September by air via Gibraltar, having been promoted to warrant officer, then commissioned, with a DFC and a score of four and two shared destroyed, three 'probables' and three 'damaged'. Varey was born in Hull, East Yorkshire, on 27 March 1920. On leaving school he had worked in the City Treasurer's Department before joining the RAF in May 1939.

James Fielden Lambert, born 8 April 1917, the only son of Archie N. Lambert and Jessie Lambert, of Winnipeg, Manitoba, had attended school in Winnipeg and worked for Sharpe, Woodley and Co Chartered Accountants as an audit clerk, before enlisting in August 1939. From April until September 1942, 'Jim' served on Malta on 185 Squadron. He was posted back to Britain as an instructor, before returning to operational flying with 416 Squadron on 23 June 1943, then to 403 Squadron on 16 October (as a flight lieutenant) and finally to 421 Squadron on 13 December, as acting squadron leader. Lambert was on his third tour of operations when he was killed in action on 20 December 1943, just over two weeks after his wedding to Miss Peggy Mabel Carpenter at St Andrew's Church, Limpsfield Chart.

Acting Flight Lieutenant Edwin Herbert Glazebrook, who would serve on 229 Squadron, was born in Outremont, Quebec, on 18 August 1918, the son of Herbert William and Ethel May Glazebrook, of Valois, Quebec. He was educated at Alfred Joyce School, Montreal, from 1924 to 1931 and subsequently, Strathcona Academy, until 1935. In civvy street, Glazebrook was employed for two months in 1934 as an office worker for T. Eaton Company, a Canadian department store chain. After taking accounting and business courses at Sir George Williams College and correspondence banking courses from Shaw Schools, Toronto, he became a teller for Royal Bank of Canada in Montreal, where he enlisted on 7 October 1940.

Other arrivals on 'LB' included 'Jerry' Smith, who had failed to reach flying altitude on 'Picket II'. He and his younger brother, Squadron Leader Roderick Illingworth Alpine Smith DFC*, born on 11 March 1922, would fly as a pair over Malta after 'Rod' landed there on 15 July in Operation 'Pinpoint', However, 'Jerry' was killed in action chasing a Ju 88 over the Mediterranean on 10 August. In the few short months spent in Malta, he was credited with three aircraft destroyed. Rod would finish the war with thirteen and one shared destroyed.

At 0940 hours on 18 May, meanwhile, twenty-five Bf 109s and Re.2001s were reported approaching Malta. Five Spitfires on 601 Squadron were scrambled from Hal Far before two were recalled and the three remaining Spitfires were jumped by 109s. At 1028 hours Pilot Officer T.W. Scott RAAF claimed one of the Messerschmitts and Sergeant Jack Nock McConnell's Spitfire was badly hit; the 21-year-old New Zealander's legs being peppered with shrapnel. His shoulder too was burned by an incendiary round, but he returned safely to Takali. At the same time, Pilot Officer Norman Ralph Fowlow of 603 Squadron was shot down off Hal Far. HSL 128, with an escort of four Hurricanes of 229 Squadron from Hal Far and two Spitfires to act as high cover for the Hurricanes, were quickly sent out to rescue the Canadian. At 1100 hours, when six to eight Bf 109s dived on the Hurricane formation, Sergeant James Richards Pendlebury, a 26-year-old pilot from Bootle, Liverpool, was shot down and killed, his aircraft crashing into the sea. 'Slim' Yarra on 185 Squadron, who attacked four of the enemy fighters, destroyed one of them and also claimed a 'probable'. At 1114 hours three Spitfires on 126 Squadron were scrambled from Hal Far to help protect the rescue launch. Pilot Officer 'Bis' Bisley destroyed one Bf 109. At 1145 hours five Spitfires on 249 Squadron were scrambled from Takali to patrol. Near Filfla, another fighter was seen to crash into the water and a parachute drifting down. The HSL crew picked up the parachutist within a few minutes of the pilot hitting the water, but, as one of the boat crew recorded later, 'it turned out to be a Hun – a cheery soul', who advised them to get back ashore before they were hurt. Unteroffizier Johannes Lompa of 4/JG 53, who was flying Bf 109F 'White 3', had been shot down by Yarra. The crew of HSL 128 resumed their search for Fowlow, and at about 10 miles out from Benghaisa Point, another figure was spotted in the sea. It was Fowlow. He was found by the crew of HSL 128 in his dinghy about 9 miles from land. Lompa insisted upon shaking hands with his adversary as he welcomed him aboard!

After his arrival in Malta, 'Slim' Yarra had had to fly Hurricane IIs pending the delivery of eleven replacement

Spitfires scheduled for 9 May. Meanwhile, he was awarded a Ju 88 'probable' after another night interception on the night of 1 May. When, on 12 May, he shot down a Bf 109 for his second confirmed victory on the Island, he was flying a Spitfire V. On 5 June he was commissioned and the award of a DFM was gazetted on 16 June. The incident for which the award was made resulted from his shooting down of one, and probably two, Bf 109s off the coast of Malta on 15 May, when, according to the citation 'a dog-fight apparently resulted in some of Yarra's fellow pilots going down into the sea. Three enemy planes attempted to continue to attack the defenceless men in the water during their rescue by a speed launch from Malta, but Yarra, although he had used up every bullet and cannon shell in his Spitfire, daringly and successfully, at great risk, made a number of feint attacks by which he held the enemy away from the launch for three-quarters of an hour.' The following day Yarra visited Kalafrana and was thanked by the crew of HSL 128.

Yarra's last flight from the Island before leaving for England was on 14 July. His final score was a dozen enemy aircraft destroyed, two 'probables' and six 'damaged'. Yarra was promoted to flight lieutenant and after leave was posted to 453 Squadron RAAF as a flight commander. He and his younger brother, Sergeant Ernest Robert 'Bob' Yarra, who had been born in 1923, was also on the squadron. A third brother, James Yarra, was born in 1925 and the family had moved to Grafton, a small coastal town north of Sydney where the brothers attended high school and their father worked at the town's newspaper, the *Daily Examiner*. Grafton at the time was with a population of around 10,000 with its economy built around farming and the nearby copper mine. 'Jack' had worked as an apprentice printer for the *Daily Examiner* until, in October 1940, at age 19, he had enlisted in the Royal Australian Air Force.

Unfortunately, 'Jack' and 'Bob' Yarra's time together was brief. On 10 December 1942, 'Jack' was shot down when a flak-ship hit his Spitfire while leading an attack with six others on a small convoy of German merchant vessels off the Dutch coast. He crashed into the sea and was lost without trace. He had long since written a letter to his mother that was to be sent only in the event of his death. It read: 'I entered this war with the knowledge that I had a rather small chance of coming out of it alive. I was under no false impression. I knew I had to kill and perhaps be killed. Since I commenced flying, I have spent probably the happiest time of my life … Above all, Mother dear, I have proved to my satisfaction that I was, at least, a man.'

Harriet would later have received another telegram telling her that 'Jack's' 21-year-old brother, Pilot Officer 'Bob' Yarra was shot down and killed on Friday, 14 April 1944 during an attack on a V-1 weapon site in northern France.

On 20 May 1942 in Operation 'Style', twenty-eight replacement Spitfire pilots made the convoy journey from Milford Haven to Gibraltar aboard the freighter *Empire Conrad*, which was carrying thirty-two crated Spitfire Vs. Arriving on the 27th, the crated Spitfires were assembled in the carrier *Eagle*, which then sailed for the flying off point 700 miles from Malta on 3 June escorted by a cruiser and five destroyers. Three experienced flight leaders and even aces – Squadron Leader 'Tony' Barton, Flight Lieutenant 'Jimmie' Peck, and Flying Officer 'Johnny'

Plagis, had days before flown in on an air transport Hudson from Malta to help guide the others in groups of four to Malta and get them safely on the ground. Halfway through Barton's tour of duty in Malta, he had survived an engine failure on take-off and a nasty crash in which he was injured and also disfigured by battery acid. Barton probably felt that the time had come to take a long rest. He had been on operational flying since September 1939, and his old enthusiasms seemed to have ebbed away.

The first three flights of eight Spitfires landed safely on airfields in Malta. The last group, led by 'Johnny' Plagis, had the misfortune to run into a dozen Bf 109s of II/JG 53 – the 'Pik As' ('Aces of Spades') – that had taken off from Pantelleria. They were led that day by 25-year-old Oberstleutnant Gerhard Michalski, who would become the highest-scoring ace in the Malta campaign on either side. He is credited with 73 aerial victories in 652 sorties, of which 59 were achieved over the Western Front. Sergeant Len Reid RAAF in Plagis' flight saw their leader suddenly rolling over and diving for the sea. 'He left us up there like sitting ducks,' Reid said bitterly.

II/JG 53 returned to Pantelleria with claims for five Spitfires shot down, though just four Spitfire pilots failed to reach Malta; two of them coming down near Pantelleria and the other two, near Gozo, where one of the NCOs that was lost circled continually for an hour. With no help forthcoming after he crashed in the sea, he tragically drowned. Flight Sergeant Thomas Francis 'Tom' Beaumont, a 27-year-old former air-sea rescue pilot, was from Soham in Cambridgeshire. Flying Officer James Howard 'Jim' Menary was a young Irishman. Twenty-two-year-old Flight

Sergeant Hugh Douglas Kingsley 'Foo' MacPherson RCAF was from Vancouver, British Columbia.

The fourth lost pilot, Pilot Officer David Francis Gaston Rouleau, who had spent almost a year of flying Spitfires on 131 'County of Kent' Squadron, was shot down at 1056 hours by Unteroffizier Heinrich Sedlmeier 60–65km south-east of Pantelleria. The Spitfire caught fire, pulled up and then rolled over, spiralling into the sea. It was Sedlmeier's first victory. He also shot another down ten minutes later. Rouleau, a 24-year-old Lisgar Collegiate graduate from Ottawa, loved badminton and in the summer would also swim and paddle in the logging route known as the Gatineau River. On 6 June David's widowed mother Gertrude received a telegram informing her that her son – an only child – was missing.

A dozen of the twenty-eight replacement pilots who flew off from *Eagle* for Malta on Operation 'Style' were Canadians. Some, like John Harvey 'Crash' Curry, who wore the shoulder flash of the RCAF, were American. Born 12 August 1915 in Dallas, Texas, after obtaining his civilian pilot's licence, 'Crash' would give flying lessons and throughout the late 1930s was also well-known as a 'Barnstormer'. He would join 601 Squadron with whom he scored one victory – a MC.202 on 26 June – before his squadron moved to the Western Desert. 'Crash' would finish the war with ten and five shared destroyed, two 'probables', twelve 'damaged' and a DFC. His commendation read: 'for displaying the greatest determination to attack the enemy, regardless of the opposition encountered, and [his] source of inspiration to fellow pilots ... This pilot is an outstanding shot and is keen to come to grips with the enemy regardless of the numbers opposing him.

The ease [with] which he gains superiority over his opponent and invariably shoots him down is an example which inspires the less experienced pilots in the squadron. He has now destroyed seven enemy aircraft confirmed, with four credited as probably destroyed in the space of three months.'

Flight Sergeant (later Flight Lieutenant) Philip Marcel Charron, who was born in Ottawa on 22 January 1917, had enlisted in the RCAF on 31 October 1940 and was posted straight from training to Malta, where he joined 126 Squadron. During three straight days in October on Malta he would destroy a Ju 88 on the 14th, damage a Bf 109 on the 15th and down another Ju 88 on the 16th.

Another Canadian on 'Style' who would quickly earn enduring fame flying from Malta was 26-year-old Flight Lieutenant Henry Wallace McLeod, a slim, moustachioed pilot on 603 Squadron. 'Wally' was born in Regina, Saskatchewan, to James Archibald McLeod and Hannah Elizabeth McLeod on 17 December 1915. When he was 3 his mother died from Spanish flu during the pandemic. The principal of Balfour Technical School wrote that he was 'a young man of excellent intelligence, ability and personality', and added, 'He possesses unusual powers of leadership and comes naturally into the first line of any assembly of young men.' Training in Canada later, he was described as 'a good pupil but inclined to be talkative and over-confident'.

'Wally' began his military career in 1928, serving with the 5th Saskatchewan Regiment and Regina Rifle Regiment until 1934. During the last years of the Great Depression, he would drive his battered 1937 Ford sedan from small town to small prairie town showing movies at night to townspeople who could afford the admission. On 2 September 1940 'Wally' joined the Royal Canadian Air Force. After graduating from training on 1 April 1941, he and Bill McRae and two other RCAF pilots left for England on the SS *Nicoya*, an elderly 5,363-ton British steamship that sailed with Convoy HX-126 from Halifax on 10 May. Ten days out the convoy came under sustained attack by U-boats. The ship directly in front of the *Nicoya* was hit and sank 'almost immediately'. In less than an hour, three more ships were sunk. In all, nine ships were lost. *Nicoya* docked at Liverpool on 28 May to be welcomed by a heavy night raid on the port. 'Only McLeod,' McRae wrote, 'with his piercing eyes and determined, almost fierce, expression, looked much like a fighter pilot, and a deadly one he would turn out to be. Little did I realize at that moment that of the four, I would be the only one to survive.'

At the end of August, McLeod began fighter sweeps over France with 485 Squadron RNZAF. His first operation over occupied Europe came on 2 September, when he helped escort three Blenheims bombing shipping near Ostend. On 23 December 1941 he was posted to 411 'Grizzly Bear' Squadron RCAF. By the end of April 1942, he had damaged three enemy fighters and claimed a Fw 190 'probable'.

It was said that 'if he has a reasonable amount of ability and enough operational experience, Malta was the place for him'. It was. Flying from Malta, 'Wally' would score his first confirmed victory on 23 June 1942, when, west of Gozo, he shot down a Macchi Folgore. He was also credited with another Macchi MC.202 'damaged'. In four months on Malta, he lost 25lb and began having nightmares about crashing but Malta became what he would call 'the Spitfire pilot's happy hunting ground' and his score would increase rapidly.

'Usually most of us came through safely, while a lot of the Huns or Italians didn't,' McLeod wrote. His first victory on the Island was a Macchi, which, he insisted, 'went into the drink from sheer fright'.

'The Italians always go in for weird and wonderful aerobatics, which is about the best thing they do. This chap was hit by my fire, but I don't think he was out of control. He just appeared to panic and hit the sea in a deep spiral dive.'

The second enemy plane he destroyed, on 17 July, a Bf 109 flown by Feldwebel Heinz Sauer of I/JG 77, was hit just behind the fuselage so the fuel tank exploded and blew the craft to pieces right in front of McLeod's airscrew. Bits of the wreckage spattered his Spitfire. 'The pilot was thrown clear,' McLeod said, 'and his 'chute opened. After he hit the water, I circled him and he waved to me, apparently quite cheerfully, so I dropped my dinghy for him to show that I had no ill feelings either. He didn't make any attempt to climb into the rubber dinghy, but one of our rescue launches came out and picked him up. He had a cannon shell through his chest, and he died in the launch.'

McLeod was shot down for the first time when a Reggiane Re.2001 hit his Spitfire in the oil cooler, forcing him to crash-land. He was shot down again when twenty-five Junkers Ju 88s came over Malta just at dusk, against the setting sun, and McLeod led a section of four Spitfires in attack. He shot down two enemy aircraft, and the other pilots between them shot down three more and damaged others.

'One of their tail gunners hit my engine, but I managed to flog the old motor long enough to shoot down another of them before I landed. Then, just to put the lid on the experience, I found that the airdrome was under a bombing attack as I was coming in.'

The engagement that gave him the greatest satisfaction was when eight Spitfires took on more than seventy attacking enemy machines at the height of the recent 'blitz' on Malta. The Canadian's mainplane was holed and his flaps blown off, but with the last burst of ammunition from his one still-firing cannon he accounted for one of the attackers.

By the time McLeod left Malta he had destroyed seven Bf 109s, three Ju 88s and three Macchi MC.202s, and had probably destroyed or damaged many others.

Flight Sergeant (later Flying Officer) James Hamilton Ballantyne on 603 Squadron, another Canadian on 'Style', was born on 14 January 1918 in Toronto. The dapper 24-year-old former insurance clerk had worked at General Accident Insurance for three years. His mother was from Ireland. His father, James Ballantyne Senior, who was originally from Scotland and worked as an aeroplane inspector at the Department of National Defence, had quickly realised that from a young age that his son was keen on flying. 'He was never in the air until he joined the RCAF, but he spent a large part of his younger days making toy airplanes in the cellar and flying them around the streets,' he said. On his first engagement on 1 July, he shot down a Bf 109 and damaged another but he was shot down into the sea and he bailed out with a slight neck wound, being rescued by an HSL. After 603 Squadron was disbanded, he was posted to

229 Squadron and in August he would receive a promotion to warrant officer. On 15 August, whilst landing, he collided with a stationary Spitfire. Although he was unhurt, both aircraft were damaged beyond repair. Later that month he was promoted to warrant officer.

On 6 June, three days after landing in Malta, and being posted to 249 Squadron, Flight Lieutenant Frank Everett 'Spitfire Man' Jones was awarded a half share in a Ju 88. Born in Cloverdale, British Columbia, on 6 September 1916, he would return home to Sherbrooke, Quebec, in 1945 with the DFC he was awarded in September 1942, and a score of four and two shared destroyed and three 'damaged'. Jones was described in the citation as a 'vigorous fighter whose fearlessness in face of odds sets praiseworthy example'. The citation said that [on 11 July] he led his section in an attack against twelve aircraft heavily escorted by fighters. Jones dived among the fighters and shot down a Me 109. 'Although he was attacked from all sides by many fighters,' the citation said, 'he skillfully frustrated them and despite damage sustained by his aircraft he succeeded in leading his section safely to his base.'

After landing in Malta, 21-year-old Flying Officer Robert George 'Bob' Middlemiss too was assigned to 249 Squadron. A strong young man, born in Montreal, he soon discovered how the siege could affect new pilots on the Island, unaccustomed as they were to the deprivations they faced. He normally weighed about 140lb but the severe shortage of food soon reduced his weight by 10 to 15lb. 'Malta's civilians, what with bombs and a food shortage, certainly took a beating,' wrote one RAF pilot. 'Though they were begging for food, they had absolutely no idea of giving up.' The armed forces did better 'but all the same the food situation was pretty tough. We called beef extract marmalade. We had marmalade soup, marmalade sandwiches, marmalade everything.'

Middlemiss had soon succumbed to 'Malta Dog' but was well enough to fly on 2 July when the first air raid alert for approaching Bf 109s was given at 0830 hours. Eight Spitfires of 603 Squadron intercepted six of the enemy fighters. Pilot Officer John Hurst DFC was reported 'missing' over the Mediterranean. At 1055–1205 hours and 1205–1245 hours, two pairs of Spitfires carried out a search for him, but it was all in vain. The day before, Hurst had claimed a Fiat BR.20 Cicogna (Stork) 'probable' (later identified as a Savoia-Marchetti SM.84 three-engine torpedo bomber) to take his final score to four and one shared destroyed, seven 'probables' and one shared 'damaged'. The 24-year-old pilot left a widow, Winifred Maud Hurst, of Strood, Kent. David Douglas-Hamilton wrote: 'Nobody saw what happened to him. But it was almost certain that he was killed outright. He was a great loss to the Squadron. He had destroyed four and probably destroyed another six Huns. He was the first of the Squadron to be awarded the DFC on Malta and it was said that he never knew about it. He was a fine fighter pilot and used to take on enormous odds all on his own. After several combats, he had come down with his machine riddled with holes, but he had generally done much more damage to the enemy.'

At 0920 hours, twelve Spitfires on 249 Squadron were scrambled to intercept another raid. In the battle with eight 109s and five Cant Z.1007 Alcione (Kingfisher) tri-motor medium bombers, 'Laddie' Lucas and Canadian Flight Sergeant Thurne

'Tommy' Parks, each claimed a Bf 109 'probable'. Born in Oshawa, Ontario, on 15 July 1921, 'Tommy' had been posted overseas on 7 September 1941. En route to England he had led a revolt against the ship's crew in protest at the 'unfavourable' food. His misdemeanour resulted in him being busted to corporal. Quickly restored to sergeant, he had been posted to Malta. Warrant Officer Charles Benn Ramsay, 22, of Newcastle, New Brunswick, damaged the starboard engine of one of the Cants and reported pieces fly off the port wing. (Ramsay would be KIA on 11 July when his squadron dived on a dozen Ju 88s at 1910 hours but were intercepted by fifteen Bf 109s.)

At 1400 hours seven Spitfires on 249 Squadron were scrambled to intercept approaching bombers. Twenty minutes later three Ju 88s escorted by four Bf 109s dropped bombs on Luqa from 23,000ft, killing two civilians and wounding two more. Two soldiers were also killed. Spitfires on 249 Squadron made their attacks and Pilot Officer B.W. 'Tex' Spradley, who was from Dallas, damaged one of the bombers; Pilot Officer Oscar Mahaffy 'Ozzie' Linton RCAF damaged another and Pilot Officer Daddo-Langlois' attacks on a third resulted in the crew bailing out 40 miles north of the Island. 'Bob' Middlemiss spotted a Macchi MC.202 Folgore on the tail of the redoubtable Pilot Officer Harry Kelly RCAF, opened fire and it dived and splashed into the sea.

At 1920 hours seven Spitfires on 249 Squadron that were scrambled spotted eight Cant Z.1007s with a strong fighter escort of Bf 109s. 'Laddie' Lucas and 'Tommy' Parks each damaged one of the fighters, which was last seen going down. On 13 August 1942 Parks bailed out for his second time, when he was shot down by the flak gunners of a friendly ship he was trying to protect during Operation 'Pedestal'. He was picked up by a destroyer, slightly wounded, and set ashore at Gibraltar not knowing he had been reported 'missing'. He received a Mention in Despatches serving on 421 'Red Indian' Squadron, on 14 January 1944. He was sent back to Canada due to 'exhaustion'.

Harry Kelly failed to return from an interception flight over Malta on 2 July when he was shot down and killed in combat with Bf 109s. On 2 July, however, there were rich pickings for Flight Sergeant C.S.G. 'Gerry' de Nancrede RCAF on 249 Squadron, who scored hits on the leading bomber and damaged one of the others. Eight Spitfires on 603 Squadron, meanwhile, spotted a Cant Z.1007 with an escort of twenty fighters. Pilot Officers Neville King RAFVR and Flight Lieutenant Edwin Herbert Glazebrook shared a Macchi probably destroyed before they were attacked head-on and they were forced to crash-land at Takali.

Early on the morning of Tuesday, 7 July, 'Bob' Middlemiss, who on the 4th had claimed a Re.2001 Falco 'probable', and Flight Lieutenant Daddo-Langlois, were held in reserve at Takali but with enemy aircraft approaching Malta, they did not want to miss out on the opportunity to shoot down some of the raiders. Their protestations soon convinced the controller that they and eight other Spitfires could take off. They flew south and then north over the sea before two Folgores escorting the bombers were spotted. However, the Spitfires had still not gained sufficient height nor did they have the advantage of positioning themselves so that the sun was behind them. 'Daddy Long-legs' asked over his radio should they 'have a go?' Middlemiss said they should and he fired at one of the Folgores that was closing in on Daddo-Langlois's tail, and it exploded. He then turned his Spitfire left to break away but as he leaned forward, he looked to his left and the pilot of the other 109 fired at him. At least one cannon shell hit the starboard side of his fuselage and his right hand left the stick with the impact of being shot in the right arm and back.

The Spitfire was in a spin and smoking. Middlemiss was unable to get out because of the centrifugal force but he managed to roll the Spitfire over and fall out. He opened his parachute and drifted down, eventually landing in the sea. He shed his parachute and pulled out his dinghy. The words went through his mind: 'Slowly turn the tap of the CO2 bottle', but to his dismay, as he frantically continued turning, he discovered that the bottle was empty. With his right arm useless, he had problems trying to attach the bellows pump to the dinghy; the chord attached to the dinghy kept getting in the way but he finally took out his knife and cut the cord while holding the dinghy with his bad arm and he screwed in the pump and began the inflation. After a while there was enough air in the dinghy to allow him to climb in and begin paddling towards Malta. He had been shot down on the eastern side of the Island but, unfortunately, his squadron was searching for him on the western side. Only when Pilot Officer Paul Brennan and Sergeant Louis de 'Ara – a former Spitfire test pilot – flew out on patrol to protect some minesweepers was Middlemiss spotted in 'the drink'. They made one pass over him and then approached again. Middlemiss thought of jumping into the sea in case they attacked the dinghy. However, they waggled their wings and he breathed again. Shortly afterwards HSL 128 reached him and he was hauled aboard, wrapped in blankets and given a shot of navy rum, which almost made his eyes pop out! Later, he saw the holes in his arm.

Had he not been leaning forward in his seat and looking around when he was hit, he would have been, as he said later, 'a goner'. Middlemiss had been hit within a quarter of an inch of his lungs.

On the ward in hospital at Imtarfa, Middlemiss went toe-to-toe with the bed occupied by Gerry de Nancrede, who after scoring hits on the leading Ju 88 from below, striking the belly and wing roots, was hit in the engine by return fire and his controls were shot away. He managed to bail out and land in the sea. Luckily, his injuries were only slight.

Comradeship played a large part in the lives of pilots on Malta. Many years later, de Nancrede wrote: 'Soon after my arrival I found I had joined a new family. Groundcrews and aircrews were drawn together in a group that was sharing the intensity of life and death. There was something in those lines of King Henry which captured it: "We few, we happy few, we band of brothers."'

Operation 'Salient', the next 'Club Run', began on 26 May 1942 when the freighter *Hopetarn* left Milford Haven escorted by the frigate *Rother* and corvette *Armeria*, with 32 cased Spitfire Vs, 13 officers and 106 NCOs and airmen to assemble the aircraft after arrival in Gibraltar on 2 June. On completion, *Eagle* embarked the Spitfires and sailed on 8 June under the code name 'Maintop', escorted by the light anti-aircraft cruisers *Cairo* and *Charybdis* and the destroyers *Antelope, Ithuriel, Partridge, Westcott, Wishart* and *Wrestler*. The following day the Spitfire pilots would make the four-hour flight to Malta led by Reade Tilley and several other seasoned pilots, who had flown to Gibraltar to get them safely to the Island.

'Salient' included the usual blend of neophytes and experienced pilots that made up most Allied denominations on the 'Club Runs'. Flight Sergeant Basil Wilfred Andrews was from Chicago, Illinois. Basil had a wife, Martha Jashelski Andrews. There were, of course, British, and Canadians, too, like 25-year-old Pilot Officer Joseph Hubert Roger Paradis, who hailed from Shawinigan Falls, Quebec. There was even an Argentinian – Flight Lieutenant Kenneth Langley Charney. Born in Quilmes, on the coast of the Rio de la Plata, in the province of Buenos Aires on 28 February 1920, Ken's father had been a soldier in the First World War and now was manager of the Anglo Mexican Petroleum Company. Because of this the family moved from one Argentinian city to another. When he was 12, Ken Charney was speeding in his father's car when he was caught by the police of Bahia Blanca city! One of his father's responsibilities was to refuel Aeroposta Argentina S.A. aircraft in Patagonia. Aeroposta was an early pioneering airline in Argentina established in the late 1920s, and a subsidiary of the French airmail carrier Aéropostale. Ken met French pilots and he fell in love with aeroplanes.

After completing his studies at Aldenham College in Elstree, Hertfordshire, for two years, 1934–36, Charney returned to Argentina and entered St George's College, where his irreverent attitude often got him into trouble. Ken left for England in the second group of Argentineans that fought with the Allies (approximately 4,000 volunteers including about 800 in the Canadian and Royal Air Forces). He received his wings in April

1941 as a sergeant pilot and his first squadron was 91, whom he flew with for fourteen months.

Another Canadian pilot on 'Salient', who, most probably, looked to avenge the death of his brother at the first opportunity, was 23-year-old Flight Sergeant Bernard Walter Reynolds, from Lake Lenore, Saskatchewan. He had lost his 27-year-old brother, Flight Lieutenant Joseph Benedict Reynolds, a Hurricane pilot on 1 Squadron RCAF, when he was killed on 18 February 1941 in a crash at Bridlington golf course. Unfortunately, Bernards' sojourn on Malta on 126 Squadron would be all too brief.

Flight Sergeant (later Flight Lieutenant) Ian Roy MacLennan DFM RCAF had already made his name in England, though not in the way he would have hoped, and was more eager than most to carve a niche for himself. Having damaged two Spitfires on 401 Squadron RCAF in an accident in England, MacLennan had fallen out of favour with his flight commander, who pointed out that 'they were looking for volunteers for Malta!' Born on 9 April 1919 in Regina, Saskatchewan, MacLennan had shot ducks near his home in Gull Lake when he was a boy and knew about deflection. He had studied engineering at Saskatchewan University before enlisting in the RCAF in October 1940, arriving in England in the summer of 1941.

On arrival on Malta, MacLennan would be assigned to 1435 Flight at Takali–Luqa, whose pool of serviceable aircraft and pilots was available for nominated squadrons to draw upon. The flight was first formed at Malta as a night fighter unit equipped with Hurricane II fighters. When 603 Squadron was disbanded on 3 August 1942, it was partly incorporated into the flight to form 1435 Squadron. With this unit, MacLennan would claim seven victories (and seven 'damaged'); the last, a seaplane, on 14 November 1942.

Pilot Officer John Frederick McElroy RCAF damaged his Spitfire's tail on take-off from *Eagle* and crash-landed on arrival on Malta. Born in Port Arthur, Ontario, in 1920, McElroy had served in the North Battleford Light Infantry and the Rocky Mountain Rangers before entering the RCAF in 1940. Commissioned in September 1941, he had left for England in November and he joined 54 Squadron at the start of April 1942. His pride was probably hurt after the take-off incident on *Eagle* but after being temporarily grounded and almost reposted to the Middle East, he soon showed his true mettle on 249 Squadron.

From the antipodes came Sergeants A.R. Richardson RAAF and C.L. Baxter RAAF, and fellow Australian, Flight Sergeant Colin Henry Parkinson. Born on 29 December 1916, 'Parky' was a former business manager in Killara, New South Wales, before the war, and he had joined the RAAF in 1940. After finishing training, and posted to Britain, he served briefly on 56 and 19 Squadrons. He took off from *Eagle* at about 0700 hours, one of eight pilots with an inexperienced flight lieutenant to lead them. His speeds varied from 100 to 200mph and soon Parkinson's long-range tank ran out of fuel. His Spitfire dropped like a stone but he managed to get the engine running again and he jettisoned the tank over Tunis. After arriving on Malta, Parkinson was posted to 603 Squadron.

From New Zealand had come Sergeant Erle Thomas Brough, who would receive the DFC and return to Owaka after his service on Malta; Pilot Officer Charles Henry Lattimer; Flight Lieutenant Alan Carthew Rowe; Sergeant Colin Lethbridge Wood of Hicks

Bay; and Flight Lieutenant Gray Stenborg, born in Auckland on 13 October 1921, the only son of Gunnar Stenborg, a Swedish emigrant to New Zealand, and his wife Ruby. Educated at King's College at Ōtāhuhu in Auckland, where he played in the school's first cricket XI, Gray was also active in rowing and yachting. In 1940 he had left college and joined the Air Force at the age of 18. In April he went to Canada and he looked back on that trip as a wonderful event in his life when he pulled away from the wharf for England, not having expected to leave just then and without having said goodbye. He got 'quite a shock' however 'the next day all was right again. We had such fun, and we all thought what a wonderful thing this war was after all.'

At Moose Jaw, Saskatchewan, Gray Stenborg and sixty-seven other New Zealanders trained on Harvards. He gained his commission in November that same year. 'What a marvellous time we had,' he wrote later in a letter to his parents at 6 King Edward Parade, Devonport, in the harbourside suburb of Auckland's North Shore. 'I look back on how hard we worked in the classroom, and how I concentrated to try and fly as well as my instructor, Flying Officer Dave Bell. He had fought in France and Britain. He was a bomber pilot.'

Gray admitted that he owed all his success in the air to Bell. 'In fact,' he added, 'I owe my life to some of the evasive tactics that he taught me. Then at last WINGS! Can you imagine that day! Poor Dave was so miserable as he waved goodbye on the train. It was with great sorrow that I had to leave for more training in Scotland (with ice skating for relaxation). Hurray, at last I was posted [to 111 Squadron]!' He was to recall how he next met Dave in London and what a great time they had together.

Flying and war are 'just what the doctor ordered', he wrote. 'On April 26th I did my first real bit of work, first time over enemy territory and I saw one of our bombers shot down in front of my nose. Well during that run, I shot down a German fighter [a Fw 190] but war, to me, was not such fun as before.' However, by 30 April he had destroyed four more Focke Wulfs. On the trip to Gibraltar in *Hopetarn* he admitted he was scared his ship would be sunk by a submarine, though he did admit 'to having a glorious six days'.

On Malta on 15 June, now on 185 Squadron, Gray Stenborg destroyed a Bf 109F for his first victory but his outlook had changed dramatically. In his letter home he wrote: 'War is no longer a "good thing". It is a horror. Flying on this island is not enjoyable, it scares one to death but I can hold my own more. My greatest desire, which increases with the days, is to return to my home in New Zealand … I am not at all pessimistic about this but even the very best of British pilots die here and so, if I happen to be "one of the good who die young" – always remember that I am proud and happy to die in such a heroes' island and in such a good cause.'

On 9 July, for the third time in the war, Stenborg claimed two enemy aircraft (Bf 109s) in one sortie. By the end of the month, he had been promoted to flight lieutenant and decorated with the DFC. But on 20 August, he wrote that it looked like his 'end' was coming close.

'I have had more shaves than I dare to think of. Three days ago [17 August] topped them off. I led my section of four Spitfires up after some 109s. Two of the boys had to return for engine trouble etc. Well, the two of us that were left attacked twelve or more Messerschmitt 109Fs. I blew one of them to pieces and the next instant chunks flew off my wing and the whole plane started shaking and shuddering all over. It went into a steep dive with smoke pouring from the cockpit. I was completely out of control: my tail must have shot away. "This is it!" I thought when I found I couldn't get the hood off. Anyhow, in sheer desperation I banged it off somehow, and undid my straps. The next thing I knew was myself flying through the air, so I pulled the ripcord and made a safe landing in the sea – about 5 miles out. I got all tangled up in the harness and shrouds, but – half drowned – succeeded in inflating my dinghy.'

Gray Stenborg had lost control at 27,000ft and his Spitfire fell 14,000ft at over 400mph before the hood came off and he suddenly found himself thrown out. He had seen a German pilot open his parachute at that speed and his harness had been ripped off, so he waited for a while before pulling the ripcord in order to slow up and then he pulled the cord and landed in the sea. He was picked up off Delimara Point by the rescue launch shortly afterwards.

'All my injuries are bruises and scratches over my left eye. Wow! Was I lucky or was I lucky?'

On Tuesday, 23 June, meanwhile, Flight Sergeant Colin Parkinson had opened his account on 603 Squadron, being awarded a one third share in the destruction of a MC.202 Folgore west of Gozo, Maresciallo Aldo Buvoli of 360° Squadriglia, 22° Gruppo Caccia Terrestre (land hunting), who had flown biplane fighters in the Spanish Civil War, bailed out. Parkinson had 'sailed in' and made one three quarter head-on attack after spotting another

Spitfire getting the worst of the exchange with the Macchi. 'The "Ity"', he said, 'flicked and turned away, presenting his tail to me. I was about 200ft behind with the bead dead on and firing. I saw something break off the fuselage and then the pilot bailed out. His kite went into the sea. I circled the pilot whose chute had opened. He looked dead to me so I eventually flew straight at him and then decided he wasn't dead because he started to wave his arms frantically.' Buvoli was taken prisoner.

Parkinson's diary entries often provide a tongue-in-cheek yet thrilling story of Malta's epic defence throughout his time on the Island. However, all too often there was also a dark side, as occurred on the afternoon of 25 June when Flight Sergeant Maurice Ernest Tomkins on his squadron nursed his damaged Spitfire home to Takali, only to crash and for his aircraft to burst into flames. 'The fire tender was about to approach,' wrote Parkinson 'but the ammo started to go off so they stopped. The kite had nearly burnt itself out before they went near it. I went over to have a look and saw the pilot caught in amongst the wreckage … I could smell his clothes burning. It was Tomkins, who sleeps next to me.'

On Sunday, 12 July, a dozen Ju 88s attacked Takali at 1000 hours. Eight Spitfires on 603 Squadron that flew an early morning patrol failed to intercept the bombers and they returned empty handed. Colin Parkinson taxied in at Takali to witness crews 'running like hell' for the (so-called) shelters and a flock of Ju 88s overhead. 'I nipped smartly out of my kite and made the world's record for a 200-yard sprint to the surface shelter. One bomb lobbed just at the back of the shelter and shook us all to our underpants.

'A stick of bombs had fallen along the dispersal pens and punctured my new kite in the wings.'

After inspecting it Parkinson was walking back to dispersal when a DA (delayed-action bomb) exploded with a terrific roar 20 yards from the Spitfire, which caused more holes and a rock 'bashed' the spinner. Five other Spitfires on 'B' Flight were also damaged which left six fighters instead of twelve remaining.

On 13 July Colin Parkinson rose at 0430. At about 0900, after he was scrambled to 24,000ft, '"Hun" bombers', he said. 'Came over, with large fighter escort. Our section did not see the bombers, but saw some fighters. An Me 109 swung in to attack a Spit, but the Spit turned towards it. They then both went in opposite directions. I put my nose down and went after the 109 with everything pushed. Got to within 150 yards, and gave a long squirt with cannon and M.G. fire. I allowed plenty for drop. Saw strikes and black smoke pour out of 109. He pulled up slightly and dived steeply. I kept on squirting till my cannon ran out of ammo. This took place 15 miles south of Filfla. Another 109 bounced me, but turned up-sun and he lost me. I headed for home at 1,000ft. Another kite dived at me and I swung up-sun and did a steep turn on to his tail. It was a Spit. Came back to 'drome and claimed one "probable"! Delayed actions have been going off all day round the 'drome.'

On 30 July there was a cool northerly wind blowing and fast-moving cloud. 'Hope I have some luck,' Parkinson wrote. 'An 88 would be nice compensation for being on this island. No scrambles until about 8 o'clock.' At 0820 hours there was an air raid alert for a thirty-five-strong fighter sweep. 'Finally took off and climbed into the sky over Gozo.'

'Reached 11,000 ft, turned south-east, down-sun, and reached the Malta coast in time to see ack-ack bursts over the centre of the island. As we drew level with the coastline in a steep dive, I saw a Ju 88 underneath with black smoke pouring out of the centre of the fuselage. I rolled on my back and dived after it. At a range of about ten yards, I opened fire. The 88 tried to gain height, but burst into flames and finally disintegrated. My machine flew right through the falling wreckage. The 88 was a definite gonner before I attacked [and it] crashed into the sea.'

The Spitfires of 503 Squadron attacked four Bf 109s but then they were jumped by six Macchi MC.202s. Parkinson broke away up-sun and saw a Bf 109 'weaving in and out among a number of Spits'. He was about to give one of them a burst, but gave a squirt in instead. The 109 continued weaving on its way westward unmolested. He was close behind. Eight miles north of Żonqor Point it evidently saw him and started a dive. 'I gave a long squirt and followed it down through light cloud to about 200ft above the water. The ME continued diving, and crashed straight in. I stooged about for another quarter of an hour, and then came down to pancake.'

At 1055 hours another eight Spitfires on 603 Squadron were airborne to intercept a reported plot of twenty-seven hostile aircraft, including bombers. One Spitfire returned early and ran into enemy fighters. One Spitfire was slightly damaged. Two more air raid alerts were plotted and 24-year-old Sergeant Colin Lethbridge Wood, of Lottin Point, East Cape, New Zealand, was killed.

Axis command was now sending only fighter sweeps in daylight, flying at high altitude in an attempt to gain the advantage over the Spitfires. Until this point in time, the Spitfires had fought defensively, but the 'Forward Interception Plan', issued on 25 July by Air Vice Marshal Sir Keith Park, who had succeeded Hugh Pughe Lloyd as the Air Officer Commanding, appeared to be taking effect.

On taking over, Park said: 'The magnificent fighting by our fighter pilots at Malta in April and May has very rightly been generously acknowledged. The courage, endurance and fine work of the officers, NCOs and men on the ground has not, however, received full acknowledgement. During the blitz in the spring, the enemy was so vastly superior in strength that our day fighters were practically forced onto the defensive. Under these conditions it was inevitable that Royal Air Force personnel on the ground, and civilians, should undergo severe bombing daily, and I now pay tribute to the courageous manner in which they kept our airfields going in spite of the lack of protection from our fighters. Our day-fighter strength has during June and July been greatly increased, and the enemy's superiority in numbers has long since dwindled. The time has now arrived for our Spitfire squadrons to put an end to the bombing of our airfields by daylight. We have the best fighter aircraft in the world, and our Spitfire pilots will again show their comrades on the ground that they are the best fighter pilots in the world.

'All fighter formation leaders are warned that the enemy will probably reintroduce bomber formations whenever there is an important operation in the Malta area. Because our Spitfires, using the forward plan of interception, have recently stopped daylight raids, does not mean that only fighter sweeps are likely to be encountered over or near Malta in the near future.

'Any signs of defensive tactics by our fighters will encourage the enemy to reintroduce formations of bombers or fighter bombers. Therefore, the more aggressively our fighters are employed, the better will Malta be defended against daylight bombing.'

On 31 July, using three squadrons, Park tasked the first to engage the escorting fighters by 'bouncing them' out of the sun, the second squadron to strike at the close escort, or, if unescorted, the bombers themselves, while the third was to attack the bombers head-on. Three fighter sweeps of six, fifteen and thirty aircraft respectively were flown on 31 July. Very few enemy fighters crossed the coast and the Malta fighters destroyed two 109s and an Re.2001. Colin Parkinson damaged a Macchi MC.202.

The plan would result in increased enemy aircraft losses and would force many bombers to jettison their bombload before reaching their targets. The Axis would have to abandon daylight raids, and the Stukas were withdrawn from operations over Malta altogether. Kesselring, Park's adversary in the Battle of Britain, sent in fighter sweeps at even higher altitudes to gain the tactical advantage but Park ordered his fighters to climb no higher than 6,100ft. Despite losing a considerable height advantage, it forced the Bf 109s to descend to altitudes more suitable for the Spitfire than the German fighter.

In response, Park ordered his fighters to remain below 20,000ft to force the enemy to drop to the Spitfire pilots' preferred altitude if they wanted to engage in combat. With improved radar and faster take-off times (two to three minutes) and improved ASR, in October more offensive action would become possible.

By the end of July, thanks to the 'Club Runs', the RAF had eighty serviceable fighters at Malta, mostly the latest Spitfire

Vcs, but the losses continued with an average of perhaps fifteen a week being shot down or too badly damaged to fly again.

On the morning of 4 August, when east of Żonqor Point, four Spitfire Vs of 229 Squadron intercepted a pair of Macchi MC.202 Folgore fighters. Lieutenant Cecil Jack Ormonde Swales – who was better known as 'Zulu' – and Squadron Leader Bill Douglas, his Scottish CO, were first to attack. Swales, who had originally trained in the SAAF as an air gunner before transferring to pilot training, had arrived on Malta after flying off the *Wasp* on 20 April. Douglas destroyed a Ju 88 on the 25th, a Bf 109 on 9 May and he got a Ju 87 'probable', shared another and damaged two more on the 10th. On 11 May Douglas got another 109 before colliding with another Spitfire while intercepting a Ju 88. He and the other Spitfire pilot both bailed out safely. He was awarded an MC.202 'damaged' on 6 July and a Ju 88 'damaged' on the 13th.

Swales fired a short burst at the two Italian fighters, which was quickly followed by a fusillade of fire by Douglas, who used up all his ammunition but could not get closer than 400 yards. No strikes were seen but 'Zulu' was not finished. He turned on the other Macchi and fired a five-second burst at 200 yards into the starboard wing and fuselage of the Italian fighter, and it began to smoke. The pilot swooped into a steep dive and Swales followed the Italian down, firing until all his ammunition was spent. The Macchi was last seen at water level, smoking badly. Swales was credited with one Macchi 'damaged'.

On the early afternoon of 11 August 1942, *Eagle*, which was carrying sixteen Sea Hurricanes of 801 and 813 Squadrons as well as four reserve aircraft for the 'Pedestal' operation, was hit by four torpedoes from *U-73* and sank within four minutes. Fred Treves, a 17-year-old junior apprentice on MV *Waimärama* who was on his first voyage wrote: 'The attacks were terrifying. I cannot think of another word. The worst for me were the Stukas, their sirens made the most appalling noise. The sky was absolutely mottled with flak from the ships … nothing had ever been seen like it. The destroyers too were simply remarkable. The worst sight of all was seeing *Eagle* go down, because you could see both planes and men sliding into the sea. You could actually hear the screams and yells. It was extremely frightening; no, it was not frightening, it was terror, absolute terror.' In the sinking 2 officers and 158 ratings, mainly from the ship's propulsion machinery spaces, were killed. Other vessels rescued 67 officers and 862 sailors. Also 16 Sea Hurricanes were lost; 4 from 801 were aloft when the ship was torpedoed and landed on other carriers.

In Operation 'Bellows', *Furious,* escorted by a light cruiser and a destroyer, set out for Gibraltar on 4 August loaded with thirty-nine Spitfires. *Furious* and *Manchester* joined the WS.21S convoy on 7 August, and the entire force and convoy passed through the Strait of Gibraltar on 10 August. Next day *Furious*, escorted by the destroyers *Laforey* and *Lookout*, detached from the main body and, 635 miles west of Malta, flew off all except one of the embarked Spitfires. One was forced to land hurriedly on the fleet carrier *Indomitable* nearby. One flight was ably led by Pilot Officer William Thomas Edward Rolls DFM, born in Lower Edmonton, north London on 6 August 1914. He had scored seven victories flying Spitfire Is on 72 Squadron in 1940. Rolls decided against leading his flight over the planned route as he expected probable enemy action and instead, he headed immediately southwest, which took them to the Algerian coast, then over the coast of Tunisia and finally, out over the Gulf of Hammamet, which avoided possible action from the Vichy French.

On 12 August at the culmination of 'Bellows', *Furious* had returned to Gibraltar to load Hurricanes from the transport carrier *Argus* and thirty-two Spitfires that had been shipped from England in crates aboard the freighter *Empire Clive* and assembled ashore. The Spitfires were destined for Operation 'Baritone', the last but one 'Club Run' to Malta. *Furious* sailed once again on 16 August under escort by the light cruiser *Aurora*, light anti-aircraft cruiser *Charybdis*, fleet destroyers *Antelope, Eskimo, Keppel, Laforey, Lookout, Lightning, Malcolm, Venomous, Wishart* and probably *Tartar*, and escort destroyers *Bicester* and *Derwent*.

On 17 August, in an undertaking whose RAF element was 'Headlong', *Furious* took up position to fly off the thirty-two Spitfires to Malta. Newly commissioned Pilot Officer Colin Parkinson, who was one of four pilots chosen to lead them to the Island, watched the first eight take off without mishap; 'the second crowd also. The third bunch were unlucky, one kite [piloted by Sergeant William Joseph Alexander Fleming] taking off, struck a signal lamp in the port navigation position as it swerved, stalled one wing, and crashed over the side after knocking the tail off. It hit the water on its back and sank immediately.' Fleming was lost with his aircraft. 'Sergeants L.J. McDougall and J.C. Sullivan could not get their wheels up after taking off and they abandoned their Spitfires en route. Colin Parkinson's section, meanwhile, had taken off successfully and they set course for Malta. 'The trip was uneventful,' wrote Parkinson. 'Bags of fuel when we arrived. Had to orbit off the Island while a raid was in progress. Sergeant J.G. McGill crashed at Luqa and was badly burned.'

The highest-ranking RAF officer on 'Bellows' was 35-year-old Group Captain Walter Myers Churchill DSO DFC, the elder brother of Peter Churchill and Oliver Churchill, both of whom were Special Operations Executive officers. On arrival on Malta, he would take command of Takali. Walter Churchill was born in Amsterdam on 24 November 1907. He graduated with a BA from Pembroke College, Cambridge and was then employed by Hawker Siddeley as an engineer. Later, he formed his own company, Churchill Components (Coventry) Ltd. In 1931 Churchill joined 605 Squadron, Royal Auxiliary Air Force, and was commissioned in January 1932. He had commanded 605 Squadron from June to September 1940, flown Hurricanes in the Battle of Britain as a squadron leader before helping form the first American Eagle squadron (71 Squadron) in late September 1940. Suffering from sinus trouble, on 23 January 1941 he relinquished his flying status and command of 71 Squadron. By July 1942 Churchill was again fit for flying.

Arthur Hay Donaldson DFC AFC was to be Group Captain Churchill's wing commander flying on Malta and he would at first be put in charge of ground training, but soon he would be given command of the three Spitfire Squadrons – 229, 249 and 185 – at Takali. Donaldson was the youngest of the famous Donaldson brothers – all three of whom would receive the DSO serving in the RAF. (It is said their mother journeyed to Buckingham Palace to attend her sons' assorted investitures on no fewer than thirteen occasions). Born in January 1915, Arthur was commissioned in March 1934 as a pilot officer and he had spent the pre-war years flying biplane fighters. He was a flying instructor when war was declared and he largely missed the Battle of Britain. In January 1941, he joined 242 Squadron, commanded by Douglas Bader. Appointed to the command of 263 Squadron in February 1941, Arthur commenced a flurry of 'hit and run' strikes to occupied France and Belgium in the unit's Westland Whirlwinds, a period of operations that witnessed his first close encounter with mortality. On 14 June he and other pilots attacked Querqueville airfield in occupied France. Donaldson's fighter was hit by flak and he was nearly killed, but he returned to England and eventually made a swift recovery. During a low-level attack on an enemy airfield at Morlaix in September 1941 his aircraft was hit by flak and an explosive round ripped apart the top of his flying helmet.

Flight Lieutenant Eric Norman Woods DFC would take command of 249 Squadron on his arrival in Malta. Born in Buenos Aires, Argentina, on 8 May 1910, his family had returned to England in 1914 and his father joined the Royal Navy. In 1920, the family moved again, this time to Victoria and then to Vancouver in 1924, where he was educated. He moved to England in 1936 and worked for a telephone company and also for the Reigate Police Force in Surrey. He enlisted in the RAF in May 1940 but was placed in reserve until August that year, when he began pilot training. In the spring of 1942, now on 124 Squadron, he shot down an Fw 190. Then, on 72 Squadron, he claimed two Fw 190s 'damaged', a Bf 109F destroyed and another probably destroyed. During his tenure as commanding officer of

249 Squadron he increased his score to nine and two shared destroyed, four probables, nine 'damaged' and one destroyed on the ground.

Pilot Officer Leo Stratton Nomis RAFVR, born on 9 March 1922 in Los Angeles, California, who was destined for 229 Squadron had, in the autumn of 1941, joined 71 'Eagle' Squadron at Debden, Essex, flying a Spitfire Mk Vb on his first operational sortie on 7 December, the day Pearl Harbor was attacked. He made his first claim in January 1942 for an enemy aircraft damaged in the Pas-de-Calais and he shared in the destruction of a Ju 88 kill on 17 April off Felixstowe. By then, Leo had acquired a personal Spitfire (BL287) and decorated it with an Indian head in honour of his Sioux ancestry (Nomis's father was half Sioux). He was no doubt aware that his squadron shared their airfield with 249 Squadron and one George 'Screwball' Beurling. Nomis, certainly, was out of the same mould as the controversial Canadian ace. After borrowing a Spitfire for an unauthorised, lone-wolf, night-time sweep of Sicily, Nomis was punished with a transfer to El Alamein in the Western Desert and assigned to 92 'East India' Squadron, where he claimed a 109G destroyed and one 'probable'.

During August 1942 Arthur Donaldson and Walter Churchill led the initial fighter sweeps over Sicily. Churchill planned the first attacks on Sicily and led the first raid on 23 August. Four days later, leading a raid on Biscari airfield near Gela in southern Sicily, he was killed when his Spitfire was hit by flak and crashed in flames. Arthur Donaldson wrote: 'We maintained complete RT silence so as to arrive unheralded. My Squadron was to attack Biscara. The flak was intense. I looked across at poor old

Walter Churchill, and at that very moment he was shot down in flames, crashing in the middle of the aerodrome.'

Air Vice Marshal Keith Park, Air Officer Commanding, RAF Mediterranean, wrote a letter to Churchill's widow, in which he said: 'It may be some comfort to you in your great loss to know that your husband met his end leading a fighter formation in a most successful attack on the enemy ... his fine example and inspired leadership will live on in Malta to the end of the war. He arrived in Malta leading a formation of reinforcing Spitfires to protect the last vitally important convoy. During his all too short stay in Malta Walter Churchill was an inspiration to the fighter squadron in the air and on the ground. If it was ordained that Walter Churchill was to give his life for his country, I feel sure he would have chosen to end it as he did, leading a fighter formation on a daring and most successful fighter sweep over enemy territory.'

Donaldson shared in a Dornier Do 217 'probable' at Biscari airfield on 27 August and on 2 September shared a Macchi MC.202 Folgore 20 miles from Cap Scaramia before the Luftwaffe mounted its final momentous attack on the besieged island in October. On Sunday, 11 October, in a spate of combats north of Grand Harbour, he destroyed a Ju 88, claimed another as a 'probable' and a Bf 109 'damaged'. Next day, between 1130 and 1230 hours, eight Ju 88s with an escort of thirty fighters were reported heading southwards from Sicily. Encouraged by the new RAF tactic of 'forward interception' – attacking raiders well before they reach Malta – the Spitfires were scrambled early, intercepting the raiders a few miles south of the Sicilian coast and 35 miles from Malta. Eight Spitfires on 249 Squadron attacked the Ju 88s and fighters head-on. Donaldson destroyed a Ju 88 and a 109, and was awarded a half share for another Ju 88. 'It was the most spectacular sight I have ever seen,' he wrote later. 'The whole sky was filled with enemy aircraft in severe trouble. I saw three flaming Ju 88s and another three flaming MEs and counted no less than ten parachutes descending slowly, three of them from a Ju 88 I had shot down ...'

On Monday, 21 September, meanwhile, Squadron Leader Adrian Warburton on 69 Squadron, flying a cannon-armed Spitfire V of 249 Squadron, undertook a special reconnaissance sortie at 1730 hours along the Sicilian coast between Marsala and Sciacca, during which he encountered a Dornier Do 24 maritime patrol and search and rescue aircraft at sea level off Agrigento. He took some shots at it and claimed to have damaged the three-engine flying boat.

'Worby' was born in Middlesbrough on 10 March 1918, the only son of Commander Geoffrey Warburton DSO, a highly respected Royal Navy submariner, and Muriel Warburton. Adrian was christened on board a submarine in Grand Harbour. He became legendary in the RAF for his role in the defence of Malta and was described by Air Marshal Sir Arthur Tedder as 'the most important pilot in the RAF'. In 1940 431 Flight was sent to Malta following pressure from the Commander-in-Chief (C-in-C) Mediterranean, Admiral Cunningham, who wanted 'eyes' on the powerful and modern Italian battle fleet. Cunningham planned to strike a blow at the Italians at their naval base at Taranto in southern Italy, but first he needed up-to-date intelligence. In November 431 Flight flew two Martin Maryland trips to Taranto. On 3 November, 431 Flight reported three battleships in the harbour. On the 7th there were four. The most important sorties were flown on 10 and 11 November, two on each day. Warburton's Maryland was subjected to intense flak and intercepted by a CR.42, which took twenty minutes to shake off. Photographs of the Italian fleet taken on this sortie proved crucial.

On Monday, 12 October 1942 Acting Flight Lieutenant Arthur Ford Roscoe RAFVR on 229 Squadron, who had arrived on Malta after flying off *Furious* on Operation 'Bellows', participated in an engagement against a force of German fighters. The 21-year-old American, who was born in Chicago, had been determined to fly from an early age. At Los Angeles Metropolitan he washed planes and took on any chores that needed doing in return for flying time. He soloed at 16 and after high school he got a job with the Lockheed California Aircraft Company. He and two of his buddies purchased a small aircraft of their own and applied to the Military Academy at West Point. Unfortunately, he failed the medical because of a slight astigmatism in one eye but, undeterred, he had sought out the Clayton Knight Committee, who were screening young potential pilots for the RAF. They were not concerned about his lack of 20-20 vision and he was accepted for pilot training in England. On completion, he was posted to 71 Squadron – the first American 'Eagle' squadron – at North Weald flying Spitfires.

Showing the grim determination that had so far served him well, Roscoe took on the enemy fighters and when one of his fellow Spitfire pilots was being attacked by a Bf 109, a burst from Roscoe's guns caused the Messerschmitt pilot to break away with pieces falling from his aircraft. Roscoe's Spitfire was then attacked by six 109s. Although he was shot through the shoulder, and had probably suffered a broken arm as well as being weak from loss of blood, he fought his way through and, in so doing, destroyed one of the attacking 109s. Whilst heading for base he was again attacked. His engine caught fire and it was only by skilful airmanship that he was able to right his aircraft, although the last thing he remembered was flying low over a blast shelter and reasoned that he must have hit the top of it. He had been flung out of the cockpit, landing some way away with serious injuries and loss of blood caused by his cannon shell wound. He came to lying on a table in the mess.

In his citation for the award of the DFC it said that, '... this courageous officer who has completed a large number of sorties and destroyed 4 enemy aircraft has always displayed great skill and determination.'

On 16 October, on seeing enemy bombers starting a shallow dive, Bill Rolls gave the order for a head-on attack. He chose the leader of the formation and gave a three-second burst and hit the starboard engine. The Ju 88 immediately started to smoke and went into a steep turn to port, glycol coming from his engine. The rest followed him and jettisoned bombs in St Paul's Bay. The last Rolls saw of the leader he was going down very steeply. The Ju 88 crashed into the sea about 10 miles east of Grand Harbour. It was his sixteenth victory.

Four enemy raids in all were launched on 16 October, the first with eight Ju 88s and a large number of enemy fighters. Spitfires intercepted them 15 miles out from Żonqor Point. Two Spitfire pilots on 249 Squadron were lost at sea. Maltese fishermen picked up 28-year-old Sergeant Martin Aloysius Lundy near the Blue Grotto at the end of the second raid but the body of Warrant Officer Peter Carter RCAF was not recovered after he was shot down into the sea. In the fourth raid a German bomber was shot down 5 miles out from Delimara Point.

Air Vice Marshal Park, only too aware of the losses on the Spitfire squadrons and their dogged defensive work, sent a message to each squadron that evening: 'Grand work fighter-boys. Your magnificent fighting in the last few days is being watched not only in Malta but by the RAF on other fronts as well as by our Russian allies. Although heavily outnumbered last May, the Malta Spitfires came out on top and I am confident that you will win the second battle of Malta. Some of the enemy bomber squadrons have already shown they cannot take it. Keep it up and in a few days the other German bombers will throw in the sponge. Replacement pilots and Spitfires are on their way but there is still some stiff fighting to finish the job. Good luck to you and good shooting. Your [maintenance personnel] part in the present battle for Malta greatly appreciated but serviceability of Spitfires continues to fall. You can and must get it up again. Where you have worked hard you must work harder and faster. Give the fighter boys Spitfires and they will drive the Hun out of the sky.'

On Sunday, 25 October Bill Rolls scored his seventeenth and final kill when he shot down a Bf 109F over Luqa. On landing he was told by one of the pilots on his squadron that the AOC's nephew, Nigel Manfred Park DFM RNZAF, who had just been promoted to pilot officer, had been shot down over the sea and was missing.

Park had been a keen sportsman and after finishing his education at Mangatu School and Gisborne High School, had worked as a shepherd at Whatatutu before joining the Royal New Zealand Air Force in May 1941. He did his initial training at Weraroa Station near Levin and then proceeded to No. 2 Elementary Flying School, first flying solo on 27 June. He went to Canada in August for further flight training with the Royal Canadian Air Force, gaining his wings in November and promoted to sergeant the same month. He flew briefly on 122 Squadron on the Channel Front before being sent to Malta in July 1942. He travelled to Malta aboard HMS *Eagle*, which was transporting thirty-two Spitfires to the Island in Operation 'Pinpoint'. He flew his Spitfire off the carrier's flight deck and landed at Malta on 15 July.

Within two weeks of his arrival on the Island, on 28 July, Park destroyed a Bf 109 and was awarded a quarter share in a Ju 88. He had further successes over the next few months. On 9 August, he was one of twenty-two Spitfire pilots scrambled to intercept a group of Bf 109s approaching St Paul's Bay and he shot down a Bf 109 despite his own aircraft receiving some damage to its wing during the engagement. Park's Spitfire was damaged again, in an encounter on 10 October with a group of enemy fighters. Despite his cannon having jammed, he was able to evade them and land back at Takali. The following day he damaged a Reggiane Re.2001. On 12 October, 15 miles north of Grand Harbour, with two other pilots, he made a head-on attack on a formation of seven Ju 88s, shooting one down immediately and then, regardless of the danger from the escorting 109s, turned and destroyed a second Ju 88. Later that day, north-west of Filfla, he claimed another bomber.

On the 14th 'Parky' destroyed a Ju 88 that had just bombed Takali, and also downed a Bf 109 15 miles north of Comino and a 109 15 miles north-east of Żonqor Point. Two days later he destroyed another Bf 109 in the same location and on the 18th 126 Squadron were attacked by a dozen Bf 109s and he was shot down and crash-landed his Spitfire Vc but escaped with minor injuries. His luck ran out on the 25th when he failed to return from the sortie.

When Bill Rolls was told that ASR would take some time to reach 'Parky' and it was getting dark, Rolls, his flight commander, asked for, and received, permission to take off and search for his friend or to protect him if he was in a dinghy. One pilot believed that he had crashed into the sea, while another thought he had bailed out. A search was mounted for 'Parky' but he was never recovered. Rolls noted in his logbook that 'Parky' had shot down a Bf 109F before he was killed, which took his score overall to ten and one shared victories. Following his recommendation, Park was posthumously awarded the Distinguished Flying Medal.

'To honour her brave people, I award the George Cross to the Island Fortress of Malta to bear witness to a heroism and devotion that will long be famous in history.'

The award to the people of Malta by HM King George VI was announced on 15 April 1942.

Chapter 7

The Fighter Pilots' Paradise

'This new blitz has relieved the monotony of the island for the time being – Malta pilots knocking them down like ninepins.'
Diary entry by Flight Sergeant Colin Henry Parkinson RAAF on 229 Squadron, whose previous victory had occurred on Thursday, 27 August when he destroyed a Ju 88 on the ground off the Sicilian coast.

On Sunday morning, 11 October 1942, Malta had been hit by heavy bombing raids for the first time in three months as the Luftwaffe sent fifty-eight bombers with massed fighter escorts over the Island. The attacks, which killed thirty-one civilians, marked a return to blitz conditions not seen since the end of April that year. The latest raids, which would last a month, would come to be known as 'the last blitz'. Charles F. 'Chuck' McLean stated 'conservatively' that at its height the odds against them were fifty to sixty to one. 'It wasn't funny pitching against odds like that, but 'ol lucky McLean came through,' he would write triumphantly.

Flight Lieutenants William Rolls DFM on 126 Squadron, Allan Scott on 1435 Squadron and Colin Parkinson and Flight Sergeant 'Jimmy' Ballantyne on 229 Squadron were particularly successful during this period. On 11 October Rolls claimed his twelfth victory of the war, and the first of seven kills that momentous month, when he shot a Re.2001 down into the sea. Mar Romano Pesavento bailed out. Rolls circled the Italian in his rescue dinghy but he refused to return his wave. Pesavento was later declared 'missing'. Rolls was also awarded another Re.2001 'damaged'.

Wing Commander Arthur Donaldson, leading 229 Squadron, claimed a Ju 88 in a head-on attack against nine of the German bombers 15 miles north of Grand Harbour. Two others were claimed 'damaged' by 'Jimmy' Ballantyne and Pilot Officer H.T. Nash RCAF, while Colin Parkinson probably destroyed another. 'I could see the Ack-Ack going up and the search lights,' he wrote. 'Decided to wait off Zonqor Point to try and catch an odd bomber on the way home. I was lucky. I caught a glimpse of one at 10,000ft, about 2,000ft below. Dived in to attack; was fired at by rear gunner, who I put out of action with my first burst. Made about two more attacks and finally the Ju 88 caught fire. Followed it down to about 1,000ft where I lost sight of it while trying to manoeuvre for another attack. It probably dived into the sea.' He was awarded a Ju 88 'probable'.

Next day, Monday, 12 October, between dawn and dusk, the enemy carried out five major raids on Malta. Bill Rolls claimed a Ju 88 of 8/KG54 over Grand Harbour. 'I saw one of the Ju 88s I had fired at diving down. I put a final burst into it, and it almost fell to pieces ... I followed to 4,000ft and thought I saw two bail out. I did not see what had happened to the others I had hit since I was too busy getting out of the mass of aircraft flying around ... I saw Ju 88s burning and going down all over the place.' He also claimed two Macchi MC.202s, one of which blew up in mid-air and the other that crashed into the sea off Gozo.

On the third enemy raid of the day, when eight Ju 88s approached the Island at midday escorted by ten MC.202s and twenty Bf 109s, they were intercepted south of the Sicilian coast and the survivors turned back after they were intercepted by eight Spitfires of 249 Squadron and seven of 229 Squadron led by Wing Commander Arthur Hay Donaldson, who earned a half share in a Ju 88 destroyed 30 miles north of Gozo and another Ju 88 and a Bf 109 both destroyed 35 miles north of Malta.

Allan Scott shot down a Reggiane Re.2001, probably destroyed another and damaged a third. Later that same month he claimed two Ju 88s 'damaged', a Bf 109 destroyed, one damaged and one probably destroyed. 'To me flying a Spitfire was wonderful,' he said later. 'You flew it instinctively. You didn't think about flying. You turned your head to go left and the aircraft followed you. It became part of you; it fitted you like an overcoat; and, especially in combat, that was very useful. It saved my life a number of times.

'We were all frightened, but you didn't show fear,' he once said of his time on Malta. 'In combat though, you'd get into a cold sweat. It trickled down and inside my mask and into my mouth (which he could still taste years later). We had a life expectancy of 15 minutes when we were in combat.'

Scott would remain on 603 Squadron until December 1942, when the squadron was disbanded and he was posted to 1435 Squadron. While on Malta he was credited with at least five destroyed, a further two 'probables' and three 'damaged'. He was awarded the DFC and in January 1943 he would be commissioned.

On 13 October, Arthur Donaldson damaged a Ju 88 north of Gozo and the following day north of Grand Harbour he damaged another Ju 88. On the 15th, he led a head-on attack on

Ju 88s, which split up their formation, and then he followed up with an astern attack on one of the bombers. 'My No. 2 and 3 could not follow me, possibly because of their inexperience,' he wrote. 'I got my sights on the Ju 88 and smoke and flames came from it. It looked doomed but because I had no one covering my tail I was all of a sudden bounced by enemy fighters.

'My Spitfire was riddled with bullets. One came through the side, took away the throttle and then entered the engine, putting it out of action. I looked down and to my horror I saw two of the fingers of my left hand lying on my lap! There was blood everywhere, petrol was streaming into my eyes and I wasn't at all happy. The controls seemed OK so I rolled over, stuck the nose down and beat the hell out of it.

'I cannot say that at that moment I felt any pain. I was in a state of shock and all I wanted to do was remain alive. As I had dived down, I was thinking of what to do. I decided to try and make Takali since if I bailed out by parachute it would be minutes before the RAF Air Sea Rescue picked me up. However efficient they were, no doubt I would bleed to death before rescue arrived; not only was my left-hand bleeding profusely but I had numerous other wounds to my head, arms, legs and face. So, I turned towards the airfield and luckily I had sufficient height to glide back to it. Luckily also the enemy thought I was a "goner" and they did not follow up the attack. I do not know what hit me but probably an Me 109. My undercarriage would not come down and anyway, in case like this, it is safer to land with wheels up. I could see a certain amount of chaos on Takali as it had received a heavy attack.

'The airfield was covered with delayed action and incendiary bombs. I had no option but to land and so put the Spitfire down as gently as I could with only one hand. The fire tender was on its way before the aircraft had come to a stop. The gallant crew pulled me out regardless of any danger to themselves. I was told that one of them was awarded a George Medal and well he deserved it. I think by that time the ambulance had also arrived.'

Donaldson was transferred to the ambulance and taken to Imtarfa hospital, where after treatment he watched the air battle from the veranda of the hospital. AVM Keith Park later visited him at the hospital and told him that he had, like two of his brothers before him, had been awarded the DSO.

'It was about half an hour before I experienced any great pain. I suppose it nature's way of dealing with a severe wound. Within minutes of arriving in the military hospital they put me under an anaesthetic and trimmed up the remains of my left hand. I was of course delirious and I know that I upset the nursing sister with my language ... I watched the reminder of the battle from the hospital veranda. We were only two or three hundred yards from Takali and there were many near misses.'

On 13 October also, Flight Lieutenant Rolls claimed another Ju 88 in a head-on attack. He recalled: 'I saw my cannon shells hit the leading aircraft; its port engine blew up and the aircraft went down. The others had also opened up at the other bombers and although it was only a couple of seconds firing, several of the bombers had been hit and the formation broke up in chaos. We pulled up above the formation and attacked the fighters which were in a turn and broken formation.

'I soon ran out of ammunition and went down on the deck to see what had happened and I saw a Spitfire hit the water and a couple of Ju 88s were floating half submerged. I could see above me two other Ju 88s smoking and coming down.'

Rolls reported meeting the pilot of the Ju 88 he hit in the head-on attack whilst in hospital later that month, Rolls having accidentally received serious leg and foot injuries when a wall, earlier damaged by a bomb, collapsed on him. On the 16th, meanwhile, Rolls claimed a Ju 88, which came down in the sea 10 miles east of Grand Harbour. On the 26th he attacked a Bf 109F at 8,000ft and again at 4,000ft, which took hits and went into a vertical dive from 2,000ft, pouring black smoke. It was his seventeenth and final victory of the war. News of the award of the DFC was announced on 4 December. His evacuation to Britain would follow soon after.

'Jimmy' Ballantyne, who had only ever taken four days' leave while on the Island, claimed a Bf 109 and a MC.202 on 11 October and a Ju 88 'damaged'. Next day, he damaged three enemy aircraft and shot down a MC.202 and a Bf 109. On the 13th, he was hit by a Bf 109 and had to crash-land at Takali. By the end of the month, the Canadian ace had been awarded the DFM. It was all a far cry from his time at Initial Training School in 1941, when he was considered to be 'slightly timid', lacked confidence and his conduct was 'doubtful'!

On Sunday, 11 October, Colin Parkinson had claimed a Ju 88 probably destroyed off Żonqor Point. The next day, 5 miles south of Gela, as well as claiming a 'Breda 205' 'damaged' and a Bf 109 destroyed, he also was awarded a half share in the destruction of a Ju 88 'probable'. On the 13th it was: 'Readiness this morning early.

Was scrambled about 5 o'clock, nearly too late. Climbed to about 7,000ft and came round south of Gozo to the Malta coast, and met the JU's coming out, about 12 of them. Attacked an 88 from beam and astern, and saw strikes on the fuselage, wings and wing roots. Cannons packed up, so came home and claimed a damaged.'

On 14 October, American Pilot Officer H.T. Nash RCAF and Flight Lieutenant Edwin Glazebrook on 229 Squadron shared in damaging a Ju 88 but the escorting fighters attacked and Nash's Spitfire was shot down into the sea. The Texan got out with a fractured upper jaw and other facial injuries and was soon picked up by HSL 128 and hospitalised. Pilot Officer Philip Dixon's Spitfire was also badly shot up but he got down safely, although his aircraft was pronounced unrepairable.

On Thursday, 15 October on the second enemy raid of the day, Sergeant Hugh (Gwyn) 'Red' Bryden RCAF on 249 Squadron was flying in a group of three Spitfires when 'Schmitts' swooped down on them from the sun. 'Six or seven cannon shells went into my plane and the last one got me in the right leg above the knee. I looked down and knew that the leg was nearly torn off, but it didn't seem to be bleeding very much. By that time, I was up to my ankles in gas', the engine had been hit and a fire was starting. I didn't feel any pain, but my brain was sort of numb. I was up about 22,000ft and going around 300mph and when I tried to bail out everything seemed to go wrong. I made a mad scramble and forgot to undo my oxygen and radio cords. Then my 'chute caught in the seat and I was dangling back over the fuselage. It looked like I was a goner, but I was able to kick the stick forward with my left foot. It sent the plane down and pitched me up into the air and away.'

Bryden floated around in the Mediterranean for half an hour and was then picked up by air-sea rescue. Six weeks later his leg was amputated. On 28 January 1943 he went to England and was hospitalised for two months. He would return home to Saskatoon in April 1943.

On 15 October also, Flight Lieutenant Rod Smith was forced to bail out after his Spitfire was hit by an Bf 109 when he was chasing a group of enemy fighters heading back to Sicily. He later recalled: 'For some reason I glanced down at my left wing and happened to see a small bullet hole in it just a few feet from me. I assumed I'd picked it up earlier, when we were sparring with the 109s high up, I then fired a few more rounds over the top of the 109 in front of me but he would not turn. I looked again at the bullet hole in my left wing and saw a second one about a foot from it. It took a long second for me to realise there must be a 109 behind. I broke violently to the left and upwards. In an instant, things began to happen. Exploding balls of fire making sharp cracking bangs appeared on the left side of my engine. The aircraft shook as if poked from behind by long metal rods. The cockpit filled with the smell of cordite.

'The engine oil pressure dropped to nothing. The oil temperature shot upwards. But the engine kept going without missing a beat. Over my left shoulder I saw the yellow nose of a 109 about 100 yards behind me and closing in. Puffs of smoke were billowing from its guns and being blown back over it.

'It came so close it almost touched me as it passed behind. As soon as I was pointing back to Malta, I straightened out and climbed at full power. We had been told that if a Rolls Royce

Merlin engine ever lost its oil pressure you should flog it, not nurse it. To my great relief I reached 600ft then 1,000ft.

'The engine kept delivering full power. I marvelled how it could do this with no oil pressure. I switched the R/T over to emergency and called "Mayday! Mayday! Mayday!" – the oral SOS. Immediately, the Malta controller responded. "Keep transmitting," he said, "we've got you!" Soon I was at 2,000ft and Malta looked closer. To my wonderment and admiration, the engine kept going till I reached 3,800ft and was almost at the coast of Malta. By then, acrid smoke was pouring through the cockpit and the power was failing. I bailed out and was rescued from the sea.'

On Friday, 16 October Colin Parkinson claimed two Ju 88s damaged. Next day he rose at 0315 hours and went to Readiness at 0445. 'Everything quiet until about 0830,' he began. 'Scrambled up to about 24,000ft, and was away, so I joined up with a nest of two who flew out to sea. We saw two 109s below us, so we bounced them. I gave one a good squirt, and saw bursts of cannon shell all over the fuselage and wings. The 109 flew level for a few seconds, and then did a slow dive, down to the sea and went right in.'

He had seen Sergeant Ron 'Dusty' Miller in his 'chute and decided to orbit but three Bf 109s attacked from 3,000ft. He broke into them and gave one 'a squirt' but his aim was off. 'They buggered off anyhow, which was the main thing,' he recalled. '"Dusty" landed in the drink.' Parkinson saw a rescue launch and he directed it to the spot before escorting it home for a while. After he had landed with 10 gallons of petrol remaining, he discovered that it was not Miller who had been rescued but a German airman from a Ju 88. Miller, who came from Leeds, was 22 years old.

On 25 October, Parkinson was awarded a MC.202 'damaged'. This took his final score to eight and one shared destroyed, three and one shared 'probables', seven 'damaged' and one destroyed on the ground. On return to Australia, the erstwhile Aussie ace found himself in trouble with higher ranks and he was sent to a posting in which he had little interest. Problems continued and before the end of the war he was court-martialled and discharged from the RAAF.

The final 'Club Run' had taken place on 20 October 1942, when thirty-one Spitfires in Operation 'Train' were embarked on *Furious* in the Clyde. Sailing under escort with three destroyers, the carrier arrived in Gibraltar on the 26th. Three days later, escorted by two cruisers and eight destroyers, *Furious* arrived at the flying off point and flew off twenty-nine Spitfires, two remaining on board with defects. Then the carrier and her escort returned to Gibraltar to prepare for Operation 'Torch', the invasion of North Africa.

On 22 October 'Wally' McLeod had scored the last of his thirteen victories flying from Malta (a MC.202 over Comino), plus two 'probables' and several enemy aircraft damaged, by which time he had earned the nickname 'the Eagle of Malta' (he was also described as 'a killer if ever there was one'. But he had become irritable and stressed. Posted home, he left Malta on the ill-fated RAF Liberator AL516 for Gibraltar, where he transferred to a Dakota for the flight to England. After a period of recuperation and instructing in Canada, 'Wally' returned to combat action, flying Spitfire IXbs on 443 'Hornet' Squadron RCAF. He was described by Wing Commander 'Johnnie' Johnson, the 144 RCAF Wing leader, as '... a cool-eyed, alert man of 28. The first time I met him he moved about the room restlessly. He had the reputation of being a deadly shot, very fast on the draw. A killer if there ever was one, I thought. Might be inclined to stick his neck out too far; I'll watch him.'

'Wally' McLeod's twenty-first and final victory came on 30 July 1944. On 17 August his Spitfire was hit by flak and he crash-landed near Falaise. On 27 September Squadron Leader McLeod DSO DFC* was KIA when he failed to return after chasing a lone Messerschmitt Bf 109 over the Nijmegen area during 'Market Garden'. Remains of his Spitfire were discovered in September 1949. McLeod was still in the wreckage of his Spitfire, 9 miles in the outskirts of Wesel, near Duisburg, just inside the German border. He is buried in the Commonwealth War Graves Commission cemetery at Rheinberg.

McLeod's score would be eclipsed only by a fellow Canadian, George 'Screwball' Beurling, whose name has gone down in aviation folklore.

'George Beurling had been on the Island little more than a fortnight,' recalled 'Laddie' Lucas, 'when we settled on his nickname. He had, by then, flown infrequently but quite enough for me to see that in this way-out individualist and eccentric, with flying and fighting qualities far above the general run, we had a find – and an oddball with it.

'By nature, fairly brash and outspoken, he was always something of a loner and, early on with the Squadron, he tended to keep his thoughts very much to himself. Later, he wasn't averse from allowing his opinions full rein. "Screwballs" became a well-worked phrase in the Canadian's vocabulary. It served every purpose … the flies, the Maltese, the Messerschmitts, the drivers of the tea cart – all became "the goddam screwballs." So "Screwball" he was named. It suited him and I think he rather liked it. It encouraged his ego to feel that he was being noticed and thought about, even with affection, by a squadron in which he had quickly developed a pride. He hadn't been treated like that, he told me, in England.'

'Every Service has its quota of romantic figures who capture the imagination of the general public and that is as true of the Royal Canadian Air Force serving overseas as of any other Service,' wrote Leonard Gribble. 'But even in the RCAF few pilots achieved the popularity of Flying Officer George Beurling. He lived a charmed life and in Malta his deeds became almost legendary. German and Fascist fliers alike went down before his blazing guns. On his day "Screwball" Beurling was a one-man air force. He was a human dynamo in an aircraft and the scourge of the Axis.

'When he was 18, he applied to join the RCAF, but was turned down. That was in the summer of 1940. He straightway signed on with the crew of a cattle boat and sailed to England, where he tried to enlist in the RAF as a pilot. He was told he must produce proof of previous flying experience and his parents' consent. This was a poser. He had logged about forty hours in civil flying, but he did not know if that record would be considered seriously. So, he signed on with the crew of another boat and went back to Canada. The money he had earned on the trip he spent taking his parents for a motor tour of the Laurentian Mountains. Then, with their consent to his flying, he signed up on another freighter and went back to England for the second time and enlisted. He duly completed his training and after making a few operational sorties over the Channel applied for posting to Malta.

"'I figured there would be more fun there," he told a friend.

'Once on the island he studied air-firing very carefully. He discovered what allowances to make for any distance at which he opened up with his machine-guns and wing cannon. Then he developed his own diving technique and went into action.'

'Screwball' neither smoked nor drank anything harder than Coca Cola when on active service and he invariably kept early hours. 'That's the reason I'm never jittery before a take-off,' he explained on one occasion. 'I got to look forward to getting up aloft. There's no better fun in the world than tangling with the German.'

By October 'Screwball' Beurling's score was twenty-nine and twelve shared destroyed, with nine damaged; all except two of them gained on Malta. During the October blitz he destroyed eight aircraft in five days and was subsequently awarded the DSO but on the 14th, when he claimed a Ju 88 and two Bf 109s, his Spitfire was hit repeatedly by return fire and his right heel was struck by a cannon splinter and he was forced to bail out. Fortunately, he was rescued by an HSL after just twenty minutes in the water. A committed Christian, invariably, Beurling carried a small Bible in his pocket. According to 'Laddie' Lucas, 'Beurling's relief at the recovery of his bible which his rescuers found floating on the water nearby was greater than his concern for the badly damaged foot which he had just sustained.' In hospital later his right leg was put in plaster.

On 31 October Beurling and others like Arthur Donaldson, who was a stretcher case, and Art Roscoe on 229 Squadron, as well as a number of time-expired pilots, boarded Liberator AL516 on 511 Squadron for evacuation to England.

Art Roscoe bedded down in the converted bomber's bomb bay together with some of the others and he slept most of the way to Gibraltar. He awoke with the dawn and, feeling hot, he clambered to one of the waist-gun positions where he could enjoy a cool draught blowing through the open hatch. Beurling joined him because he wanted to watch the landing at Gibraltar. But their arrival at the Rock coincided with a thunderstorm. Flight Lieutenant R. Walton, the B-24 pilot, landed too far along the runway and then attempted to go around but the Liberator stalled and sank in the sea off the end of the runway. Walton was one of six crew who were injured. Flight Sergeant Kenneth Robert Mitchell RAAF suffered abrasions to his face and ankle. Art Roscoe and George Beurling escaped through the open hatch. Arthur Donaldson emerged from the wreckage with burns to one of his arms. Art Roscoe clung desperately to a large piece of wreckage and when he saw a couple of rubber dinghies on the water, he swam over to them and inflated them. He helped another pilot into one and pushed him towards the shore. Beurling, who was nearby, offered to help but Roscoe told him that he could manage. Somehow, Beurling and Roscoe both managed to make the shore.

Six pilots died. Flying Officer Hetherington DFC, 24 years old, was trapped in the rear half and he was drowned. Twenty-year-old Kamloops, British Columbia-born Pilot Officer John William Williams DFC, affectionately known as 'Willie the

Kid', who since 6 May, had shot down six enemy aircraft, scored a 'probable' and damaged eleven more, also perished. Educated in Kamloops and Chilliwack from 1936 to 1940, he had been so keen to enlist that he took a six-month ground course in aviation by correspondence and enlisted in Vancouver on 24 October 1940. Twenty-three-year-old Flight Lieutenant Edwin Herbert Glazebrook of 126 Squadron and Flight Sergeant Charles Edward 'Rip' Mutch of Clinton, Ontario, also perished. Warrant Officer II Rupert Henry Davey RCAF and 24-year-old Sergeant David William James Spencer, two members of 511 Transport Squadron based at RAF Lyneham, who flew regularly to Gibraltar, were drowned. Spencer's wife, M. Carrie Spencer, of Msida, Malta, was one of two women who were injured. A husband and wife and four other women civilians, including Isabella Josephine Aston, the Maltese wife of an FAA pilot, and their 2-year-old son, and Mrs Edna Patricia Chase and baby son, died too.

All six crew of the Liberator, two of whom had already survived after a Liberator had been shot down off Norway in February 1942 and they had to walk to Sweden, survived, although Flight Lieutenant R. Walton, the pilot, and Pilot Officer G.W.R. Frampton, the navigator, were injured.

Eighteen air force pilots also survived. They included Flight Sergeant Eric Livingstone Mahar DFM on 185 Squadron, who had a fractured right leg; Flight Lieutenant L.G. 'Ping' Pow RCAF, who had ferried one of the first two long-range Spitfire Vcs to Malta on 25 October; and Flying Officer 'Gord' Farquharson from Corbyville, Ontario, on 126 Squadron, who had a foot in a cast after receiving a splinter wound in his heel on

15 October. He survived by clinging to the broken leg of another pilot who had managed to grab a piece of floating wreckage. Flight Sergeant Arthur William Varey, who had five and one shared destroyed, four 'probables' and seven 'damaged' to his name, was temporarily knocked unconscious before scrambling through the torn fuselage and swimming to shore. Sergeant F.W. Clewley RAAF, also lived to tell the tale. He had crashed on take-off from Hal Far on 13 August when his vision had been impaired by a dust cloud created by the leading Spitfire taking off. Temporarily blinded, he had crashed into a stone-built dispersal pen and suffered a badly lacerated chin and concussion. The aircraft had to be written off.

Pilot Officer 'Joe' Bush, who on 12 May had been wounded in both legs and had belly-landed his Spitfire at Luqa, crashing through some stone walls at the perimeter of the airfield; Flying Officer Frederick Raymond Johnson RAAF, and Johnny G.W. Farmer on 249 Squadron, too were fortunate. On 17 September Farmer had just managed to bail out of his Spitfire at 450mph after his flight controls had been shot to pieces by a Bf 109 of 1/JG 77. He pulled his ripcord too soon and the jerk of the parachute had given him a slight rupture, dislocated shoulders and a broken arm. He came down in the sea and was soon rescued by HSL 107.

After landing back in Britain, George Beurling was sent to Canada to join a Victory Loan Drive, selling war bonds, being the guest of honour at a parade in Verdun and meeting Prime Minister Mackenzie King. He did not enjoy the war bond campaign. Also, he often said things that embarrassed the RCAF, such as that he enjoyed killing people. The leg wound Beurling had received over Malta, combined with his poor general health, returned him to hospital for several weeks. He completed his promotional work in mid-1943 and in Vancouver also met his future wife, Diana Eve Whittall of Westmount, Quebec. Returning to Britain, Beurling was posted as a gunnery instructor to 61 OTU. On 27 May 1943 he was posted to the Central Gunnery School at RAF Sutton Bridge. On 8 June, during a mock dogfight, Beurling was forced to bail out of his Spitfire II when the engine caught fire after being hit accidentally. It is alleged that while stationed at RAF Sutton Bridge, he actually flew under the Cross Keys swing bridge that crosses the Nene.

The fact that Malta's stubborn defenders and its stoic citizens had valiantly refused to capitulate during the siege was due in no small part to the bravery and dedication of the never-to-be forgotten pilots and the largely gutsy gunners and ground crews; the gallant 'Club Runs' and the defiant supply convoys, which operated consistently throughout despite mounting losses.

In all operations during the Siege of Malta, that had begun on 11 June 1940 and effectively ended on 20 November 1942, a date on which the Axis Powers were routed at the Second Battle of El Alamein, the Royal Navy had transported 756 aircraft, of which 719 (a little over 95 per cent) arrived on the Island.

In letters to his girlfriend, Joan, in Staffordshire in November 1942, Leading Aircraftman Ray Roberts, a 20-year-old engine fitter attached to 69 Squadron, who had spent two years on Malta under siege conditions, provided some indication of life on the Island, while saying little about the dangers and deprivation.

Thursday, 4 November. 'Everyone is starving here … We are being raided day and night. Gosh! Are we hungry.' On Saturday,

7 November, he revealed that 'the Aussies who brought us were shot down into the sea last night. They are posted "missing presumed killed …"' As the weeks' unfolded, news was worse. 'We get about three crashes a day and we have no equipment to repair them. Gosh, it really is terrible here. Work from dawn till dark and after, and hardly anything to eat. How these RAF lads here have stuck this for twelve months is beyond me. But when you look in their faces you can see that they are underfed and should all be sent home … You know Joan, I never thought I would end up like this but I am actually billeted in a poor house, so I guess it will be Christmas Day in the Work-house.' He deliberately did not mention that he would spend a cold and hungry Christmas Eve because the house had no roof.

During 8–16 November, when the Allies landed forces in Vichy French Morocco and Algeria, the Axis diverted their forces to the Battle of Tunisia, and attacks on Malta were rapidly reduced. 'Unternehmen Herkules' (Operation 'Hercules') – the proposed invasion of the Island, which had been set for mid-July 1942, was postponed and then cancelled. To quote Albert Kesselring: 'To guarantee supplies to the Afrika Corps in Libya the capture of Malta was necessary. The one fatal blunder to the whole undertaking in North Africa was the abandonment of this plan. When this happened, the subsequent course of events was almost inevitable.'

In December 1942, air and sea forces operating from Malta went over to the offensive. 'The 11th of December,' Wing Commander Stan Grant wrote: 'It really was a day to remember. Six of Wing Commander John Kenneth Buchanan's Beaufighters from Takali and eight Spitfires from Qrendi, a runway perched alongside a cliff, took off for a long patrol, and at the end of it, west of Lampedusa, we suddenly saw those 24 Junker 52s, escorted by one Ju 88 and four Me 110s. We took a heavy toll.'

When the Spitfires and Beaufighters attacked, the Spitfires dealt with the German fighters. The Beaufighters shot down six troop-carrying aircraft, with the Spitfires shooting down another two, a Junkers 88 bomber and four fighters. Many more were damaged, for the loss of only two RAF aircraft.

Grant, however, could not hide his frustration and fury when the Beaus and Spitfires, out of ammunition and low on petrol, had to turn for home, to see in the distance, another smaller air convoy heading towards Africa. Even so, AVM Sir Keith Park was delighted with the day's work and three days later he wrote to Arthur Donaldson: 'Since you left, Malta has changed immensely, and we have for some weeks been carrying out an all-out night bombing and shipping offensive with five new Squadrons from Middle East. Qrendi Strip has blossomed forth into a two-squadron station, and we expect the arrival of a Mosquito Squadron from UK shortly.

'In fact, we have now doubled the number of Squadrons we had when you arrived here in August, and the Mediterranean Fleet and Convoys make the harbour look extremely busy. We have done everything possible to invite the enemy to blitz us again, but at the moment he seems to be too busy in Tunisia.

'The Spit-bomber has been a great success, but our fighter sweeps rarely meet the enemy, though occasionally they slaughter an Air Transport Convoy trying to sneak past Malta, but well out of range of short-range fighters.'

In Operation 'Stone Age', round the clock air cover was possible and the Mediterranean convoys were resumed to supply the advancing British forces, from which ships for Malta were detached and escorted to and from the Island. Erwin Rommel's prophesy in May 1941 that, 'Without Malta the Axis will end by losing control of North Africa,' was now reality.

In January 1943 Wing Commander Alexander Vallance Riddell Johnstone, better known as 'Sandy', the new Wing Leader, commanded the two squadrons at Qrendi. He frequently led his squadron over Sicily, hoping to shoot down Luftwaffe aircraft, but they refused to sally forth to fight. After experimenting with two 500lb bombs fixed under the wings of each Spitfire, Johnstone learned that the fighter could readily be transformed into a bomber.

For the first raid on 16 January 1943 Johnstone led his two squadrons in an attack on a chemical factory at Pachino in Sicily. Twelve Spitfires each carried two bombs, with twelve more Spitfires acting as fighter escort. When they arrived in sight of the factory, the escorting Spitfires flew to one side, while each Spit-bomber made for the target. In his book, *Where No Angels Dwell*, Wing Commander Johnstone gave a gripping description of both the onslaught and his own emotions:

'In each Spitfire, with his 500lb lethal weapon under each wing, the pilot kept his screaming dive under control while he zeroed the bombs on target by using the normal gunsight. One after the other the bombs rained down on the target area, dropping at regular intervals and exploding with frightening velocity. At least three made direct hits on the factory, sending tons of masonry hurtling through the air to join the twisted metal of the gutted machinery. As the last bomber began its dive, I swooped down to ground level with my eleven escorting companions and raced in on the scene of destruction, raking the smoke and flames with cannon and machine-fire.

'The vibration set up by the firing of the guns was like the tingling of newly awakened nerves ... It was a strange overwhelming feeling of excitement that made your mouth dry with the taste of it; your heart beat faster and your body tensed itself in its firm and unrelaxed grip.

'Your hands gripped the controls as you put your fighter through its paces, and the quick responses to your demands seemed to mould you more firmly into the very heart of the machine until you were not merely there with it. When fighter and pilot were as one like this you felt invincible.

'But it was a feeling which only took possession for a few fleeting moments when the thrill of the chase, the dog-fight, or the attack was at its height. Once it had ebbed away your brain told you once again that you were but a man – a mere microcosm of humanity – and that the fighter you flew was but a machine of nuts and bolts, of metal subject to all man's frailties. Back to reality you felt vulnerable; even lonely ... I swept towards the wreckage of the factory ... As I pulled back on the stick to lift the Spitfire above the smoke, there were clear indications that my fire power had struck home. There were signs of a large explosion and judging by the clouds of steam, followed by dense black smoke which billowed from the tall chimney and burst outwards from several of the factory windows, I was certain that I had hit a massive boiler.

'Re-forming, the bomber aircraft, now shed of their loads, acted as escort to the twelve "straffers" whose ammunition was spent. We set course for Malta and were back on the ground, ready to refuel without any retaliation from the Sicilian-based enemy aircraft.

'Back on the Island I discovered that owing to the speed which the bomb-carrying Spitfires had accumulated in their vertical dive on the factory, a number of seats had collapsed through the immense pull of gravity, exerted when they were pulled violently out of the dive. The pilots had been forced to crouch or adopt semi-standing positions in their cockpits throughout the entire flight back to base.'

This RAF offensive, which was likened to the 'flashing sword of Achilles' was a welcome boost to the morale of the fighter pilots and the Maltese. The Luftwaffe was now concentrating on flying food and equipment to the Afrika Korps by Junkers Ju 52 transports. Knowing their vulnerability to attack from Spitfires, they flew from Sicily to Tunis at sea level, below the radar screen. The Malta-based Spitfires were fitted with extra fuel tanks, enabling them to fly for up to five-and-a-half hours, and they intercepted some of these transport aircraft. Not many got through to the Afrika Korps, which was now on the point of collapse. As a result of the islanders' self-sacrifice, the dedication of the Malta Garrison, and the advance of the Allies on 12 May, the Afrika Korps surrendered, and 291,000 Germans and Italians became prisoners of war. When the Maltese heard the news, the church bells started to ring, and there was dancing in the streets.

On the next day, Air Marshal Park wrote to 'Sandy' Johnstone, saying that John Joseph Lynch Jr of 249 Squadron, in the Qrendi Wing, had shot down the 1,000th Axis aircraft from Malta.

Of all the enemy aircraft that attacked Malta; on 17 August 1943, Editor of the *Times of Malta*, The Honourable Mabel Strickland singled out just one – the Ju 88: 'The hideous German Junkers 88 no longer possess the sky, instead there is the continuous drone of the British fighters and bombers heading out for Italy, speeded on their mission by the Maltese with a fierce and furious delight. They are the first liberators of oppressed Europe.'

'It was with a great deal of satisfaction and pleasure,' wrote Don McLeod, 'that each of us heard of the diminishing supplies to Rommel and of the increased supplies to the British 8th Army. We even got so well off that we sent a squadron to help pursue Rommel through the hot sticky desert and it wasn't many months, not more than four, before the allied pincer movement started at Cairo on one end and by the invasion of North Africa on the other end ended up in wiping out Rommel in Tunisia.

'Little Malta, just a spot on the ocean, just the half-way-point on the Mediterranean Highway, remained unconquered, badly battered, but certainly proud.'

On 31 July 1942 Don McLeod was posted to 53 OTU Llandow as instructor. That September he transferred to the USAAF, was promoted to captain and posted to the 4th Fighter Squadron, 52nd Fighter Group at Goxhill on 9 October. He was then shipped overseas, to Gibraltar on 24 October. After arrival, on 6 November, the next day he led the 4th Fighter Squadron on a redeployment to Oran in North Africa but he lost all instrumentation and flew back to Gibraltar. Five pilots were lost, two were safe and three were interned in French Morocco. McLeod spent two weeks in Algiers awaiting orders before being sent home to the USA on 23 November to rest. In 1943 he returned to England when he was posted to the 83rd Fighter Squadron, 78th Fighter Group at Duxford, which was equipped with the P-47. On 10 June 1944, he was shot down in his P-47 Thunderbolt and crashed near Argentan. He evaded capture, helped by the French Resistance.

Meanwhile, Don McLeod's best buddy, 'Jimmie' Peck, had left Malta with four kills and one enemy aircraft 'shared destroyed', three 'probables' and ten 'damaged'. Transferred to the USAAF, he joined the 52nd Fighter Group, becoming a flight commander in the 2nd Squadron. In North Africa during the winter of 1942–43 he saw action on Spitfire Vs once more, and on 2 January 1943 shot down an Fw 190 for his fifth victory. Promoted to captain, Peck was appointed CO of the 394th Fighter Squadron in the 367th Fighter Group, which formed in mid-July at Hamilton Field in the San Francisco area of California. In early March 1944 the 367th set off by train to New York to embark on the Duchess of Bedford, a Canadian Pacific liner converted to a troop ship; destination unknown. On 3 April the 'Drunken Duchess' as she was known, berthed at Greenock, where the group boarded a train for southern England.

The pilots and ground crews learned that they were now in the 9th Air Force and their new home would be RAF Stoney Cross, in the New Forest. All the pilots' flying experience had been on single-engine fighters and they were expecting to fly the P-51 Mustang, so they were shocked when told that they would be flying twin-engine Lockheed P-38 Lightnings – and they had less than one month to be ready for combat missions!

Some of the P-38s were war weary, having been passed on from other units and many required engine changes. After every engine change and upgrade, each P-38 had to be test flown by an experienced pilot. On 11 April, at the end of a test flight, one of 'Jimmie' Peck's engines cut out; the P-38 stalled and he crashed into the perimeter track. Thrown clear, 'Jimmie' suffered a fractured skull and died on the way to hospital. He was 22 years old.

On 22 September 1946, his great friend, Don McLeod, now domiciled in Norwich, Connecticut; died while undergoing surgery (probably) meant to repair his long-standing neck injury. He is buried at Blackstone Cemetery.

Appendix I: The 'Club Runs' Hurricanes 1941

Date	Operation	Details
19 May	'Splice'	48 Hurricane IIs flown off *Furious* and *Ark Royal*
6 June	'Rocket'	44 Hurricane IIs flown off *Furious* (20) and *Ark Royal* (24). One Hurricane returns with defects
13 June	'Tracer'	46 Hurricanes flown off *Ark Royal* and *Victorious*. 2 crash on landing, one ditches, 1 has to land in N. Africa
27 June	'Railway I'	22 Hurricanes flown off *Ark Royal*. 1 crash on landing
30 June	'Railway II'	35 Hurricanes on *Ark Royal* and *Furious* (7 not launched due to deck accident on *Furious*)
9 September	'Status I'	26 Hurricanes on *Ark Royal*. Only one guide Blenheim makes the rendezvous so only 14 are flown off
13 September	'Status II'	46 Hurricanes are flown off *Ark Royal* and *Furious*, one crashing on take-off
12 November	'Perpetual'	*Argus* and *Ark Royal* fly off 37 Hurricanes to Malta. Three Hurricanes fail to arrive. On 13 November, during the return to Gibraltar, *Ark Royal* is torpedoed by *U-81* and next day sinks in tow within sight of base

Appendix II: The 'Club Runs' Spitfires 1942

Date	Operation	Details
February	'Spotter'	*Argus* loads 15 Spitfire Vbs, the first for Malta and the first sent overseas, and sails with *Eagle* in convoy on 16 February to Gibraltar, arriving on the 24th but defects in the fuel tanks are discovered and the operation is aborted
7 March	'Spotter'	The 15 repaired Spitfire Vbs aboard *Eagle* are flown off and are guided the 700 miles to Malta by 7 Blenheims
21 March	'Picket I'	9 Spitfires from *Eagle* arrive in Malta but the other 8 return with the carrier to Gibraltar
29 March	'Picket II'	8 Spitfires embarked, 7 fly off *Eagle*; 6 Albacores unable to fly off *Argus*
20 April	'Calendar'	47 Spitfire Vcs flown off USS *Wasp*. 46 arrive
9 May	'Bowery'	64 Spitfires: 47 Spitfires flown off USS *Wasp* and 17 from HMS *Eagle* (4, all from *Wasp*, are lost en route)
19 May	'LB'	17 Spitfires (including 1 remaining from 'Picket II') flown off *Eagle*; 6 Albacores again fail to fly off
3 June	'Style'	32 Spitfires reach Gibraltar 27 May. Flown off *Eagle*. 28 arrive safely, four are shot down en route

9 June	'Salient'	32 Spitfires reach Gibraltar 2 June. Flown off *Eagle* on 9 June, all reach Malta safely
15 July	'Pinpoint'	32 Spitfires reach Gibraltar on 25 June on 3 freighters. Flown off *Eagle* on 15 July, 1 providing cover for *Welshman*
21 July	'Insect'	32 Spitfires shipped to Gibraltar from Britain on 3 freighters. Four are damaged in transit
11 August	'Bellows'	39 Spitfires flown off *Furious*. 1 forced to land on *Indomitable*
17 August	'Baritone'	32 Spitfires flown off *Furious*. 29 arrive
29 October	'Train'	29 Spitfires flown off *Furious*. Two remain on board with defects

Index